D1084403

The Western Frontier Library

Medicine Man

Medicine Man

BY OWEN TULLY STRATTON, *1868-1950*

Edited by Owen S. Stratton

University of Oklahoma Press : Norman and London

Library of Congress Catalog Card Number: 89-40224

ISBN: 0-8061-2241-2

The paper in this book meets the guidelines for permanence and durability of the Committee on Production Guidelines for Book Longevity of the Council on Library Resources, Inc. ∞

Contents

Illustrations

Editor's Foreword

By Owen S. Stratton

Medicine Man is a book of reminiscences by my father, Owen Tully Stratton, mostly about his life in the West as a medicine show grafter from 1898 to 1904 and his years as a country physician from 1906 until his death in 1950.

Between the late 1920s and 1950 he spent hundreds of evenings and odd hours during the day in his office over the Penney Store in Salmon, Idaho, pecking out his reminiscences on an old Underwood.

In a 1949 letter, he wrote, "I have bet the postage on the manuscript covering my medicine show days [apparently sending it to a publisher]. Though I have revised it many times, I am afraid it is a flop. Am now awaiting the sad news. But I am still working on my horse-and-buggy days. If the manuscripts have served no other purpose, they have kept me occupied and, possibly, out of Blackfoot [the location of the Idaho state insane asylum]."

I thought his manuscripts had been lost, but in 1985, thirty-five years after his death, I found them in a box of family papers and photographs my nephew had sent me. They consist of more than six-hundred typed pages that range from rough drafts to drafts that are apparently the products of much revision.

One manuscript of 102 pages is about my father's medicine show days, and another of 192 pages is about his years in medical practice. A shorter piece describes his family background, his childhood and adolescence, and some of the people with whom he grew up. Another tells of his venture to Alaska in the Klondike gold rush. And a third is mostly about his experiences in Washington state from 1889 to 1894. There are also several short sketches on various subjects.

As the core of *Medicine Man*, I retained almost all of the manuscripts on the medicine show business and the practice of medicine, eliminating only a few case descriptions that seemed repetitive. On the ground that it was unrelated to the medicine show business or the practice of medicine, I left out almost all that he wrote about his experiences in Washington state from 1889 to 1894.

I provided the title, *Medicine Man*, divided the material into chapters, arranged the chapters in their present order, wrote the chapter headings, revised the paragraphing and punctuation, and recast a good many sentences while trying to retain my father's anecdotal style. All the footnotes are mine. My father used fictitious names for his medicine show associates, but I believe that the names of all the others mentioned are their real ones.

Some readers may find offensive some of the language my father used in referring to Indians, blacks, and members of other ethnic groups. I have let the language stand, trusting that readers will be aware that my father was a man of the nineteenth century, who was born in Illinois three years after the end of the Civil War and inevitably acquired the language and many of the prejudices of the people among whom he grew up.

In what follows, chapters 1 and 2 take my father to Washington state in 1897, to Alaska in the gold rush, and back to Tacoma in 1898. Chapters 2 through 7 are about the medicine show business and end with my father's return to medical school. Most of chapter 8 on his family background, upbringing, and marriage comes from his manuscript on the same subject. The position of the chapter in the middle of the book reflects his arrangement in which he referred to his family for the first time on page 101 of his 102-page medicine show manuscript. Chapters 9 through 20 contain the manuscript on the practice of medicine. I have added an epilogue.

I believe that my father wrote entirely from memory without benefit of diaries or other contemporary records. It is true, however, that tucked away in a photograph album I have found a small leather-bound notebook in which he recorded medicine show income and outgo from August 13, 1899, to the end of June 1900. Most of the entries for 1899 give both place names and dates and directly support his manuscript account of that period. His entries for 1900 are dated, but in most of them he omitted place names. The dates as well as the few place names he recorded fit his account of the first six months of that year. No doubt the notebook would have aided his memory for the period it covers, but I am almost certain that he had forgotten its existence by the time he came to write his reminiscences. If I am correct, the notebook testifies to the accuracy of his memory.[1]

But anyone's memory is selective. For example, my father probably remembered his good deeds better than he remembered his sins, and cases in which his patients recovered may have stood out more saliently in his memory than those that furnished business for the undertaker.

Medicine Man is not scholarly history, but it does paint a vivid picture, surely accurate in its main outlines, of what it was like to run a medicine show around the turn of the century. And it describes in personal terms a process that must have been fairly common early in the twentieth century

---

[1] Sometime in the 1930s he sold an article to the Spokane *Spokesman Review* that was mainly a list of the people he had known in Yakima from 1889 to 1894, and he often remarked that no one had written to the paper to correct him.

when poorly educated doctors consulted books, observed surgery, analyzed their mistakes, and thus trained themselves to become reasonably competent physicians.[2]

[2] My father's medical library filled a glass-fronted bookcase in the living room of our house in Salmon. I can remember him standing by the bookcase studying an open book held in his hands as he tried to solve some diagnostic puzzle or prepare for surgery that he had to perform the next day.

Introduction

By Owen S. Stratton

Before my father went to Winona, Minnesota, in 1897, where he begins *Medicine Man*, he had led a varied life. He was born in October 1868 in Litchfield, Illinois, a town of around five thousand people fifty miles northeast of St. Louis. After a short and quarrelsome marriage, his parents divorced each other when he was two, and not long after that, his father, who had practiced medicine in Litchfield, moved to California, leaving no imprint on my father's memory.

He remembered his childhood as one of poverty, occasionally relieved by a ten- or twenty-dollar donation from a maternal uncle named Singleton D. Cave, a professional gambler in St. Louis.

My father worked at various boy's jobs until the end of his first year in high school when a druggist hired him as an apprentice at a salary of four dollars a week. His mother and grandmother debated whether he should go back to high school for a second year or drop out in order to continue in the drugstore. The drugstore job won out, and he dropped out of high school.

His mother died when he was seventeen. In the absence of her spur, the contrast between the hard work, long hours, and low pay of the drugstore job and the apparent ease and splendor of his Uncle Singleton's life as a gambler made my father abandon the idea of becoming a druggist in favor of becoming a gambler like his uncle.

He aped his uncle's dress and profanity but was never able to walk with his feet turned out or chew fine-cut tobacco as his uncle did. He played poker with other "youthful Litchfield outlaws," as he called them, and tried to act like a big shot when he visited St. Louis.[1] His Uncle Singleton tried to discourage his gambling aspirations and to that end paid his tuition for two years at the St. Louis College of Pharmacy. Although my father's mind was more on poker than pharmacology, he managed to pass the school's final examinations a few months before his twenty-first birthday.

Just after that birthday, in 1889, he went west to North Yakima, in what was then Washington Territory, where some cousins lived. He stayed in Washington from 1889 to 1894, playing some poker but mostly earning a living in more respectable pursuits, ending with a year and a half as a deputy U.S. marshal in Yakima, engaged mainly in arresting bootleggers for selling liquor to Indians.

In the fall of 1894, when he was twenty-six, he went back to Litchfield, where he loafed and played poker until the fall

---

[1] In a 1949 letter, he wrote, "Litchfield was a hotbed for grafters. It had five railroads, coal mines, and car shops and was a tough town from every standpoint. It produced Madame Mosely, the Cherokee Queen, who ran a medicine show. I had known her as Mrs. McGown before she married Mosely, an understudy of Dr. J. I. Lightfall of Peoria, the first medicine man I ever saw in action. With the blare of a band as an anesthetic, he pulled enough teeth to pave the sidewalk in his Peoria yard. Then there were my contemporaries: Jim Ferrell, who started out as a banjo plunker for Madame Mosely, and Oliver Larson, who swung a baton in the same show. Oliver's brother, Willard, worked western carnivals with a pony and dog show. Skinny Miller made his mark, running a penny arcade in Minneapolis. Kent Rudolph became a bigmitt artist with the police fixed in Oakland, California. Peck Butler traveled as a fixer with McMahon's circus. They all came up via pink lemonade stands, striking machines, weight-guessing, peanuts, popcorn, taffy, spindles, shell games—anything to snaffle an unwary dollar. If they had worked as hard at legitimate business as they did at grafting, they would have got somewhere."

of 1895, when he enrolled in Barnes Medical College in St. Louis, giving a promissory note for his tuition.

Living close to the rind, he made it through the year until the spring of 1896 and then got a job in the Litchfield post office, where he worked until he had earned enough to pay off his tuition note. Then he quit the post office job, loafed, and in a newspaper contest won a prize of fifty dollars, which he and his Uncle Singleton used to start a poker game in the Litchfield Hotel.

In the late fall of 1896 he married Kate Palmer and then was unable to support her. As he later wrote, "I simply could not devise any method of steadily bringing in the sheaves. We finally reached such a low point that my wife insisted on taking in some of her relatives as boarders. That touched my pride as the end of the limit." Leaving his wife with her family at Hilltop Farm near Litchfield, he went to Winona, Minnesota, where he begins the story of *Medicine Man*.

Chronology

1868   Born in Litchfield, Illinois.

1889   To Yakima.

1894   Returns to Litchfield.

1895–96 First year of medical school in St. Louis.

1896   Marries Kate Palmer.

1897   Back to Yakima. To Alaska. Elder son born in Illinois.

1898   Alaska to Tacoma. Becomes medicine show spieler. Summer with Ferrell and Berry in Portland. In the fall, to LaGrande and Boise.

1899   In the spring, begins to work on his own. Forms partnership with Dr. Park. Summer with Park in northern California. Park gets drunk in San Francisco. Leaves Park and joins Berry in Portland. They work Spokane and Rossland, B.C. Teams up again with Park, and they work Anaconda and other Montana towns. Fall vacation in Litchfield. With Park, works towns along the Columbia.

1900   Trip by stage from The Dalles to Susanville, California. Leaves Dr. Park and forms partnership with Dr. McMillan.

1901   They work towns in northern California and Montana.

1902   Changes partners from Dr. McMillan to Dr.
            Gregg. Works towns in Montana and South
            Dakota.
1903   With Dr. Gregg in South Dakota.
1904   With Dr. Gregg in South Dakota. Returns to
            medical school.
1906   Receives M.D. Opens practice in Toppenish,
            Washington. Moves to Tacoma and then to
            Puyallup.
1907   In the spring, sends family back to Illinois and
            leaves Puyallup. Opens practice in Bridgeport
            but leaves Bridgeport in the fall.
1907–8   Operates houseboat hospital on the St. Joe River
            in Idaho.
1908   Leaves St. Joe in the spring and locates in Mans-
            field. Family joins him.
1909   Mansfield.
1910   Younger son born in Mansfield. Postgraduate
            work in Chicago.
1911   Moves from Mansfield to Salmon.
1918   Moves from Salmon to Great Falls, Montana,
            then to Cascade. Commissioned captain in Army
            Medical Corps. Discharged soon after the ar-
            mistice. Returns to Salmon, accompanied by
            elder son, who enters the grocery business.
1919–24   In Salmon. In 1924 visits Tilden Health School
            in Denver. That fall, moves to Kalispell,
            Montana.
1925   In spring, to Camas Hot Springs. Joins staff
            of Tilden Health School and moves wife and
            younger son to Denver.
1926   In June, leaves Tilden Health School and re-
            turns to Salmon.
1930   Elected to Idaho Senate.
1932   In Democratic primary, runs for U.S. senator.
            Continues practice in Salmon until death in
            August 1950.

Medicine Man

Chapter 1

The Give

In the early summer of 1897, about halfway between my twenty-eighth and twenty-ninth birthdays, I went from my hometown in Illinois to Winona, Minnesota, where I hoped to get a job as pharmacist in a drugstore. After learning that the drugstore had gone broke, I went back to the hotel and sat in the lobby while I debated what to do next, a question that was a stumper since I had just about enough money to pay my hotel bill if I checked out right then.

I hadn't got far in my deliberations when I saw Jim Ferrell come in the door. Although we had grown up together, we hadn't seen each other for several years, and neither of us had any idea that the other was within a thousand miles of Winona.

After a little catching up, Jim explained that he was working a graft called "the give" and proposed to make a pitch in Winona that evening. A practical psychologist named Big Foot Johnson had invented the give, and, as I soon found out, Jim had perfected it until it was as deadly as a shell game.

Jim had started out as a banjo plunker in the medicine show of Madame Mosely, the Cherokee Queen, had left her, and had become a spieler in his own right. He was six feet tall and must have weighed about a hundred and eighty. He had a keen blue eye, brown hair, and a protruding underlip. He had big well-shaped hands, usually decorated

3

with diamonds. Jim's gall would have filled a ten-pound lard pail, but when he wasn't on a platform, he didn't have a lot of nerve except when cornered. He preferred blondes or brunettes, and I used to say about him that he could enter any town, throw up his nose, and walk straight to the nearest piece of tail. But he wasn't the best picker in the world and was likely to fall for a floozy with dog tracks on her belly.

In Winona, Jim was lonesome, as grafters often were, and offered to pay my expenses if I would stick around and keep him company. With that, I agreed heartily. "Nothing to do," he assured me. "Just stick around."

That evening, Jim hired a one-horse cab with a throw-back top and in it seated a boy whose head he had wrapped in a red bandanna. Then, with Jim standing up and waving a huge butcher knife, the ballyhoo went forward, the cab covering all the downtown streets while Jim announced in tones that made the windows rattle:

"Everybody hurry down to the park corner. If you hurry down, you can see the biggest free show on earth. The great decapitation act, which has mystified millions and caused more hair to stand on end than all the three-ring circuses in the world. It's free for everybody. Hurry, hurry, or you'll be too late."

By the time Jim had made his rounds, a considerable crowd had gathered at the corner of the park, while others hurried to join them.

Jim had the driver swing the cab around and back it through the crowd to the curb. Then, slowly and deliberately, in plain view of everybody, he began to arrange the props for his act. First, he picked up an obviously heavy shot sack and poured from it a ringing stream of silver dollars into a bowl. Then he pulled out a roll of bills big enough to choke a bull, fanned the bills out so the crowd could see them, and tossed them into the bowl on top of the silver. Next, he assembled a jointed pole, hooked it to the cab, and hung from it a gasoline torch. After he lit the torch and it began to throw its flickering rays over the crowd, Jim addressed them.

"My friends," he began, an opening which I later learned was the signal for suckers to come to the surface. "My friends, I wish you would step closer. That is, if you are not afraid of the sight of blood. I'll do my best to keep from spattering you, but if you don't faint easily, step a little closer."

Hearing that, many in the front of the crowd moved as close to the cab as they could get, demonstrating their callous bravery.

"Thank you, my friends," Jim went on. "Now some of you may be wondering just who and what I am. Well, I'll tell you. I am known from coast to coast as the Silver King. The man who knows not the value of money and scatters it with a prodigal hand. The poor and needy, the poverty stricken, the ones who have a hard time making ends meet, they never go from me with empty hands.

"'But what is your object?' some of you may ask.

"I have an object, of course. A man without an object is like a ship without a sail, a boat without a rudder, a kite without a tail. Such a man may show signs of life, but he will not get very far.

"My object is this: to turn all of you into my friends. So that wherever I may go, I will be followed by your best wishes. As for money, I have more of the world's goods than I will ever need. That is why I am able to give it away without stint. What I want more than anything else is for you to be able to say truthfully when I depart from your community, 'James, we are sure glad we met you.'

"My second object is that of advertising. Not the kind of advertising that anybody can buy from newspapers, but that which is founded on experience. When you tell your friends about the benefits you receive from my invention, they will believe you, and my sales are bound to increase. Here it is! The most wonderful therapeutic discovery of modern times!"

Jim then held up one of his belts, a primitive galvanic battery made of thin strips of zinc and copper, separated by blotting paper and encased in a cheap oilcloth imitation of a belt. Although the gadget cost Jim only eight cents, it would generate electricity when the blotting paper was soaked with vinegar.

"It looks like a belt," Jim announced, "and it is a belt. But beneath its trappings, there is a powerful galvanic battery. Worn next to your skin, it will generate a life-giving current, which will restore to your glandular system all the virility of youth! Not only that, but if you are afflicted by any departure from health, which you have not neglected for too long, the belt will produce a cure."

Then Jim described the symptoms of a list of diseases, extending from pip to leprosy and not neglecting "female trouble." If written down, it would have read like a page from a patent-medicine almanac, but as he recited the list, Jim put into his voice that appeal which enables the successful hog caller to convince the hogs that he really has something delicious to give them.

When he had his audience more or less hypnotized like a rooster with a chalk mark drawn from the tip of his bill, Jim addressed a nitwit in the front rank. "Here, you," Jim said. "Come a little closer. Now, while I hold one end of my belt on your forehead, touch the other end with your tongue." When the fellow obeyed, he received a shock that made him bat his eyes and almost lose his hat.

The crowd laughed, and Jim went on, "See, my friends, the power my invention contains! With that life-giving current always entering your system, you will have the fountain of youth!

"Now, my friends, some of you may be wondering just how expensive my invention is. And here's where I surprise you. While my belt would be cheap at any price, I'm going to let *you* decide what it will be. Could you ask for a fairer proposition than that? I know you couldn't, and so do you.

"So, in order to keep my belts out of the hands of whistlers, whittlers, and spitters, who will accept anything if it's free, here's what you do. Hand me anything you like, and the belt is yours. But bear this in mind: If you hand me anything less than a dollar, I'll throw your money back in the crowd.

"Now I want you to stand right where you are, and watch what I do for the good and honest man who has the courage to hand me a dollar. Then you'll know just what I mean when I say I'll make a stingy man hate himself. Now who's the first friend and neighbor who would like to try one of my belts?"

A man close to the cab accepted a belt and passed up some small change. Away it went into the crowd. Another handed Jim a half-dollar, which went the way of the small change. A third loosened up with six bits, and when Jim threw that back, it produced a scramble.

Then somebody handed up a silver dollar, and Jim not only gave him a belt but rewarded him with praise. "Thank you, my friend. Thank you. You're a man after my own heart, and I want you to stand right where you are, and see what I'll do for you. I said I'd make a stingy man hate himself, and if I don't do it, I'm not the Silver King."

Jim looked over the crowd and picked out a substantial looking old man, who was standing a little back. "Come here, my friend," Jim said, beckoning to him. "I'd like you to help me a short time, and I'll pay you well for it. Let the gentleman through, brothers and sisters. Thank you.

"Now, my friend, you look like a man who can be trusted, and I'm going to trust you. Give me your hand so I can help you, and up you come! Now be seated, and hold your hat in your lap just like that. Here's your pay in advance."

The old man looked puzzled, but he pocketed the two dollars Jim gave him. When the old man was properly arranged with his hat upside down in his lap, Jim continued.

"Now all you have to do to earn your pay is just sit there,

hold your hat in your lap, and listen to every word I say. Then if you hear me tell one lie, make a single misstatement, or make a promise that I do not keep, all the money that goes into your hat—and there's going to be more in it than there ever was before—all that money is yours to do with as you see fit. Keep it, give it to charity, or throw it into the street, whatever you think best. Do you understand?"

The old man nodded, and Jim turned to the crowd. "Now, where's the liberal citizen who had the courage to trust me with a dollar? Oh, yes! There you are. Stand right there, and see what I'm going to do for you! There's your dollar, and here are two of mine." He tossed three dollars into the hat. "I've said I'd make a stingy man hate himself, and that's just what I'm going to do! Now, where's the next good citizen who has the nerve to exchange a dollar for a belt?"

For the next few minutes, Jim was as busy as an Oklahoma land-office clerk, exchanging belts for dollars and putting each dollar received along with two more dollars into the hat. He received each dollar with a "thank you" and the admonition, "Watch what I do for you. I'm going to make all these stingy men hate themselves and go off and hide."

When the sale began to slacken, Jim picked up a belt and said, "Watch what I do for the man who buys *this* belt, with some shorthand written on it." With a lead pencil, he scribbled something on the belt. "Do any of you read shorthand?"

A smart aleck standing back on the sidewalk and wanting to get into the show called out, "What shorthand system do you use?"

I doubted that Jim knew there was more than one system of shorthand and wondered how he would sidestep the question. But he didn't hesitate. "Our friend out there wants to know what system of shorthand do I use. Well, I'll tell him. A few years ago, I had a brother who worked in a sawmill. One day he got careless while monkeying around the buzz saw and had a hand sawed off. Always afterward, he was a shorthand writer. Is that the same system you use, my questioning friend?"

The questioner didn't reply, and the crowd laughed. A purchaser handed up a dollar for the marked belt, and with that dollar, Jim threw a five dollar bill into the hat, declaring, "This is *really* where I make a stingy man hate himself!"

He sold several belts bearing different marks, and with each sale, five extra dollars went into the hat.

Then he picked up a belt and bellowed, "Watch what I do for the man who buys this belt with the word Tully written on it."[1]

I judged that to be my cue to come up to the cab, and I worked my way through the crowd. Jim leaned down and whispered, "Go up to my room at the hotel, and get me some more belts out of the trunk." I was on my way, but before I cleared the crowd, I heard him yell, "Wait a minute. W-a-i-t a minute." I looked back and could see that he was holding the trunk key up to his lips. I went back for the key and set off on my errand. I was soon back with more belts and feeling surprised that the crowd seemed to pay no attention to the interruption.

With his stock replenished, Jim went on with the sale. Before long, it began to drag again. Then he picked up a belt and said, "Watch what I do for the good, honest man who has bought one belt and now buys a belt for his wife. This is where I *really* make a stingy man kick himself."

With each belt sold for a wife, Ferrell put a ten dollar bill into the hat along with the dollar from the purchaser. But it was apparent that he had the crowd pretty well cleaned out and was nearing his "blowoff." I wondered how he would manage it.

He picked up the hat, now nearly brimming over with money, and addressed the crowd. "I know that many of you good, honest neighbors are not stingy men because you

[1] My father's middle name—OSS.

have bought my belts. But I am wondering if there be any speculators among you. Next to a stingy man, I hate a speculator who tries to take advantage of my beneficence. If I find a speculator who has bought a belt, I'll take it away from him. Now, my friend," pointing at a man holding a belt, "why did you buy that belt?"

"Because I wanted it."

"Then you didn't buy it with the expectation of receiving a present?"

"No, *sir*!"

"And you? And you?" Jim pointed at others and received the same answer.

Then, addressing the old man who had held the hat, Jim asked, "My friend, during all the time you have been sitting there, have you heard me tell one lie, make a single misstatement, or break a promise?"

"No, sir," came the emphatic reply.

Jim then put it to the crowd. "Well, if I have done none of these things, who do you think this money belongs to?"

"It belongs to you!" the answer came in a chorus so close that it sounded rehearsed.

"Well, if this money belongs to me and you were in my place, what would you do with it?"

"Keep it!" came the answer in a roar.

"Well, that, my friends, is just what I'm going to do." Jim emptied the hat into a satchel. He unhooked the gasoline torch and handed it to me. With the satchel in his hand, he hopped out of the cab and was on his way to the hotel before the crowd realized the show was over.

And there I was, left holding that damned torch, which I didn't know how to put out. Making the best of it, with the torch blazing, I followed Jim toward the hotel. A few members of the crowd accompanied me, and although they looked threatening, they apparently couldn't figure out where I came in, so they didn't tackle me. As I hurried along, I could hear the shrill voice of a street gamin asking, "Where is the good, honest man who bought a belt for him-

self and one for his wife?" As I heard no reply, I assumed
the good, honest man was on his way home with his therapeutic treasures.

Back in the safety of the hotel, Jim explained that one
drawback of the give, aside from risk of dismemberment at
the hands of disappointed hopefuls, was that it burned up
the territory. That was his problem right then, he said, and
he wasn't sure where to go next.

I had spent five years, from 1889 to 1894, in and around
North Yakima, Washington. I could recall seeing only two
street fakers there, which indicated that the territory wasn't
overworked; so I asked Jim why he didn't try the Pacific
Northwest.

To my surprise, he showed interest in my suggestion and
wanted to know how much street licenses were out there. I
had no idea. Jim thought it over for a minute and then said,
"I tell you what. I'll give you fifty dollars if you'll go back
out there and find out about the licenses."

"You've got a deal," I said and held out my hand. Jim
counted fifty dollars into it, and the next morning I was on
my way.

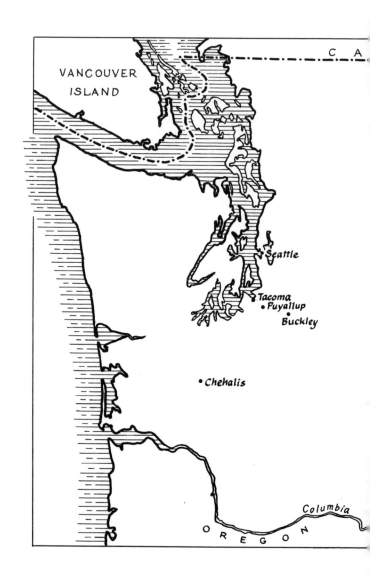

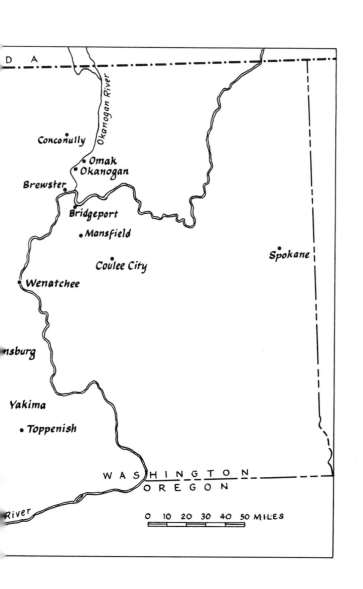

CANADA

Conconully

Okanogan River

Omak
Okanogan

Brewster

Bridgeport

Mansfield

Coulee City

Wenatchee

Spokane

nsburg

Yakima

Toppenish

W A S H I N G T O N
O R E G O N

River

0   10   20   30   40   50 MILES

Chapter 2

I Join the Klondike Rush

My second-class ticket to Yakima cost forty-five dollars, leaving me five dollars out of Jim's fifty to spend on incidentals. By riding in day coaches and carefully rationing myself on lunchroom sandwiches, I was able to pay six bits for a tourist sleeper for my last night on the train. That enabled me to clean up, but when the train pulled into the North Yakima station, I had only sixty-five cents left in my pocket.

I gave fifteen cents of that to the porter, who pawed over the tip to show what a cheap screw he thought I was. I wanted to kill him, but I was afraid the law wouldn't agree with me that it was justifiable homicide to slay a porter for sneering at a tip that represented nearly a quarter of the passenger's total assets.

At the Yakima Hotel, where I registered as though I had money and amounted to something, the personnel greeted me effusively because the last time I had stopped there I had been dragging down three thousand a year, which was important money in that place and time. Fortunately, the hotel operated on the American plan, giving me a week of meals before the showdown.

After I carried my bag to my room, I took a look around, and in the cardroom back of the bar, I found the same old gang, their eyes looking like holes burned in a white blanket, finishing up an all-night poker game.

After I shook hands all around, one of the players asked

me to play his hand while he took care of some legitimate business in the grocery store he ran. He was stuck and very much a loser, but Lady Luck was on my side, and in a short time, I had him even and then winner.

When he came back, the game broke up, and he handed me two dollars, apologizing that he was awfully hard up. I, of course, was a bloated bondholder with half a dollar in my pocket, but I accepted the two dollars, though I knew, as did the groceryman, that I was entitled to half of what I had won.

I fulfilled my agreement with Jim Ferrell by interviewing the city clerk and wiring the information back to Jim. A week or so later, he showed up with a dentist named Anderson and two performers, and they were soon making pitches at the corner of Yakima Avenue and First Street.

One evening, as Ed Reed, editor of the Yakima *Herald*, and I stood on the sidewalk listening to Jim's harangue, I remarked that he and I had gone to the same school in Litchfield. Just then, Jim introduced Anderson as "the little giant tooth puller who has pulled more than ten thousand tooths." That prompted Ed Reed to remark, "That must have been a hell of a fine school you guys went to."

I knew nearly all the white men and half the Indians around Yakima, but nobody was in the market for my services. I managed to pay my hotel bill, however, by spending most of most nights sitting in the poker game back of the bar.

The big subject of conversation among the rounders with whom I associated was the Klondike gold rush, about which they had firsthand information. The year before, in 1896, four local adventurers had gone to Alaska, and three of them had returned with tales to tell. They had gone to Dyea and crossed the Chilcoot Pass to Lake Linderman, where they built a boat. Then they floated down the Yukon through White Horse rapids to the mouth of the Pelly River and claimed they had gone up that stream for nine hundred miles. I think their account of that lap was a little exaggerated, although no doubt it seemed like nine hundred miles because they were constantly soaked to the hide and fighting gnats and mosquitoes all the way. A year later, I. H. Dills, a Yakima clothing merchant, who was one of the party, showed me his legs, spotted with remains of mosquito bites that looked like tattoo marks.

He told of floating through stretches of the Yukon where the river was ten miles wide, of lassoing fish in the clear water by working a wire fiddle string back of their gills, of using oars to kill wild geese that had shed their wing feathers and couldn't fly, and of panning coarse gold on some of the benches along the Pelly River.

Three members of the party had interests in Yakima that required their return. To get back to Dyea, they had to hike all the way and could take only as much of their supplies as they could carry on their backs.

The fourth member of the party, S. O. Morford, had no inducement to return because he had left Yakima mortgaged to the hilt, with creditors about to foreclose on a fine ranch he owned near Yakima City. So, when the party reached the mouth of the Pelly, Morford declared his intention of going on down the Yukon.

The others tried to talk him out of it, but when they found him determined, they put the boat in the best condition they could, loaded it with the supplies they couldn't pack, and shoved it off with Morford aboard.

Only God knew where Morford was headed, but Lady Luck rode in the boat with him, and he landed at Dawson Creek just after Joe LaDue discovered the Klondike. The rest of the story I heard a few years later, how Morford staked some valuable claims and then, because he was a lawyer, LaDue appointed him manager of the townsite of Dawson City at a salary of one thousand dollars a month. So, going from rags to riches, he was able to return to Yakima with a sackful of gold nuggets and redeem all his property except his wife, who had got a divorce and married another lawyer.

Jim Ferrell, of course, had heard all the talk about the Klondike, with the result that he offered to grubstake me to the tune of five hundred dollars if I would join the gold rush. Once more, I held out my hand.

Although I knew nothing about gold rushes, I wasn't a tenderfoot, having lit in North Yakima in 1889 when it was still in Washington Territory. I knew every trout stream in Yakima County and all the best places to find brant, ducks, and geese. I was one of the first to navigate the Yakima River in a skiff and had the dubious distinction of firing the first smokeless powder ever fired in Yakima County. I doubt that the solid citizenry, those who kept their change in purses fastened with brass knobs, thought very highly of me, but my experience as a nimrod was more useful than the experience of a good many others who joined the Klondike rush.

When news of my grubstake got around, the poker-playing grocer offered to join me. His business was about to go on the rocks, and the gold rush looked as good to him as going broke in Yakima.

He had more money than I did, but neither of us had enough to finance what we were undertaking. We more or less knew that, but went anyway to Tacoma, where we assembled the kind of outfit we would have put together for an extended hunting expedition in the winter. We bought a lot of mackinaw[1] clothing, woolen underwear, blankets, gum boots, and other footwear. We also bought a 16-by-24-foot sidewall tent, which turned out to be the most useful thing we took with us.

We took steerage passage for Skagway on the steamer *Queen*, leaving Tacoma on August 21, 1897. The ship put in at Seattle, Port Townsend, and Victoria, picking up other adventurers, so she was loaded to the gunwales when we were finally under way. Our tickets entitled us to two bunks in the hold, where the bunks were arranged in tiers of three. Most of the way, the ship followed the Inside Passage, which

[1]Heavy, tightly woven wool material.—OSS.

was smooth as a mill pond; but when we crossed Queen Charlotte Sound, and the ship hit the Pacific swell, the effect on some of our fellow voyagers made us glad we had picked top bunks.

We steerage passengers ate at long tables set up in the hold, and the food was shot along in dishpans from one diner to another. The food was substantial, well-cooked, and palatable; the service was rough and ready, but we were not finicky.

The *Queen* stopped at Fort Wrangell, where we went ashore to look around. What we saw was rain, a forlorn village, many totem poles, and a camp of wet prospectors, with the carcass of a cub bear hung up in a tree.

We stopped next at Juneau, arriving about daylight. We walked uptown through the rain, and the only thing of interest we found was a poker game, which had been running all night. The players seemed to have plenty of money, with many hundred dollar bills in sight.

From Juneau, we went through Lynn Canal to Skagway, where the steamer anchored offshore. In the absence of a pier, lighters carried the passengers and freight ashore. We had trouble finding our outfit but eventually located all of it.

While we stood considering our first move, a stranger offered to give us a lot he had staked on the beach. We moved our outfit onto it and exercised squatter's rights for a short time until we moved elsewhere and abandoned the lot. Not long after that, another squatter sold the lot for five hundred dollars.

Skagway was a village of tents except for one large wooden building, which housed the Pack Train Saloon, a deadfall equipped with a long bar and a complete gambling casino, where every evening a full house of gamblers sought their fortunes at faro, roulette, blackjack, and chuck-a-luck.

We found out right away that we didn't have a bankroll big enough to take us to the Klondike. The Canadian Northwest Police had established customs houses and post

offices along both the Skagway and Dyea trails and would
let no one pass unless he had two thousand pounds of grub,
which was worth a dollar a pound at Lake Bennett or Lake
Linderman, where the voyage down the Yukon began.

When we learned that a so-called wagon road had been
cut through the timber to the foot of the Skagway trail, we
hired a man with a team and wagon to haul our outfit there.
We set up our tent and began buying outfits from discouraged adventurers who had found the trail too tough for
them. It was a gamble, because nobody knew how long the
gold rush would continue, but we took a chance.

The prices we paid were ridiculous. We paid seventy-five
cents for a sack of flour, provided it was dry and in a canvas
bag that cost thirty-five cents in Seattle. We bought hams,
bacon, beans, rice, tea, and coffee at comparable prices and
soon had our tent nearly full of such provender. We refused
to buy picks and shovels, but people gave us enough of them
to dig the Panama Canal.

One day a man showed up carrying a canvas bag of tea
and a dozen cans of beef extract. I felt the tea, found it dry,
and, mostly to hear him holler, offered him two dollars for
the tea and the extract. To my surprise, he snapped at the
offer, and when I gave him the money, away he went. The
tea weighed twenty-two pounds, and we sold it to a store in
Skagway for eleven dollars.

When we found out what our clients were up against, we
stopped wondering why they sold their stuff so cheaply. To
call the loblolly of water, mud, chuckholes, and tree stumps
a wagon road was rank flattery; and to call what took off
from it a trail was even more flattering. Compared to the
Skagway trail and the road, the pioneers who traveled the
Oregon Trail were on a boulevard.

I recall two young men who packed their outfits on their
backs in relays of about half a mile. They would accumulate
it at one station and then take off for the next. Whenever I
passed one of them, he wouldn't even speak to me, he was
so sore at the world and everybody in it. They relayed past

our tent and disappeared up the trail. A month later, they came dragging back empty-handed. Where they left their outfit, I don't know.

One popular means of transportation was an axle with a buggy wheel on each end. Two pieces of two-by-four, lashed across the axle, extended fore and aft, providing shafts for two men; and across these, they lashed their outfit in canvas bags. One man pushed and the other pulled the rig along the so-called wagon road. When a wheel hit a stump, which happened frequently, the rig would lurch, and the men were lucky if one of them didn't get knocked into a mudhole.

A story went the rounds about two preachers operating such a contraption. One became a victim of a lurch, and after he arose and clawed the mud out of his eyes and ears, he expressed his exasperation. "I have never sworn in my entire life," he declared, "but right now I want to say that this is the most unChristly, God damnedest country I have ever set foot in!"

Men's inhumanity to themselves, however, did not amount to shucks compared to what they did to horses. I have heard it said that more than five thousand horses were killed on the Skagway trail, and I can believe it. It was common to see a man beating a horse as the horse slipped, floundered, and fell on granite boulders as hard as the Rock of Gibraltar. If there is a hell, I hope horses are tending the fires to roast the men who treated them the way they were treated on the Skagway trail.

The ox was the only pack animal remotely suited to that trail. Oxen never got excited, as horses and mules did, and when an ox was dead, he was worth thirty cents a pound.

In the woods below our tent, a fellow named Ed Webster, whom I had known in Yakima, broke some steers to pack. When he had them trained, he contracted with the Canadian Northwest Police to move five thousand pounds of supplies to Lake Bennett. I know the weight because I got five dollars for serving as the neutral weigher, weighing the freight on a steelyard hung on a tree. Webster loaded the freight on his steers and packed it through in a single trip, for which he collected five thousand dollars. The last time I saw him, he was pooping off his hard-earned money in a dice game in the Pack Train Saloon.

Somebody once hired me to lead a packhorse loaded with baled hay for twelve miles along the trail. On my way, I passed many poor horses who had been abandoned to starve. When I came in sight of one of those derelicts, I could see him prick up his ears when he spied the hay. Though I knew I did wrong, I couldn't keep from slowing down as I passed and letting the poor fellow have a couple of mouthfuls of hay. That couldn't have helped him much, and it would have been more kindly to shoot him; but you didn't dare do that because if you did, some son of a bitch would show up and accuse you of killing a good animal. Then you might have to burn more ammunition to get out of the difficulty.

When I arrived at my destination with the hay-laden packhorse, I had to sit out in the rain and eat my supper from a frying pan. Then I tried to sleep in wet blankets. Next morning, my employer urged me to continue, but I had had enough of it and wouldn't have sloshed another twelve miles for his entire outfit and all his future prospects.

One day a man came along and wanted to sell his outfit, which he had loaded on a horse. We bought the outfit, and the seller offered to give us the horse, which we declined. But the man walked off, leaving the animal, and we were saddled instead of the horse.

At one time, he had been a pretty good horse, but now he was badly stove up. Not knowing what else to do, we built a brush corral on the bank of a creek and began feeding the horse hay and chop we had bought from a discouraged argonaut. The horse soon knew me by sight and would nicker whenever he saw me. His flattery made me attached to him, but then we ran out of feed. There was only one thing to do, but I didn't like the job; so I violated cowboy etiquette which requires every man to kill his own horse and gave an ex-prizefighter a dollar to shoot the animal. It took him three shots to kill the horse with a Colt's .44, and the sound of each shot felt to me like a kick in the belly.

A couple of days later, a bear found the carcass; and the next evening, while reading by candlelight, we heard a fusillade of shots from the direction of the dead horse and guessed that somebody had built a crows nest in a tree and had waylaid the bear.

I dressed, headed toward the scene of action, and on my way met a little Englishman named Harry Hampton, who was built like a Brownie and was toting a sourdough lantern with which he lighted our way.

When we arrived, we found the shooters sizing up the results of their marksmanship, which consisted only of some blood on the rocks. While we guessed about the amount of damage done to the bear, we heard a loud crashing in the brush across the creek, and everybody decided it was the wounded bear, returning for vengeance.

What a scattering then took place! Harry, with his lantern, took off like a bat out of hell. His short legs must have made a blur as he picked his feet up and laid them down. Now and then, he paused and turned the light of his lantern behind, which would give me clear sailing for a few feet. But in one of the intervals of darkness, I took a header over a boulder and decided I'd rather meet the bear than flounder around any further. It turned out that the noise in the brush was made by a belated arrival trying to find his way in the dark to the scene of the shooting. The bear was probably a mile away and going in high gear.

Early in October, it began to snow, and we could see that our outfit buying was finished. We had what we had bought hauled to Skagway and made a fair profit peddling it to the stores there. Then we invested $250 in a squatter's right to a lot, on which we set up a knock-down wooden house, which, for comfort, wasn't as good as our tent, although it looked more respectable.

We decided to open blackjack and poker games, on which we didn't do too badly until two Canadian cardsharps came along. One, named Cal, was tall and had a lantern jaw, with a mouth so full of gold crowns that it looked like a brass bedstead. The other was said to have been a participant in Riel's half-breed rebellion.

It didn't take them long to clean us out of what we had on the table, and when they left, I gave the deck of cards a deep study. It took me awhile to dope out how we had been taken, but I eventually found that the gentleman from Riel's had pricked all tens and face cards with some sort of sharp point, maybe a sliver of glass glued to a thumb nail. Playing blackjack in those days, the deal passed, and whenever Riel, who was an expert second dealer, came to a marked card, he held it for Cal. Every time Riel dealt, Cal would hold two cards that added to twenty.

When Riel didn't have the deal, they still did all right because they could see by the pricks when a hand added to twenty, when they would bet a chunk against the house. On a hand that came to less, they would bet only a quarter. It had more finesse, but their play was as deadly as a blackjack applied to the base of the skull. Subsequently, I saw Cal walking along Pioneer Square in Seattle and still wearing his brass bedstead, so I knew he had yet to meet the right guy to knock it out of his lantern jaw.

One day I came in and found my partner stuck up to his neck in a poker game,; and not only that, but he had been playing the check rack, which means that he had issued more checks than he had money to cash them. He was playing with five strangers, who looked as though they might not be able to see the humor in the situation.

When I arrived, my partner got up from his seat, took me to one side, and explained his problem. He also asked me to play his hand while he undertook a doubtful attempt to raise some money.

I discovered that he had been tightwadding it with only a few checks in front of him. I decided that if I was going to get killed, it had just as well be for a sheep as a lamb; so I took out a stack of yellow chips, each of which, with the proper gold reserve, would have been worth $12.50.

Pretty soon, I picked up a hand with which I beat a good one held by the player with the most chips. A little later, I gave the same treatment to two others, and when my partner returned—without the money—I was sitting pretty, with more money in the till than there were checks out against it. I have a sort of hunch, however, that if Lady Luck hadn't been with me and I hadn't held those top hands, my story might have ended right here.

We held on with our gambling enterprise, getting nicked a little here and a little there, hoping to make a scratch. Like most amateurs, however, we never succeeded in doing so. On New Year's Day of 1898, we sold our building to a man named Neece from Roseburg, Oregon, for one thousand dollars and a lady's gold watch. I can't remember what became of the watch nor did I ever hear how Neece made out on his investment.

From then on, it was financially pretty much touch and go, with most of the accent on the go. I staked some lots and had carpenters build cottonwood log cabins on them. The cabins were chinked with moss and had shingle roofs. My carpenter made a bedstead, table, and four chairs for each cabin, and I completed the furnishings with a sheet iron cookstove. The cabins appealed to prospects who had women with them, and I would let a cabin go when I could sell it at a profit of fifty dollars. When the boom flattened out, I thought I was stuck with the last one, since nearly every cabin in the woods had a "For Sale" sign on it. But my shingle roof lured a victim through the maze, and I never left his tail until I had landed him.

One day, I decided to take a look at Dyea, which was the place of entry for the experienced sourdoughs on their way to the Yukon. I crossed the bay in a steam launch and was impressed as soon as I landed by the lack of hoopla in Dyea, where everybody seemed to know what he was doing, in contrast to Skagway. I met a man I had known when he was Yakima Indian Reservation agent and found that he was now operating a fleet of bobsleds, hauling outfits over a snow road toward Chilcoot Pass.

I hooked a ride on one of his bobsleds, which took me to Sheep Camp, from where I hiked to the Scales at the foot of the pass. When I arrived there, it was nothing like what I had expected. Instead of frowning cliffs with a narrow gap between them, the Chilcoot was a smooth, snow-covered mountain, with a stairway cut in it, extending upward beyond my sight. On nearly every step there was a man with a pack on his back, slowly plodding toward the top.

Parallel to the stairway, I could see several breaks in the snow and wondered what they were until I saw what looked like a miniature snowstorm coming down the mountain. When it arrived at the bottom, a man emerged, evidently having slid on his back all the way from the top and now ready to take up another load.

The stairway was something I had no desire to tackle, even without a pack. But I was told that only the day before a Siwash had climbed it, carrying a canvas boat that weighed a hundred and forty pounds.

The Indian was as good as two Swedes I heard about on the Skagway trail, each of whom was said to make thirty dollars a day by carrying four fifty-pound sacks of flour in each load over the uncertain footing of a cut-off half a mile long and doing it without setting the load down.

The stories about the Siwash and the Swedes were hard for me to swallow, since I once undertook to carry a sixty-pound pack for twelve miles and thought I would die before I got to the end of it. After that, I swore they would have to chloroform me before they got pack straps on me again.

Although my trip to Chilcoot amounted to nothing more than a sightseeing trip, I was impressed enough with Dyea that my partner and I returned there about a week later, hoping to make a scratch of some kind. We met a man named S. C. Henton, whom I had known in Yakima, who turned out to be superintendent of the Dyea freight yards for the Pacific Coast Steamship Company. When I asked Henton if he had two jobs he could give a couple of hard-working guys, he studied a little and then said all he had was one job of checking freight at five dollars a day.

"Give that to my partner," I said. "Now, what have you got for me?"

"Not a thing that you would do."

"You don't know how bad I want a job," I replied.

He shrugged and said, all right, but all he had was a stevedore job, unloading scows at fifty cents an hour.

"Lead me to them," I said, and he led me to the beach where a gang of men were unloading lighters that had been brought in on a high tide from a steamship offshore and were then high and dry on the beach.

It had been a long time since I had bowed my back at anything like that kind of work, but I went at it and began wrestling boxes, barrels, crates, and bags. It wasn't long before every muscle in my body, with the possible exception of the one that underlay my scalp, was protesting and had me looking hopefully toward the bunkhouse where the stevedores slept.

When quitting time came, however, and I had gone to bed without supper, I found little relief. I had a bunk and plenty of blankets, but I couldn't find a soft spot anywhere. I tossed and tumbled all night, and next morning at six o'clock, I was hitting the collar again. I survived that day, slept better that night, and the work was easier on the third day. After that, my muscles began to behave, and I felt as though I could lift anything I could get under.

After awhile, I got promoted to a job as night watchman at eight dollars a day. I carried a six-shooter and maintained a patrol among the piles of freight out in the open on the beach. One night while walking along a row of piles that had been driven into the sand to make the beginning of a pier, I thought I heard footsteps behind me. I halted, but could hear nothing. Then, as soon as I went on, I could hear the crunching noises again. That was repeated several times, and I concluded that somebody was trying to sneak up on me.

I got my back against the next pile and unlimbered my artillery. After quite a wait, the crunching began once more, and I remained motionless. Finally my pursuer came close enough for me to make him out in the darkness, and he turned out to be a big billy goat with a long beard. Somebody had abandoned him, and the poor fellow seemed to be lonesome and seeking company.

As time went on, I could see the end of my job not far ahead. The Klondike rush was about over, the argonauts were pinching out, and the steamers with freight became fewer and fewer. Anyway, I had got a bellyful of Alaska.

One day, I saw smoke rising from a steamship coming into Skagway, and I decided to get going. After hustling to the bunkhouse, where I got my pack and distributed my blankets to my stevedore friends, I was kicking up the sand toward a rowboat, which was pulled up on the beach waiting for passengers. In my haste, I lost a mitten, which I painfully missed as I hung onto the gunwale of the skiff as it ferried me out to the old coastal steamer *Yukon* waiting offshore. The *Yukon* reminded me of the Sangamon River steamboat, which, according to Abraham Lincoln, had a six-foot boiler and a one-foot whistle, and every time the boat whistled, it stopped. While the *Yukon*'s whistle slowed her a trifle, she retained enough steam to get me to Skagway.

There, I found that the incoming steamer was the *Centennial*, due to leave for Tacoma that night. Although somebody told me she had been condemned by the maritime authorities, I was ready to sail in a cast-iron teakettle if there was any chance it would get me out of Alaska. Instead of taking the Inside Passage, the *Centennial* stood boldly out to sea. That saved both time and coal, which was all right with me.

One day in the passageway leading to my cabin, I detected the odor I had smelled around Chinese laundries, which indicated that a worshipper of the opium poppy was

making obeisance to his goddess and didn't have his cabin
door well chinked.

Another incident of the voyage was finding a cootie making buttonholes across my belly. I caught him, then lost
him, and he must have transferred to another passenger. He
was the only member of his tribe I met during my sojourn
in Alaska, where everybody was supposed to get lousy.

Although I didn't miss a meal during the rough passage,
the voyage was boring, and I was glad when the *Centennial*
turned into the Strait of Juan de Fuca between Vancouver
Island and the Olympic Penninsula. We traversed the sound,
and at last I went ashore on a wharf in Tacoma Bay.

Chapter 3

I Become a Grafter

Since I was nearly broke when I landed in Tacoma in April 1898, I had to find a job in a hurry and was lucky enough to run into an acquaintance from Yakima days who had got himself elected on the Populist ticket as auditor of Pierce County. He offered me a job figuring taxes on the night shift at three dollars a clatter, and I didn't delay about lighting on his payroll.

One night, while adding up the bad news for taxpayers, I heard some of my co-laborers talking about a medicine man operating on Pacific Avenue. To hear them tell it, he was a wonder and selling so much medicine that he had the undertakers scared.

The account aroused my curiosity, so the next afternoon I scouted around, and at the Donnelly Hotel, sure enough, I found Jim Ferrell. He was tickled to see me and not at all critical of the flop I had made with his grubstake. On the contrary, he gave me credit for steering him into the fat territory of the Northwest, where he had been cleaning up.

Jim was working with Dr. J. L. Berry, an M.D., who had starved out in general practice in a little town near San Jose, California. For years after that, he had sold Dr. Berry's Mineral Water Salts up and down the Pacific Coast. He was about fifty years old, stood six feet tall, and wore a long coal-black beard. Dressed in a Prince Albert and a silk hat, he was a sight to behold.

Jim and Berry had a show of three performers and were doing a big business with evening pitches in Tacoma. In the afternoons, Jim had nothing to do, and neither did I, since I was on the night shift, so we did a lot of walking together around the Tacoma waterfront.

Jim didn't think much of my job and said so, pretty much in these terms:

"Where do you think you're going to get, working for three dollars a day? Now this is virgin territory out here, and these rummies'll fall for anything. I've got some electric belts and a velvet suit old Doctor Sykes used to wear, and I'll stake you to them. Learn a spiel, and get yourself a banjo plunker, and you can make some real money working water-tank towns around here. All you need's a little nerve."

Jim tried hard, but he couldn't convince me. The thought of facing an audience scared me almost as much as it had when I was in grade school and pupils had to take part on Friday afternoons in what were called declamations. My horror at having to stand up and declaim was so great that I played hookey every Friday afternoon, and rawhide and rattan applied vigorously by my mother and my teachers had no effect except to raise welts.

But Jim kept up his argument. In his attempt to persuade me to become a faker, he brought forth his electric belts and old Dr. Sykes's suit, made of blue, purple, yellow, and plum-colored velvet and decorated with a couple of yards of gold lace.

It wasn't necessary for Jim to tell me that my job had no future. I knew he was right, but the job paid my room rent and board bill until I could find something better. However, Jim kept at it until finally I gave in and could have paraphrased what Agrippa said to St. Paul: "James! Thou hast persuaded me to become a grafter."

Jim put me in touch with a blackface comedian named Tom Murray. We went to Buckley, a little town about thirty miles east of Tacoma, where I got a "reader," as the grafters called a license. Then Tom blacked up and I put on the toreador suit. Standing up in an open hack, we rode around while Tom plunked his banjo. The ballyhoo attracted a small crowd to a street corner, where we lit our gasoline torch. After Tom had sung a couple of songs accompanied by his banjo, it was up to me to make my pitch.

If I live to be two hundred and eight, I'll never forget how I felt. My voice, coming from some unknown source, made a sound utterly alien to me. My legs vibrated like fiddle strings as I forced a little air over my vocal chords and molded the air into something sounding like words, with my tremolo stop pulled clear out and my mouth as dry as a powder horn.

Most spielers began with a story, and the less truth the story contained, the better, since it was a foundation for bigger lies. For no reason that I can remember, if indeed I had a reason, my opening contained the harmless statement that I had been born in Kentucky. After my blow-off, an old man came up to me and said that if I had been born in Kentucky, he had something to show me. I was pretty tame right then, so I let him lead me to a yard that was well lighted by an arc light on the corner.

The old man pointed at a tree and said, "Now, if you're from Kentucky, you tell me what that tree is."

I had one guess coming and made it as positively as I could summon the strength for. "It's a black haw," I declared.

The old man slapped me on the back, exclaiming, "By God, you're from Kentucky all right! If you weren't, you'd have never known the name of that tree."

I made two pitches in Buckley and two in Chehalis, with my biggest sale coming to eleven dollars. It surprises me now that I did as well as I did, for my sales talks must have been terrible and the belts I sold even worse. However, the intake didn't equal the outgo, so I folded and dragged back to Tacoma to take up tax figuring again, much to Jim's disgust.

After Jim and Dr. Berry had done all they could for the

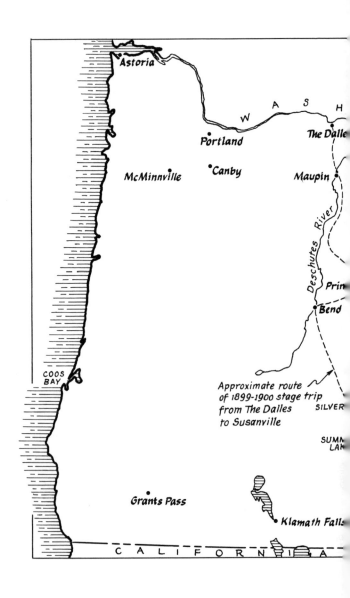

Astoria

W A S H

Portland

The Dalle

Canby

Maupin

McMinnville

Deschutes River

Prin

Bend

COOS
BAY

Approximate route
of 1899-1900 stage trip
from The Dalles
to Susanville

SILVER

SUMM
LA

Grants Pass

Klamath Falls

C A L I F O R N I A

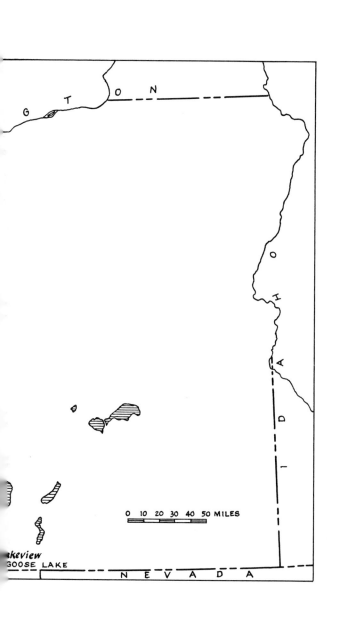

G   T   O   N

O

H

A

D

I

Lakeview
GOOSE LAKE

0 10 20 30 40 50 MILES

N E V A D A

health of Tacoma citizens, they moved to Portland. Not long after, Jim wired me a railroad ticket and said in an accompanying telegram that if I would join him, he would pay me twenty dollars a week and take a chance on what I could produce. I thought it over for awhile and decided that if Jim was willing to gamble, so was I.

As soon as I arrived in Portland, Jim insisted I put on one of his suits, which were modeled after what he thought Quakers wore. Then I tumbled to why Jim had been so anxious for me to join him: he was fed up playing "Injun" all by himself.

The reason for the getup was that the panaceas Jim and Berry were selling bore labels of the Quaker Medicine Company, an organization that owed its existence to Jim's imagination. The Quaker suit consisted of a long-tailed coat, a vest that buttoned on the side and came up to the throat, and barn-door trousers, topped off by a wide-brimmed, flat-crowned hat. All in Quaker gray, of course.

As a way of attracting attention, the suits and hats were wonders. I could pick Jim out three blocks away on a crowded street. Our getup also attracted the attention of wisecrackers, whom I ignored unless they got too personal. If one of them did get too personal, I blew back at him, and discovered that he would accept even a reflection on his birth. Some looked like tough customers, but they were always short on sand.

There were times when Jim tried to use the plain language of the Quakers, with its thee and thine, yea yea, and nay nay, but he generally made a mess of it, as he once did when he asked a performer, "Where is thou's baggage?" He accounted for such slips by explaining, "I have lived so long among the world's people that I have had much of my orthodoxy wore off of me."

As I have said, Berry was the originator of Mineral Water Salts, which were among the remedies he and Ferrell recommended for catarrh, which of course afflicted almost all tobacco smokers. The salts came in wooden boxes, each box said to contain the residue from the evaporation of forty gallons of water from a secret mineral spring in Mono County, California. When the lucky purchaser dissolved the salts in forty gallons of spring or well water according to the recipe printed on the box, he would have an elixir identical to that which he might have had if he had drunk directly from the secret spring.

The tale about the Quaker remedies was a little more complicated than the one about the Mineral Water Salts. In it, Jim spoke of a Botanical Garden, the site of which was a little indefinite. Sometimes it was in Bucks County, Pennsylvania, and at other times on the outskirts of Cincinnati. Wherever it was, it was supervised by "old Dr. Josiah Baker, a Quaker botanist one hundred and four years of age, as hale and hearty as the average man of forty." In his marvellous garden, Dr. Baker raised all the herbs, barks, leaves, gums, and berries from which the magical remedies were made. Among the reasons given for the remedies' efficacy was Dr. Baker's refusal to allow their components to be picked until they were ripe, some in the spring and some in the fall.

The main remedy was the Quaker Botanical Herbs, put up in three small cartons, contained in a larger box. By adding the contents of one of the cartons to eight ounces of alcohol, whiskey, or gin in a quart jar and then filling the jar with water, the fortunate patient would have a quart of medicine. The medicine tasted like hell, which attested to its strength, and if the patient took it according to directions, he would soon not be able to keep his bowels from moving to save his life.

Other remedies were a liniment known as Quaker Oil, a salve which was usually given away, and a soap "made from Mexican pinole, soap weed, soap bark, cottonseed and olive oils, and containing no animal fat whatsoever."

In Portland, Jim and Berry were working with three performers, Ed Young and Pat and Fanny Kelly. Before each pitch, they made a ballyhoo by riding on a dray along the downtown streets, with a portable organ playing and Pat in

Owen Tully Stratton at age thirty-one in 1899, dressed as the pur-
veyor of Quaker remedies.

Irish makeup, which consisted of a flat-crowned plug hat and a piece of sponge under his upper lip. They made most of their pitches at the corner of Sixth and Washington streets, where the Raleigh Building provided shade in the afternoons. The show consisted of songs by Fanny Kelly, what was called monkey-face Irish comedy by Pat, and slapstick comedies. There was always a good crowd.

Pat could dance a little and sang Irish songs such as "Oh, Mrs. Flaherty, what did you mean to do when you sat down on me hat? That was the hat me father wore, and if you were only a man, I would wipe the floor wid you."

In a mild soprano, Fanny sang popular ballads. She wore no paint and usually dressed in a shirtwaist and dark skirt.

Fanny didn't drink, but Pat did, and she was always trying to make him quit. Some years later, I ran across Pat in Portland and after I had bought him several drinks, he suggested, "Let's go up to the cabin and see the colleen."

The cabin was a couple of light housekeeping rooms. Fanny hugged me and then said, "I've got good news for you, Doc. Pat's quit drinkin'." When I laughed, she went on, "You needn't laugh. It's true. He hasn't drank for months." Right then, Pat was half loaded and winking at me furiously. They were fine people.

To go back to Portland in 1898, Jim didn't like afternoon pitches because the sales were small, but he made them because they maintained interest, and the ten-dollar-a-day license covered them as well as the evening pitches. I went with him, but all I did was stand around, posing, and handing out packages as they were sold. I knew I wasn't worth the twenty dollars that Jim paid me each week, but I didn't know what to do to earn it.

One day, when the dray drew up to the Hotel Perkins to take us off on the ballyhoo, Jim told me to go along with it and said he would meet us at Sixth and Washington and make the spiel.

When the dray arrived at the corner, the performers put on their usual show, toward the end of which, I began anxiously looking for Jim, who was nowhere in sight. When the show ended, I sat there on the dray, looking more and more like a damned fool. The performers were amused and the crowd seemed puzzled. I stood it as long as I could and then got to my feet and tried to imitate Jim and managed to make a small sale. As I floundered along, I saw Jim standing in the crowd with a grin on his face.

From then on, it became my job to make the afternoon pitches, at which I kept getting better and better until I made one of thirty-five dollars at the corner of Third and Morrison streets. Then Jim and Berry decided to organize another show and send me with it to Albina, a sawmill town across the Willamette River. With two performers, who were about as funny as a crutch, and some discarded paraphernalia, I opened on a platform built on a vacant lot.

In spite of being a rank novice with a rotten show, I drew good crowds, which may be hard to believe today. But it becomes understandable if you remember that I was making my pitches in Albina in 1898, the year Admiral Dewey won the battle of Manila Bay, when there were no automobiles, no movies, and no radio. There were saloons in Albina as well as variety shows and a music and beer hall, where a coon shouter named Dolline Cole was packing them in. But those joints were off limits for women and children, who flocked to my lot and did their best to find wisdom in my spiels and amusement in my show.

I began to make sales in Albina which were bigger than Jim's sales in Portland. That soon got to be too much for his ego, and one day, he said, "Here, you take the downtown show, and I'll go over to Albina tonight." Of course, I obeyed, but Jim doubled my salary.

Naturally, I was pleased, but I had sense enough to know I was still a tyro. You might think that my two years in pharmacy school and a year in medical college would have helped me, but I believe it was probably true that the less a spieler knew about basic sciences, the easier it was for him to talk language the patent-medicine buyers understood. They seemed to know just what Jim meant when he said, "The blood is the life of the flesh thereof. Without good blood, thee and thine can't have good health. But if you will take this wonderful blood purifier, which contains no mineral poisons whatsoever, it will clean and purify your blood and drive all the impurities out of your system."

If I had tried to make that statement, it would have thudded like a lead dollar. But Jim, in his ignorance of physiology, materia medica, and therapeutics, could make it ring like a twenty dollar gold piece. A listener, handicapped by advancing age, depressed spirits, and the inequities of society, knew just what Jim was talking about and would shell out for the remedy.

Consistency or, rather, the absence of it did not seem to matter at all. When Jim sold blood purifier, he condemned mineral poisons, and a few minutes later he would be extolling the virtues of mineral salts in the treatment of catarrh.

One evening, I made a pitch on the corner of Third and Burnside. Since the location was on the edge of the skid-road district, the crowds usually contained a few hecklers and drunks. They never bothered me much as long as they refrained from grabbing my legs, but when they did, I discouraged them with a hickory cane which I carried as an equalizer. On the evening I mentioned, I had finished a good sale, and the performers were ready to put on their slapstick, which always ended the show.

Just then, Jim, with his performers, arrived from Albina and drove through my crowd. He hopped out of his wagon, strutted to my dray, and climbed up on it. "Let me at 'em for a few minutes," he whispered.

"There they are," I replied. "Help yourself."

With that, Jim was off to a running start, went on for fifteen minutes, and then pitched his sale. While he "ginned" the crowd, the performers obediently canvassed them without making even one sale. When Jim saw that he was skunked, something that had never happened to him before, he hoarsely asked me, "What's the matter with them?"

"Nothing," I answered, "except that just before you got here I sold them fifty packages of herbs and a lot of other junk."

"Why the hell didn't you tell me?" he demanded to know.

"Why the hell didn't you ask me?" I replied.

He grinned, but ever afterward when I wanted to stop his bragging, I could always do it by asking, "Remember that swell pitch you made at Third and Burnside?"

We continued in Portland until along in September when the rainy season was approaching. Jim and Berry then decided to move to eastern Oregon. They got an old doctor to serve as my office man and sent me to La Grande while they went to Pendleton. I considered this my acid test to tell whether I could work alone or only as second fiddle to Jim. Up until then I suspected that I might be like one of two duck hunters entering a big marsh. He never saw the other hunter all day but felt as though he had company.

I made my first pitch on Thursday evening and took in about thirty-five dollars. On Friday I got fifty and on Saturday, nearly a hundred with two pitches. That almost convinced me that I had arrived, but Jim was still too close for me to feel sure. He didn't seem to have any doubts, however, because he raised my salary to fifty a week.

My sales continued good in La Grande, but the office was a blank. My doctor couldn't take a fee, and I didn't know enough to tell him how.[1] From La Grande, I jumped to Baker City, which was to be my last town in the open air. In Weiser, Idaho, I had my first experience working in a hall and didn't do very well. Then Jim told me to join Berry in Boise, where we worked in an opera house with four hundred seats and did a little better. After about a week of that,

[1] See chapter 4.—OSS.

Berry heard that the Wizard Oil Company had invaded the Willamette Valley, and we jumped there to head them off.

Business continued poor, and in the spring of 1899, I took Jim's hint that it would be all right if I worked alone. I tackled Canby, Oregon, a little town a few miles south of Portland, where I worked two weeks without a doctor and did better than when I was on salary.

Chapter 4

Some Fundamentals of the Medicine Show Game

Medicine sales were almost always greater on the street than on a lot or in a hall. A pitch on the street would halt a loiterer and keep him standing on his feet, which made him attentive. But let him sit down in comfort, and his mind would wander to all sorts of things besides the pitch. When we worked on lots, people would bring boxes to sit on; but we dealt with that by breaking up the boxes after each show, a tactic which quickly exhausted the town's supply.

We always made sure to have our platform well lighted. At first, we used gasoline torches, but they were sputtery and undependable. Eventually we discarded them for electric lights, on which we spared no expense.

People are generally more interested in what they perceive as the personality of a speaker than in what he says. If he speaks from a poorly lighted platform, he might as well have his speech canned and play it on a phonograph.

Another rule was not to have the platform too high. Distance may lend enchantment, but it doesn't make listeners more responsive. The greater the distance, the less the persuasion, which was why Jim, when he worked the give I have described, urged his audience to move up close to him.

I found that speaking in the open air night after night taxed my strength. I did, however, discover ways to conserve energy. Pronouncing vowels distinctly will make a speaker's voice carry and reduce the need to force it. Wearing a broad-brimmed hat will keep his voice from flying off into space and will help to keep him from talking louder than necessary.

There's a vast difference between oratory and selling. Most eloquent orators can't sell a thing. They may be able to soar "from the rockbound coasts of Maine to the golden sands of sunny California," but that kind of speaking will neither sell much medicine nor put across many ideas. Oratory may yank an emotional sinner to the mourners' bench, but it will put very little into the contribution box.

Before a high-pitch salesman can become a success, he has to know when he has made his "joint." He must not make his sale before his prospects are ready nor delay it beyond that point. There is such a thing as talking a potential customer out of making a purchase.

No sailing eagle scans the earth more closely for a jackrabbit than the spieler watches the changing expressions of his crowd. When his extra sense tells him that his joint is made, then he gathers in his sheaves. And there really is something—call it telepathy, magnetism, or what you will—that tells a good pitchman when he has made his joint and tells him as clearly as if his prospects had shouted it to him.

Another rule of the medicine game was, "Tell it to them. Tell it to them again. Tell it to them until the telephone and telegraph poles know it by heart. Then you'll start doing business."

Now that's all right as far as it goes. Every successful spieler stereotypes to some extent, but if he depends too much on a set spiel, he handicaps himself. He should have several lines of approach and be able to ad-lib when necessary.

Berry was a rigid stereotyper. When anything unusual occurred, like a dogfight in his crowd, he had to begin all over again.

Sometimes when I was feeling a little cocky and not too worried about making a big sale, I experimented with repetition. I would select a member of the crowd who looked like he might be tough to convince, and I'd direct my spiel right at him. The next evening if he appeared, I'd do the same thing with the identical spiel. Time and again, I have talked the snarl off such a man's face and watched him buy a package of herbs.

To keep order in our crowds, we hired a policeman when we could get one. It was easy money, and if there were several on the force, the chief usually rotated them. While I was working in Albina, Mrs. Berry always asked me on my return from the lot, "Did you sell your policeman tonight?" And mostly I had done so, mainly I think because he had to stay there, and while he was there, he usually had nothing to do but listen.

To get that kind of attention, we used what was called "the stall." When we made long stands, we often had trouble holding our crowds. We changed the program each evening, but the audience soon learned the sequence of entertainment and spiel. They would stick for the show, then sidestep the sale.

We had a variety of stalls, one of which was to start an announcement while remaining seated and then go right into the spiel without getting up. Another was to halt a performer in the middle of his act and while he stood at attention, deliver the spiel.

In Huron, South Dakota, we had an Irish policeman who gave away my stall. He was trying to earn his money, and when he thought it was time for the sale, he'd spread his arms and address the crowd. "Everybody keep still," he would say. "The doctor's goin' to talk." That tickled the crowd, so I never corrected him.

You couldn't blame people for avoiding the sale. It was pretty repetitive, and after they'd heard it a few times, it got boring. One evening in Lead, South Dakota, I heard a little girl tell her companion, "The show's all right, but I don't like the preachin'."

With medicine shows, as with lifeboats, women and children came first. We needed the men, of course. They usually had the money and could be landed on the spot. But in order to succeed, we had to attract the women and children. For that reason, we insisted that our performers avoid anything the least suggestive of dirt. The horselaugh of an oaf who thought he had detected something off color was deadly.

Of course, children could be a nuisance with their loud talk, pinching, pulling, and chasing each other through the crowd. I remember one of Jim's more touching appeals, which went something like this:

"You parents should never punish your little ones when they are cross, crying, and fretful. It is natural for them to be happy and playful like the little lambs on the hillside."

Then Jim roared in a voice like thunder, "Here! Here! If you boys down there don't stop that noise, I'll break your necks!"

In dulcet tones, he continued, "The dear little children! Maybe the reason why they are sometimes cross and fretful is that they are afflicted with hypo-headed, monster parasites, known as ascarades or stomach worms." Here, he held up a bottle filled with worms. "And you should give them some of our wonderful medicine to make them happy again."

Around the turn of the century, a good many people had tapeworms, and a good many more thought they might have them. Tapeworms were especially prevalent among foreigners, possibly because they were given to the consumption of raw foods and were careless about their supply.

Some said that there were different types of tapeworms— beef, mutton, fish, etc.—but they all looked alike to me. They varied in length from a few feet to several yards. I remember one tapeworm that we took from a woman in Grant's Pass, Oregon, that filled a pint fruit jar to the top and made a fine display.

Some grafters faked the taking of tapeworms. This they did by giving the patient a drastic purgative and "ringing" a tapeworm into the slop jar. During an interlude in the patient's agony, he would discover the tapeworm and cry the equivalent of "land ho!" as he pointed into the slop jar.

Neither I nor any of my associates ever attempted such ringing. We didn't think it was cricket and classified it with the use of boosters. Besides, and more important, it wasn't necessary.

When we separated a host from the host's unwanted visitor, we always had a jump in sales. In Lead, South Dakota, we captured tapeworms from members of just about every Balkan nationality, from Albanians to Serbians. When one of them expelled a tapeworm, he would put it in a tin can and carry it to our office for inspection and to be sure that he had the head, which it was necessary to capture or the worm would grow again. If the capture was complete, we exhibited the worm that evening to the gaping multitude, giving the patient's name and address. Then we landed every member of the patient's nationality who was on our lot.

I soon learned that the office was the most productive part of our business. That was contrary to appearances because the medicine sales were spectacular with the hullabaloo created by the spieler and the cries of "Sold out, Doctor!" by the performers canvassing the crowd when the joint was made. But a sale seldom exceeded two hundred dollars.

The real importance of the sale was its relation to the office. With each package of herbs went a card, entitling the holder to a physical examination if presented at the office between 10:00 A.M. and noon on any day except Sunday. In the office, the cardholder found a physician registered to practice in the state in which we were operating.

During the sale, we always emphasized that the examination tickets were included with the purchase to make sure that the medicine was what the purchaser needed. Should it be found that the medicine was unsuited to the ailment, the purchaser's money would be returned.

We blew up the importance of the examinations the way

the modern disease societies blow up the importance of the checkup. We told them something like this:

"The ticket enclosed with the herbs entitles the holder to a full, complete, and scientific examination performed by a qualified physician. When he has completed his examination, he will explain his diagnosis in words you can understand. Furthermore, he will locate your trouble be it no bigger than a pinhead, and he will do it without asking you a single question. If he fails to do that, he will make you a present of the finest suit of clothes or, if you are a lady, the finest silk dress that can be purchased in your city; and I want you to make him live up to that obligation. But I know he will not fail! He has a marvellous, uncanny ability acquired from making thousands of examinations in almost every state of the union, and this is a rare opportunity of which you should take full advantage and at no cost to you!"

Naturally, the proposal to make a diagnosis without asking a single question proved of intriguing interest to local physicians. But it was easy when you knew how. Dr. Berry did it by making a hasty inspection for obvious pathology and if he found none, reciting the following rigamarole:

"The whites of your eyes are a little yellow, showing a sluggish condition of your liver. In your nasal tract I find evidence of catarrh, which affects your throat and produces a pharyngitis. Your tongue is coated, which denotes faulty elimination. While your bowels may act each day, the evacuation is not complete, as it would be if you were normal.

"Your lungs are all right, and your heart shows no organic disease. But it has a slightly irregular rhythm, due to a nervous imbalance which should be corrected at once.

"Your liver is slightly enlarged, and you no doubt have occasional indigestion manifested by gas, bloating, or eructations of sour food, which may lead to ulcer of your stomach or duodenum. You see, you're tender in the region of your stomach." Here, Berry would poke the patient with an index finger that had the rigidity of a billiard cue and could not fail to find tenderness. "Your stomach problem should have proper treatment.

"While all this is important, your main trouble is that sometime in the past—it may have happened years ago or only recently—you have had an injury to your back. It may have come from lifting, from a blow, or from a jerk or strain. But whatever it was, it damaged your sacral plexus of nerves.

"Now this sacral plexus functions as the governor of your urinary and sexual organs, and its injury may produce a multiplicity of symptoms based on the one cause. Of course, the medicine you have bought should help you, but what you need is a special treatment before you can expect to be entirely well."

The diagnosis varied to fit the patient, but its tenor was about the same from one patient to another. It usually left the patient confused about everything except the back injury, which almost everyone could remember having suffered. Most accepted Berry's identification of the back problem as evidence of great diagnostic skill.

Once, however, in McMinnville, Oregon, a skeptic applied a test. When he first appeared, he wore a full beard while he listened to Berry recite his diagnosis. Then, when Berry dismissed him, the patient went to a barbershop where he had himself shaved as slick as a peeled onion. With another ticket, he returned for a second examination.

Berry didn't recognize him but repeated his former diagnostic statement almost word for word. That transformed the skeptic into an enthusiastic booster, who related his experience all over town.

Although Berry's method saved time, it was not so good for a patient who had a real ailment. Later, I worked with physicians who stripped their patients and went over them with the equivalent of a fine-tooth comb, requiring all of them to submit to a rectal examination and, if a woman, to a gynecological examination. If they refused, they were sent on their way.

In making a thorough examination, the physicians discovered many easily relieved minor ailments, which had been overlooked in slipshod examinations by other examiners. Relief of such ailments produced much gratitude as well as money.

Although some examiners would accept fees in hopeless cases, we never did so. Occasionally, we would undertake to treat a borderline case and then, in order to create talk, refund the fee.

Once in a South Dakota town, my examiner took on a patient with dropsy and collected a substantial fee. While I didn't know enough to hurt me, I was certain the symptom indicated a serious condition, and I insisted that the examiner return the fee. He didn't want to do it, but finally gave in. However, when he attempted the refund, the patient rebelled because he was sure he was getting better. A compromise was made. The guarantee was withdrawn, half the fee returned, and the treatment continued. Before we left town, the patient's dropsy had disappeared, and he thought he was cured. For quite awhile after that, I had to listen to yelps from the physician about the refund; but I was better satisfied, although short some money.

This physician took big fees and would quote odd amounts like $72.50, $112.60, and $234.75, which he laboriously calculated on a piece of paper. When he had figured the fee to the last penny, some prospects would depart, never to return, but enough of them came back to make it pay.

One patient the doctor thought he had lost unexpectedly returned and pulled out a sheaf of bills. The doctor tried to recall the fee he had quoted but was unable to do so. The patient, while counting down his money on a table, halted and asked, "How much did you say the fee was, doctor?"

The doctor, who could see that the patient still had money in his hand, replied, "You know damned well how much I said. Just keep on counting." The patient, smiling, then counted out the rest of the money.

Our proposal to make a diagnosis without asking questions sometimes prompted local doctors to send in a stool pigeon to find out how it was done. But this same physician who quoted the odd fees seemed to be gifted with second sight which enabled him to recognize such a bird as soon as he fluttered into the office. The doctor then gave the fake patient the works. When he came to the rectal examination, the physician would insert a bivalve speculum and, in spite of the subject's groans and protestations, stretch his sphincters until they would almost admit a team and wagon. After the victim had departed with flushed face and elevated blood pressure, the physician would say, "I'll bet that son of a bitch won't have much to tell when he gets back to the gang waiting in the drugstore."

There were a lot of angles to working the office. One was the guarantee, which stripped to its essence, was nothing except an agreement to provide enough medicine to effect a cure, with the patient paying carriage charges on the shipments. We lived up to it and sent medicine until the patient agreed that he or she was cured or had lost a taste for the medicine. No doubt, others beside the original patient were cured of whatever ailed them, and, in that way, we effected cures for which we were not paid.

One office trick I considered the equal of a trout fly which I named Lynch's Assassinator after its originator, Digby Lynch. At the end of an examination of a patient who seemed to have nothing the matter except a hyperactive imagination, the examiner would say, "It would be an easy matter to cure you if the indicated treatment wasn't so expensive. But you can't afford it; so there's no need to discuss it further." The examiner would then open the office door in dismissal. If the trick worked, the patient would demand to know how much the treatment would cost. The examiner would state the fee and say, "See, it's much too expensive for you." It was surprising how many returned with the fee, partly to show how badly the examiner had underestimated their financial status.

When we boosted the office while making sales, we always tried to capitalize on the animosity of local medicos. Occasionally, one would be asinine enough to shoot off his mouth, and, when we heard of that, we would take his hide off and tack it on the barn. In towns where the local doctors were too canny to criticize us publicly, we would roast an imaginary one. That would please the knotheads and deadbeats, as the best of physicians have their enemies.

When our office business dragged, we could often revive it by waving diplomas and certificates and challenging the local doctors to a competitive examination. The challenge made no sense, and nobody ever took us up on it, but it impressed the knotheads.

One time when I was working Fort Jones, California, I tested the effect of diploma flaunting. Fort Jones was a small town, and our main reason for being there was to work the kinks out of a new show we had organized, rather like opening in Philadelphia. We hadn't done much business with our sales, and our office take was worse.

The night before we intended to close the town, I sat on the platform watching the crowd. A man wearing a plug hat was circulating through the audience and visiting with the members, who seemed to be amused by what he said. I pegged him to be the local physician, wearing the plug hat as part of his insignia of office in the Masonic Lodge which met that evening.

I judged that he was panning us, and that made me sore; so I sent one of the performers for the tube containing our doctor's credentials. While making my spiel, I waved the documents and blasted all doctors except ours, domestic and foreign, past and present, while the audience listened attentively.

The next day our office was jammed with patients, far more than had appeared all week, which convinced me that the stunt was a good one, although I had never thought so before.

Chapter 5

Ups and Downs with Dr. Park—We Work Montana

Not long after I started working on my own in the spring of 1899, I met Dr. Berry in Portland, where he introduced me to a Dr. Park, who was willing to team up with me. Park was about sixty years old, big and portly, with keen blue eyes, thick curly gray hair, and a limp which compelled him to walk with a cane. Dressed in a broad-brimmed hat, a gray suit, a snowy shirt with a pleated bosom, and polished black Congress gaiters, he looked like a substantial gentleman of the old school.

We went down to Astoria at the mouth of the Columbia and didn't do too badly there. Then, with our performers, we boarded the coastal steamer *Alliance* for Eureka, California. The boat pulled into Coos Bay and moored at Marshfield, Oregon, for a day. The town looked dead, but I made two pitches while Dr. Park worked the office, and we took in more than a hundred dollars.

When we got to Eureka we found Dr. Sykes, the original owner of the velvet suit, and Anderson, the dentist who had come west with Ferrell. They were pulling teeth and selling snake oil and weren't happy about our arrival. So we moved on to Ferndale in the Eel River Valley.

We made expenses there, but that was about all. We closed after three weeks, returned to Eureka, and took passage on the steamer *Pomona* for San Francisco. We stayed there briefly at the Golden West Hotel, then jumped to Grass Valley.

Grass Valley was an old placer camp that had switched over to quartz mining. The streets were narrow and winding, presumably following the original burro tracks made in the days of '49. The hotel where we stayed was built on a lot too short to permit a veranda, so the guests lounged on the wide board sidewalk in front.

On the afternoon of our arrival, I sat on the sidewalk in one of the chairs the hotel provided. Almost immediately, a stranger sat down in the chair next to me and introduced himself. He seemed to be a native and was extraordinarily friendly. After visiting for awhile, he left, and the chair was shortly occupied by another friendly citizen. After he departed, a third visitor sat down, and then a fourth came along.

They spread it on with a shovel as though they had never before met anyone as wonderful as I. Their cordiality didn't ring true, as I was frankly a medicine man, accustomed to being regarded with a degree of hostility by the home guard.

As I tried to figure out what was going on, my first acquaintance returned and invited me to have a drink. I declined, saying I didn't drink, which was a lie. Then he asked me to have a cigar, and I said I didn't smoke, which was another lie. Then he suggested that I go with him down the street to a place where he would show me some wonderful high-grade quartz gold specimens. The only gold specimens that interested me had milled edges, but I didn't want to seem too ornery, so I consented to take a look.

Down the street we went, and before I realized where my guide was taking me, we were in a saloon, which appeared to be crowded with friendly strangers, to whom my guide introduced me.

We seemed to have entered the saloon in the midst of an argument based on the declaration of one man that he could guess within three pounds the correct weight of any three men in the house. Some thought he could do it; others were sure he couldn't; and they were backing their beliefs with a lot of money, which they handed to the bartender, who served as stakeholder and referee.

When the money was all put up, the bartender designated the three men whose weights were to be estimated, and, of course, I was one of them. When the estimator had carefully hefted the other two and had recorded his estimates on a sheet of paper, he turned to me. He asked me to take off my long-tailed coat, and when I had done that, he stepped back to estimate the weight of the bone and muscle in my carcass and, as I afterward concluded, the weight of the ivory in my head. Then he had me stand behind him and put my arms over his shoulders so that he could heft me. He took me by the wrists and hoisted me from the floor, and while I was thus suspended, some husky accomplice took me across my rear elevation with a barrel stave hard enough to nearly knock my back teeth loose.

When the estimator let me back down to the floor, his accomplice presented the barrel stave to my view. In spite of my state of dazed confusion and the roars of laughter from the crowd, I could make out that the stave bore the painted words, "IT IS YOUR TREAT." With that, I agreed and was immediately separated from a gold specimen in the shape of a ten dollar gold piece, which helped to quench the thirst of many thirsty spectators.

I accepted my humiliation with the best grace I could muster and afterward, got a little run for my money. During the balance of my stay in Grass Valley, almost every day a messenger would race to the hotel and announce, "Hurry up, Doc! Get there quick! We're goin' to weigh a guy!"

In spite of my admission to the inner guard, Grass Valley turned out to be a bloomer. So we closed and went back to San Francisco to regroup. There Dr. Park introduced me to his dominating weakness by showing me how drunk he could get.

I have described his impressive appearance, but now he sat in my hotel room, drunk, broke, dirty, smeared with tobacco juice, and with an attack of katzenjammers coming on.

Gus Leonard, our Dutch comedian, was lifting tapeworm bottles out of a case and examining them as though he hadn't seen them a hundred times before. Before long he got a rise out of Dr. Park. "Gus, I wish you would leave those tapeworms alone. I can damned near see them without your lifting them out of the case."

Park then turned to me. "Boy, loan me ten dollars."

"Nothing doing."

"Then loan me five."

When I made the same answer he reduced the amount to three dollars, then two, then one. Finding me still adamant, he exploded, "Then, Goddamit, buy a drink!"

I wouldn't even go for that, although I could have used one myself. This was the first time in my life when a drunk had knocked the props out from under me, and, with my bankroll as slender as it was, San Francisco was about the last place I would have picked for such a predicament.

Unable to think of anything else to do, I wired Dr. Berry. Jim was in Honolulu, but Berry wired back, asking me to join him in Portland where he was organizing a new company to work in Spokane.

I went to Portland, where Berry hired the actors, engaged an office man, and sent me with them to Spokane, where he would join us later. The office man, an M.D. registered in Washington, had one of the handsomest seal-brown beards I ever saw and, when rigged out in a Prince Albert and a glossy silk hat, was a sight for sore eyes. But that was the only ailment he was good for. He was an absolute flop and couldn't take a fee unless the patient knocked him down and shoved it into his pocket.

Before long, Berry joined me, and we worked Spokane without doing much business. Berry then decided to move to Rossland, British Columbia. There, we had to depend entirely on sales, since Berry wasn't registered in British

Columbia. Fortunately, our sales were sizeable since Rossland was enjoying a mining boom based on the War Eagle and La Roi gold mines.

The Rossland police were different from any that I'd had anything to do with in the United States. When I took out our street license, I asked the chief of police where we should work. He pointed to a prominent corner on which stood a hotel. I was sure our crowds would block the hotel entrance and said so. "Well, you've got your license, haven't you?" the chief responded. "You work there, and if anybody kicks, send them to me."

One day as I entered the lobby of our hotel, I found a moocher passing the hat. He had lost his legs at the hip and traveled on a leather pad mounted on rollers which he propelled with his hands. He was drunk as a lord, and when he tackled me, I refused to contribute. Then he cursed me as I had never heard anyone cursed before. All I could do was walk away, but the desk clerk went to the door and called a policeman.

The officer looked in, then had a delivery wagon from a nearby grocery backed up to the curb. When the wagon was in place, the policeman came into the lobby, grabbed the moocher by the collar and hauled him outside, where he threw him into the wagon and had him hauled off to jail.

In Rossland, when you ordered a drink, the bartender set out a bottle of whiskey, along with a highball glass and a siphon of soda water. The thought occurred to me that Dr. Park would quickly have broken them of doing that because he would have shoved the siphon to one side and filled his glass to the brim with whiskey.

Although our sales in Rossland were big and the Canadian one- and two-dollar bills looked imposing, the overhead was too great without our office. So we closed and beat it back to Spokane, where Jim joined us from Honolulu. He and Berry went into a huddle and decided to tackle Montana with two companies.

With him from Honolulu, Jim had brought two performers, known as the Armond brothers. They were assigned to me, but I had no office man and didn't want a dub. I knew that Dr. Park was good if I could keep him sober, so I began to burn the telegraph wires to San Francisco, trying to locate him. I finally did so and, when he agreed to come, wired him transportation.

Jim and Berry then left for Butte, leaving me to come on to Anaconda, if and when Dr. Park arrived. He came all right, but it was easy to see that he was in the aftermath of a drunk.

Before getting on the train in Spokane, I bought a bottle of whiskey but kept it hidden until I judged that Park had reached the edge of Katzenjammerville. Then I brought out the bottle of whiskey.

My, how Park's eyes snapped! He would have emptied the bottle at one go if I had let him, but I doled it out in homeopathic doses. Park had to go to Helena, the state capital, in order to get registered in Montana, and by the time we reached the point where he had to change trains, my homeopathic treatment had him almost on an even keel.

Before he left me and my performers, I gave him enough money to pay his registration fee and to cover his expenses in Helena and back to Anaconda. I also added the warning that if he spent any of the money on whiskey, he could just keep on going, as I would never want to see him again.

Park was due in Anaconda on a Sunday, and Jim, who had never seen Park, came over from Butte in order to meet him. I wasn't at all sure that he would show up, and when the train was due, Jim and I sat in my hotel room, hoping for the best and looking out the window at a cold rain falling. Then we heard the clop, clop, clop of a horse's feet on the pavement and the rattle of what we assumed to be a cab.

In a few minutes, there came a soft knock on the door. When I opened it, there stood the landlady, with Dr. Park gently weaving by her side. He was soaked to the gills, but he held out his hand to me and said, "Just as I promised you, my boy, I didn't take a single drink." Which, of course,

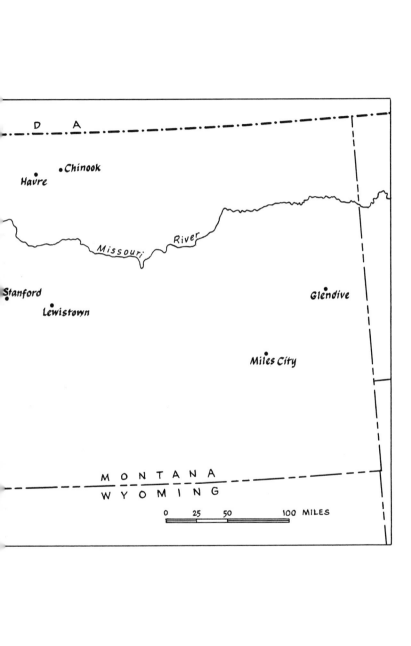

was literally true, since it must have taken at least twenty-five drinks to get him into the shape he was in.

I thought Jim would have hysterics as he rolled on my bed, but I had a hard time seeing the humor in the situation because it was up to me to get Park sober. I did so, however, and he stayed on the wagon during the rest of our season in Montana.

Jim made the first pitch in Anaconda with such success that I would have had a hard time equaling him during the ensuing four weeks, even if my old nemesis, acute appendicitis, hadn't caught up with me.

I had my first bout with appendicitis when I was seventeen, and the doctor to whom I went prescribed a dose of epsom salts. The salts did the job, and I took them when I had subsequent attacks. Now, I would as soon give a patient with appendicitis a stick of giant powder with a lighted fuse as I would a dose of epsom salts.

My attack in Anaconda was a beaner, and today, if I had a patient with my symptoms, I would be flipping my death certificates. Afterward, Dr. Park acknowledged that he had given me up, but that outcome never occurred to me as a possibility. I am now certain that I had an abscess which ruptured and drained into a gut instead of into my general peritoneal cavity. I will make a bet that I haven't an appendix, since I never had an attack after the one in Anaconda.

Jim had to pinch hit for me several times, but I wasn't sidelined for long, although at first I worked considerably bent over.

Dr. Park had no use for Jim, largely, I think, because of one of Jim's grandstand plays. When he saw Park entering the crowd during one of his spiels, Jim interrupted himself and called out, "Open up there, brothers and sisters! Here comes the grand old doctor! Open up, please!"

The crowd respectfully separated, leaving an aisle through which Dr. Park limped, his face turning scarlet. When I reached down and helped him up onto the dray, he whispered to me, "The God-damned son of a bitch!"

We stayed in Anaconda for only four weeks, which I later realized was too short a time. I was a slow starter but a good finisher, unlike Jim, whose first pitch might be his biggest. As he went along, his contradictions became too apparent.

We jumped to Great Falls, a considerable Montana town east of the continental divide, and opened on a lot with our two performers.[1] The elder of the two Armond brothers was a comedian who could fake accompaniments on an organ while the younger, in a splendid baritone, sang ballads and other songs. He knew so many songs that I never saw him stumped when a member of the crowd asked if he knew a particular one. It was evident that our show made a hit because the local variety theater had no customers until our show closed each evening.

Dr. Park and I stopped at the Great Falls Hotel, which was run by Will Clark, who was then about forty years old. He wore long hair and a moustache and Van Dyke and looked like Buffalo Bill. He was supposed to have a rich father who lived in Helena, and he once told me that he had never earned a dollar in his life.

He was an inveterate gambler and was always after me to play cards during the daytime when I loafed around the barroom which served as the lobby of his hotel. I got to playing seven-up with him at five dollars a game, and the honors were about even until, one night after the show, Clark got me into a poker game with him and several other players and I lost sixty-five dollars.

The next afternoon, as Dr. Park and I took our usual walk, he turned to me and asked, "Gambling last night, were you, young fellow?" I acknowledged that I had been and asked him how he knew. "Clark told me," he replied. "You better leave those sharks alone or they'll take all your money."

That evening I sat again in the poker game, and that time

[1] The first entry in the leather-bound notebook described in the Editor's Foreword is headed "Great Falls 8/13/99."—OSS.

I won all the money and a stack of yellow checks Clark couldn't cash. As a result, I took the receipts of both the hotel and the bar for the next few days.[2]

The day after that game when Park and I took our walk, I asked, "Did Clark tell you anything about me today?"

"No. Why?" The old man looked startled. "Have you been gambling again?"

"Yes," I said, "and when we get back to the hotel, you ought to ask Clark why he didn't tell you about it."

In Great Falls, I was on salary, and Park got half the office receipts. He imagined that the medicine sales came to more than they did and proposed that we form a partnership and work independently. I took it up with Jim and Berry, and they had no objection. So Dr. Park and I decided to tackle Lewistown on our own.

To get from Great Falls to Lewistown, a place just about in the center of Montana, we had to take Concord stage-coaches for a hundred and twenty miles on a route that went through Fort Benton and then bent southeast to Lewistown. We moved right along because they changed horses every ten miles or so. I had heard that there was good prairie chicken shooting around a stage station called Stanford; so I bought a secondhand shotgun, and the two performers and I stopped off to hunt. All we found, however, were groundhogs and rattlesnakes, so we soon went on to Lewistown.

When we arrived in Lewistown about five o'clock in the morning, the driver woke us up by banging the top of the

[2] In October 1949, my father wrote, "I think I was a pretty good poker player, an art I had learned the hard way. I could soon size up a player and tell whether he was inclined to call. If he was, I would let him catch me in a bluff and then break him when I could beat his hand. I could lay down when I thought I was beaten and have laid down four kings and four deuces. But that was when I was playing against tyros who tipped off that they had hell in their hands. Uncle Singleton never tried to teach me poker, but I learned a lot from watching him. He used to ask me to go easy on some of the players in our game, but my reply was that they could quit if they didn't like it."—OSS.

stagecoach with the butt of his whip and damned near scaring me to death. We signed into the hotel, and at breakfast, Park, who had gone on ahead while the Armonds and I stopped at Stanford, gave me some bad news to the effect that the town council intended to meet that evening and pass an ordinance that would keep us from operating. They had received news of us from Great Falls, and the home guard had rallied to protect their reserves.

Right after breakfast, I went to the city clerk's office and applied for a license. The clerk was an old man with a long gray beard who looked the way Moses must have looked when he smote the rock. When I told him what I wanted, the old boy seemed startled, probably because he wasn't expecting me so soon; but he issued the license.

The council met that evening as scheduled and passed a hold-up ordinance, which raised the license fee to a hundred dollars. I paid no attention to it, but a few days later the city marshal sidled up to me and said, "Doc, you'll have to take out that new license."

"Oh, no, I don't," I answered. "I've got all the license I need."

"But you haven't taken out the new one."

"I know that, and you'll be older than Methuselah before I do take it out."

"Well, if you work any more without it, I'll have to arrest you."

"If anybody's willing to buy, I'm going to sell. And do it without that damned license. And I'll tell you another thing: if you monkey with me, I'll make this town jump through a hoop."

I had them, and they knew it because Montana had a law that compelled us to take out a county license and specifically prohibited any incorporated town from charging more than that amount for a city license.

Occasionally we ran into an attempted hold-up like the one tried in Lewistown. One time in Everett, Washington, Jim Ferrell wasn't as lucky as I was in Lewistown. The locals in Everett tried to hold him up, and when he worked without paying, they arrested him and Pat Kelly, the Irish comedian, and locked them up. Jim had plenty of money but refused to put up bail because he wanted fast action through habeas corpus procedure, which couldn't be used if he was out on bond.

Jim and Pat were in the same cell, and Pat was plenty sore. "God damn it!" he wailed. "I didn't join this show to get thrown in jail! All I agreed to do was Irish comedy!"

"Well, why the hell don't you quit, then?" Jim replied.

Pat, being a true son of the old sod, saw the humor in the situation and stopped his bellyaching. Anyway, they were soon out on a writ of habeas corpus.

When we were sure of our ground, we welcomed a license fight. It gave us a chance to capitalize on injustice by roasting somebody, and the people were always with us because they wanted our free show. Local doctors and druggists were ill advised to start anything with us because we couldn't possibly land all the ailing, and our constant suggestions that people suffered from ill health must have put a good deal of barley into the local medicos' soup.

Once our license difficulty was out of the way, we found Lewistown to be a typical frontier town, dispensing the usual Montana friendliness and hospitality. I got to know a good many of the local citizens, and among them was one named Bill Denton, whom I will never forget. Bill liked our show, and each evening before it started, he hitched a team of mules to a three-seated hack and picked up a crowd of younger boys and girls. With his hack loaded, he would drive around town and then, before going to the show, pull up in front of a store. There, he would turn around and ask his little passengers, "What do we want?"

In a chorus, they would yell, "Candy!" After Bill supplied their want, off they would go to our show.

In Lewistown, we made our usual to-do about our ability to take tapeworms. Bill Denton learned that a saloonkeeper called Frenchy had a tapeworm but was shy about coming to us for relief. One evening while he was the only customer in Frenchy's saloon, Bill brought up the subject of tapeworms and our ability to remove them.

"How do you suppose they do that, Bill?" Frenchy asked.

"They use a tapeworm trap," Bill answered. "I think I might be able to borrow it from them if you want to try it."

Frenchy did want to try it; so the next day Bill went to the office of a Dr. Lindsey and asked if he could look at Lindsey's instruments, which were laid out in a glass-fronted case. Bill spotted a Murphy button and asked the doctor if he could borrow it, to which the doctor was agreeable.

The Murphy button is a device invented by Dr. John B. Murphy of Chicago and is useful in intestinal surgery. It is made of German silver and comes apart into two halves, each of which has holes around the edge. When one half is sutured into each end of a severed gut, the two halves can be snapped together, and they will hold the tissues in contact until they unite. Then the button sloughs and passes out of the intestinal tract.

Armed with his button, Bill watched Frenchy's saloon until all the late customers had gone. Then Bill went in and said he had borrowed the tapeworm trap from me. He showed the Murphy button to Frenchy, who was interested and asked how it worked. "Get me a piece of string," Bill said, "and some cheese, and I'll show you."

Frenchy brought the string and a piece of cheese. "Now," Bill said, "I'll tie the string in one of these holes, like this." He tied the string. "And now I'll put a little cheese in these other holes." He put cheese in the holes. "You swallow the trap, see. Then we'll wait a little bit while the tapeworm eats the cheese out of one of the holes and gets his head in it. Then I'll yank on the string, and we'll fetch old Mr. Tapeworm up out of you fine and dandy. Get some water to wash this down with."

Frenchy nearly waterlogged himself trying to wash the tapeworm trap down, but it was too big for his gullet, and he and Bill finally had to give up. In a day or two, it dawned on Frenchy that he had been the victim of a practical joke, and it took half a dozen people to keep him from taking a six-shooter and going on the warpath after Bill.

Shortly after Bill failed to get Frenchy's tapeworm, we closed in Lewistown, jumped to Fort Benton, then to Chinook, and finally to Havre in northern Montana on the main line of the Great Northern. Havre, a place in 1899 of about nine hundred people, had the reputation of being the coldest place in the United States in winter. When I was there, however, it was about the hottest as far as gross immorality went. I am willing to bet that it had more dives, dumps, and doggeries per capita than any other place in the country, and if you took your eye off any property you possessed, it was likely to turn up missing.

We closed our season in Havre, and leaving there was the only time I was ever afraid to get on a train. The Great Northern was trying to win the mail contract to the Northwest, and the management had abandoned safety for speed. As one trainman expressed it, "We're running by headlights and smoke, and if we see a headlight, we all jump." But we had a choice between staying in Havre, walking, or riding the train, so we rode it.

In Chicago, Dr. Park and I stopped at the Great Northern Hotel and hadn't much more than registered when he renewed his acquaintance with John Barleycorn. When I came back from a walk, I found him lit up like a torchlight procession. Since we were splitting up in Chicago, this particular drunk wouldn't affect me much, personally, but I knew he had a lot of money, which wouldn't last long. Through a lot of arguing and wheedling, I got him to give me $1,200 which I put in a money envelope at the hotel desk. I didn't know how much more money he had, but he brandished a sheaf of bills, saying, "I'm going to spend every damned cent of this!" I believed him and knew it wouldn't take long, but I told the hotel clerks not to give him a cent of the deposited money until they were sure he was sober. I thought I was wasting my breath, but Park told me afterward that he tried many times to talk them out of the money, but they followed my orders exactly.

I had to stay overnight in Chicago, and along in the afternoon, I noticed a passing wagon that carried a canvas banner announcing a prize fight that evening at Tattersall's, a boxing arena. I went to the cab stand in front of the hotel and asked a driver if he thought he could get me to and from the arena without losing me. He thought he could and told me when to show up.

I was right on time, and the driver took me to Tattersall's, in front of which a big crowd milled around. When I asked my driver how much I owed him, he waved me off, saying, "Hell! Don't show any money around here. Don't worry. I'll be right here when you come out."

For two dollars, I got a seat not far from the ringside. As I worked my way down the aisle, somebody with leather lungs saw my western Stetson and bellowed, "Jesus Christ, pardner! Where in hell did you get that hat?" I waved at him, and to my surprise the crowd roared.

The preliminary was a good fight, but the main event didn't amount to much, and when I saw that it was about over, I began edging my way to the door to avoid the jam. Out in the street, I could see my driver waving his whip at me over the heads of the crowd.

Several men seemed to follow me, and after I got into the cab, they ran alongside until they were outdistanced. I couldn't figure it out until I was paying my driver, when he said, "You didn't think I knew you, did you?"

"No," I replied, "and I still don't think you know me."

"Oh, yes, I do," he insisted. "You're Kid McCoy."

While I knew that I wasn't, I have often wondered if I did look like the real McCoy.

The next morning, I took the train for my hometown in Illinois and heard no more from Dr. Park until I received a letter from Washington, D.C., where he seemed to be sober and all right.

During the following six weeks, I celebrated my thirty-first birthday and put in most of my time shooting quail over a splendid Llewellyn setter named Don and often at night hunting 'possums and 'coons with Nigger Bill and his hounds along Shoal Creek. I am certain that was the finest vacation I have ever had; but, like all good things, it had to come to an end because my bankroll was getting thin. So I met Dr. Park in St. Louis and began again the chase for dollars.

Chapter 6

Nine Hundred Miles by Stage—A Change of
Partners—Bitterroot Valley

When I met Park in St. Louis in the fall of 1899, I discovered that he had taken on a wife about half his age. She was a very pleasant lady, but I didn't think much of her judgment. However, since she didn't intend to go with us, I considered that their business. "Everybody to his taste," as the old woman said when she kissed the cow.

Times were bad in November of 1899, and almost any technique for separating people from their money was going to be hard to work. We decided to try it without a show, I serving as advance man, renting office space, putting ads in the papers, and nailing up posters, while Park followed in a few days and worked the office.

We went to Wenatchee in central Washington, from which place we went on to work the little settlements along the Columbia. We had tough picking, as wheat was worth only thirty cents a bushel at the river landings. But we kept on until just before Christmas, when we jumped to San Francisco for the holidays.

Park refused to go with me to the Golden West Hotel and went instead to a cheap one on Montgomery Street. The day after Christmas, I decided to look him up and went to his hotel, where a guide led me through a maze of rooms that could have been renovated only by burning the dump down, which, of course, was what happened to it in the great San Francisco fire six years later. Just as I expected, I found

Park in the wind-up of a drunk that must have been a hum-dinger. As far as money went, he was as clean as a snowbird. His sole possession seemed to be an enormous watch dangling from his watch chain.

I was tempted to leave him to the dogs, but I needed him, so I enlisted the aid of a cabdriver, and we took him to my hotel, where I sobered him up.

When we came to San Francisco, we had our minds, such as they were, set on working central Oregon. It was stock country, far from the railroads, and it held out no promise of being a Golconda, with sheep worth three dollars a head, steers worth twenty, and hogs bringing two cents a pound. But anyway, when I got the old doctor looking almost human, I loaded him on a train and we started for The Dalles, Oregon.

Travel in those days was not as it is now, when every pin-head is hell-bent to travel from where he is sitting down to some other place where he can sit down. With two lowers in a Pullman, we almost had a private car. When I got Park settled, I left for the smoking car, afraid I might yield to an urge to break his neck.

Since he was broke, I thought I had him caught as far as booze was concerned; but when I came back to the sleeper several hours later, I found him six or eight sheets to the wind. "Where did you get it?" I asked.

"In the diner," he replied, knowing exactly what I meant.

"How the hell did you get it without any money?"

"Hell!" he said, with a lofty wave of his hand. "They don't ask a gentleman to pay his tab until along towards evening."

Then I learned that as soon as I had gone to the smoker, he had the Negro dining car waiters hotfooting it to him with those two-ounce bottles in which dining cars dispensed whiskey in those days. I think he must have ordered them in braces, one to make him feel like another man and the other to treat the newcomer. I put a stop to that by paying his tab and declaring that if they extended any more south-

ern hospitality to the gentleman, they would be left holding
the bag.

I got him through Portland all right, and in The Dalles,
we put up at the Umatilla House to await the departure of
the stage next morning for Prineville. My room must have
been previously occupied by a lady who had departed without giving notice to her customers because, along in the
middle of the night, somebody woke me up by knocking on
my door. I called out, demanding to know what was wanted,
and the knocker replied, "Sorry, honey. I didn't know you
was busy."

The stage was due to leave at 6:00 A.M., Saturday, January
6, 1900, and Park and I arrived at the station right on time,
in a drizzling rain. The stage turned out to be a three-seated
mountain buckboard, without a vestige of cover, and it was
being loaded with passengers, most of them women and
children, dragging back from a Christmas excursion to The
Dalles. I drew a precarious perch at the end of the rear seat.
Then we pulled out at a snail's pace through adobe mud.

I was tucked where the mud from the right rear wheel
flew off and hit the center of the cape of my overcoat. I
stood it as long as I could, then got out and walked. That
was easier and faster, but it indicated I was traveling on a
second-class ticket. If it had been third class, I would have
had to carry a pole.

Stored somewhere in my memory are a couple of lines
from the chorus of an old song that went something like
this:

> 'Blige a lady, 'blige a lady, suh.
> But if she don't want to sit on a big fat lap,
> Let the lady ride outside.

On the stage from The Dalles to Prineville, we were all
outside in the cold rain.

Several changes of drivers and horses occurred. I'm vague
about how many. But I do recall being served an alleged

meal at ten o'clock at night at a station on the Deschutes River called Bake Oven. The rain must have put out the fire under the oven because the food was only half cooked.

We had nothing more to eat until we arrived in Prineville at two o'clock Sunday afternoon and went to a sizeable house that served as the hotel. There, we were right on time for a Sunday dinner of chicken and dumplings cooked in an iron pot. We were well tuned by our thirty-two-hour, hundred-and-twenty-mile trip on the stage, and what we did to that dinner was disgraceful. Then, stuffed to the gills, we fell into the hay, where we remained until Monday morning.

After breakfast, I tried to salvage my overcoat cape by hanging it on a line and beating it with a carpet beater and sweeping it with a broom. But after about thirty minutes of making no progress with the caked mud, I gave up and threw the cape away.

The stage ride seemed to have been the right remedy for Dr. Park's katzenjammers, and after several days of recovery, I left him in Prineville and started off as advance man on a stage journey that was to extend for nine hundred miles, south through Oregon into northern California.

At each stage station, I heard the local gossip, which seemed mostly to be about schoolteachers and gunmen. I heard about how a local celebrity named Til Glaze got his when a crippled jockey he had offended kicked open the door of a saloon and with a blazing six-shooter blew Glaze to Kingdom Come. As for the schoolteachers, they seemed to have come west, looking for husbands on the order of Owen Wister's Virginian and then had to settle for sheepherders when they scored at all.

At intervals, I backtracked to see how the old doctor was doing and always found him on the job. He was having tough picking in territory where the natives seldom got sick unless shot or hung, but he was panning a little all the time by practicing psychosomatic medicine.

As I led the way through Silver Lake, Summer Lake, and

Lakeview in Oregon and past Goose Lake to Alturas, Canby, and Bieber in California, Old Man Winter was holding Spring at arm's length, and the temperature several times went to near zero.

The next stage station after Bieber was a little mining camp, known as Hayden Hill, where we changed drivers and horses. While the hostlers made the change, I got my dinner in a miners' boarding house. After I ate, I came out and stood, smoking a cigar and looking across the road at a building that had a low porch in front and a big sign over it reading "SALOON." Suddenly, the stage, a two-seated hack, appeared with the horses at a high trot. When the driver saw me, he pulled them to a halt and yelled, "Are you the passenger?" When I said I was, he said, "Well, git your grip, and git in, and we'll be on our way." He seemed a little exuberant, but I obeyed. While I was still getting seated beside him, he cracked his whip and whirled the outfit around in a U-turn and drove up onto the porch in front of the saloon. He put on the brakes, and out of the saloon came three merrymakers, who threw several demijohns into the stage and then climbed after them into the back seat. And away we went along the mountainside, just hitting the high places.

When the new passengers soon got out at a mine, they left us a present of two of their demijohns. By then, I had realized that my driver was lit up like a church, but there was nothing I could do about it except hang on. The horses were fresh, and he kept applying the whip as we sped around sharp corners and down steep grades. I finally suggested that if he drove a little slower, he might avoid turning the rig over and killing us both. That only made him hoot and yell, "Keep your seat, Mr. Greeley, and I'll put you there on time."

Every little while, he would divert his attention from driving, reach back behind the seat for one of the demijohns, and offer it to me. When I refused, he would take a big snort from it and fall to applying his whip once more. I

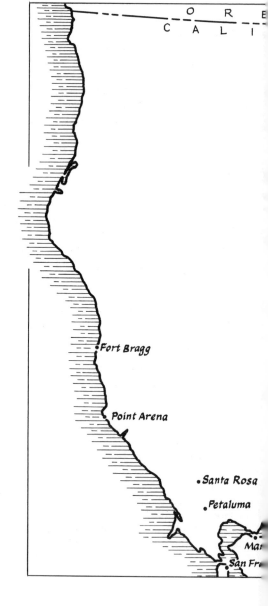

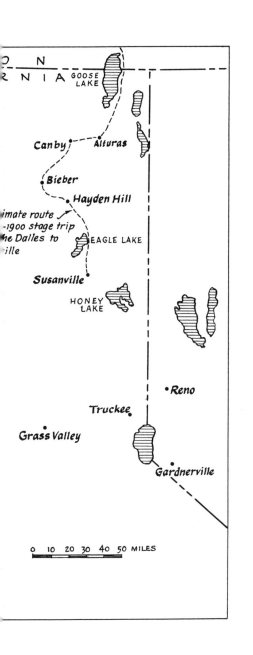

GOOSE LAKE

O N
R N I A

Canby
Alturas

Bieber

Hayden Hill

imate route
-1900 stage trip
he Dalles to
ille

EAGLE LAKE

Susanville

HONEY
LAKE

Reno

Truckee

Grass Valley

Gardnerville

0   10   20   30   40   50 MILES

had more than sixty miles of the ride ahead of me, so I went into a huddle with myself and decided that if I was going to get killed, it might as well be drunk as sober.

The next time the driver handed me a demijohn, I took a drink out of it. Then a second and a third. When the booze got into my bloodstream, the stage seemed to be going a little slower than I thought it should, so I took over the whip and applied it whenever there was any lag. An accident seemed no longer possible as the landscape flitted by and we paused only long enough to give a wayfarer a drink or trade mail sacks at a post office.

After awhile we came to a wide place in the narrow road called Eagle Lake. The post office was housed in a neat, white cottage set in the midst of an old-fashioned flower garden, surrounded by a white picket fence.

When we pulled up, the door of the cottage opened and the postmaster emerged. He seemed to take our arrival calmly until I handed him a demijohn. Then his ears perked up, and he accepted the demijohn without hesitation, balancing it on the crook of his arm as he leaned way back to take a snort out of it. I was afraid he might not come up for air and thus die of suffocation right there in the road. But at last he breathed again and handed the demijohn back.

The driver picked up his lines as he yelled, "Good by, Bill," and we moved off. But we hadn't gone more than fifty yards, when the driver called out, "Whoa," and pulled the horses to a stop. We motioned to Bill to come and have another whack at the demijohn. He gave us another exhibition of how long he could hold his breath. We started again, halted once more, and Bill repeated his act for the third and last time. As the stage surmounted a little hill, I looked back and saw Bill, hanging on and feeling his way along the picket fence as he tried to balance the load he had taken on.

By the time we arrived at the last stage station before Susanville, our demijohns were dead soldiers, and our previous elation had subsided. While we ate supper about ten o'clock, Hank Monk proposed holing up until morning. But

I would have none of that and declared that while I might be a lot of other things, I was no quitter. So, mumbling and grumbling, he hitched up and we began the last lap.

He was grumpy and for quite awhile confined his conversation to "Yes" and "No." As we neared Susanville in nearly pitch dark, I could sense that there was a considerable declivity to the left of the one-track road. "This must be quite a canyon along here," I remarked.

"It sure as hell is," the driver growled, "And if we hit a rock along one of these grades, we won't hit another God damned thing for half a mile."

The next morning, I took another stage along the shore of Honey Lake to a flag station on a narrow-gauge railroad that ran to Reno, Nevada. From Reno, I went to San Francisco, where I hired a couple of performers. Then Dr. Park joined me in Reno, where we worked for a little and then jumped to Gardnerville, a place in Nevada just east of the Sierra, seventy miles or so south of Reno. Gardnerville was the fightingest town I have ever been in, with one or two street battles every day. The atmosphere must have infected me because there I got into a fight for the first time since childhood.

We were showing in the only hall in town, when the advance man for Zamlock the Magician came along and wanted us to give way to his show on Saturday evening. I refused, which made him sore, and he then went all over town, knocking us. When I heard about that, I went looking for him and met him almost in front of our hotel.

He weighed about a hundred and eighty to my hundred and fifty, but I told him at some length exactly what I thought of him. I thought he might swing on me, and I was ready to belt him in the solar plexus. But instead of swinging on me, he grabbed me and threw me down on a patch of grass to one side of the board sidewalk. I tried to get up for fear that he might kick me, but he fell on me, and I found myself in a wrestling match.

I turned him onto the sidewalk. Then he turned me.

Then I rolled him over again until he landed flat on his
back between the sidewalk and a tree. He tried to bite my
hand, but I called a halt to that by sticking a thumb in his
eye. Then he held his mouth as far away from my hand as
my hold would let him, lest I might misunderstand him.
The bartender from the hotel was dancing around, yelling,
"Punch his head off, Doc!" but I just talked to him, and
when I let him up, he was ready to eat out of the hand he
had tried to bite.

Gardnerville must have loved winners because our business boomed for the rest of our stay there.

After a short stay in Truckee, California, we jumped to
Santa Rosa, a place in the Napa Valley not far north of San
Francisco. We were doing a lively business there, but I
scented trouble when Park's wife arrived from Washington, D.C.

A day or two later, when I went to our hotel, I found our
reception room filled with patients and Dr. Park drunker
than a lord. His wife seemed to think his condition funny,
but I was fed up with drunks and couldn't see the humor in
it. I had had enough and paid our performers two weeks'
salary more than they had coming, shipped my stuff to San
Francisco, and followed it. I never heard how the doctor and
his spouse got out of Santa Rosa nor did I give a damn.

I was confronted by a real challenge—no doctor and not
much of a bankroll. If I had been able to see a way to get
out, I think I would have quit the medicine game right
there. But then I met Dr. McMillan.

McMillan, an M.D. registered in California, had recently
been on the staff of Dr. Hudson, a newspaper advertiser,
who had gone on the rocks. McMillan looked pretty seedy
and admitted to being broke, but I thought I could detect
in him a personality I could work with.

As a desperate venture, I suggested that we join forces.
He was willing, but he didn't even have streetcar fare. I had
about fifty dollars, a stock of medicine, show props, and

three performers willing to take a chance that I could make the ghost walk. So, when one of McMillan's friends staked him to a new suit, we tackled Petaluma.

We opened on a lot, but the weather turned bad, which meant going into a hall if we could get one. I found a hall with four hundred and fifty seats and talked the manager down from thirty dollars a week, paid in advance, to five dollars a night payable each evening just before our show.

We all stopped at a little American-plan hotel, and when our first week ended, we didn't have enough money to meet our board bill. Dr. McMillan and I then fell to trying to persuade each other to brace the landlord for an extension. We were doing so in McMillan's room, which served as our office, when we heard a knock on the door. I opened it and nearly collapsed when I saw the landlord standing there because I was sure he had come for his money. But he looked right past me and spoke to Dr. McMillan. "Doctor," he said, "there's a couple downstairs who've just come from Penn Grove. I told them it was after your office hours, but they'd like to have you examine her, and I said I'd ask you. Would you do that?"

Would he? I'll say he would! He'd have examined her if it had been three o'clock in the morning and she looked as though she had as much as four dollars. But McMillan feigned reluctance, then consented.

The landlord led the couple up the stairs while I went down to the lobby. I sat there for quite a while without much hope, and when the couple came downstairs and left, I went up, expecting to renew the argument with McMillan about who would give the bad news to the landlord. But when I entered the room, McMillan tossed me a roll of bills that came to fifty dollars.

Since anybody could have been pardoned for lowering his sights at such a time, I thought then and still think that McMillan showed monumental courage when he stepped out after that fee. In a long life of many ups and downs, I have never beheld as much money as that fifty dollars seemed then. With that in our hands, both of us became anxious to see the landlord.

With the landlord paid, the rest came easy. At the end of four weeks, we had settled up with everybody and had five hundred dollars in the bankroll. On our last night, we jammed almost nine hundred people into our hall, a count of which I am sure because we took in $89.90 at the door at ten cents a crack.

After Petaluma, we spent the winter working towns in Sonoma and Mendocino counties, including Fort Bragg and Point Arena. We made a little money in all of them, but not enough to get excited about; so, along in the spring of 1901, we decided to jump to Montana.

Dr. McMillan went ahead to get registered while I continued working in Martinez with another doctor, named Gregg, of whom more later. Before long, McMillan wired me to come to Hamilton, a Montana town of a couple of thousand people, located in the Bitterroot Valley about forty miles south of Missoula.

I'd never heard of the place before, but I didn't question McMillan's judgment and headed north with a blackface comedian named Harry Holmes, Harry's wife, and their high-diving dog, Dandy.

After we landed in Hamilton, it didn't take me long to figure out why Dr. McMillan had picked the place. He was a gourmet, and Hamilton had one of the best American-plan hotels it has been my good fortune to stay in. It was called the Ravalli, after the county in which it was located, and had been owned by Marcus Daly, the Butte mining magnate, about whom it was said, "Ten thousand Micks laid down their picks, when Marcus Daly died."[1]

[1] Marcus Daly was born in Ireland in 1841. In 1856 he arrived in California, where he worked as a pick-and-shovel laborer and through hard work, sagacity, and luck became a wealthy mineowner. In Butte in 1891 he founded the Anaconda Copper Mining Company. Daly died in 1900.—OSS.

A white man managed the hotel, directing a staff of Negro cooks, waiters, and porters, imported from Nashville. Nothing was spared in the preparation of the daily menu, and the hotel operated at a loss in spite of charging four dollars a day.

Dr. McMillan was a heavy drinker, but in contrast to Dr. Park, McMillan could handle his load. I used to say that if I knew when he had got out of bed and how many drinks he had had, I could tell the time of day, since he took a drink every eleven minutes. Although that was an exaggeration, McMillan did get up about daylight and drink whiskey all day, getting tuned up for the evening meal, which was all he ate except on special occasions. The Ravalli Hotel was made to order for him.

The reason Daly supported the hotel the way he did was that he used it as a kind of guesthouse for his nearby stock farm, where he raised racehorses as a hobby. The farm had a half-mile circular racetrack and a quarter-mile straight-away track, the latter under cover. When we were there, Daly had a prized stallion, named Tammany, housed in a steam-heated stable known as Tammany Hall.

We did fairly well in Hamilton and then moved to a nearby small town called Victor, where we stayed a week. The hotel there, a considerable comedown from the Ravalli, served some of the toughest steaks I have ever tried to eat, but the menu improved when I discovered there was good fly fishing in the Bitterroot River. I bought a secondhand lancewood pole in a drugstore and got up every morning at daylight to fish the river. I kept our company well supplied with trout and caught one beautiful four-pound redside that made even the natives sit up and take notice.

We made our next stand in Stevensville, where the hotel had no dining room, and we ate in a restaurant run by a woman who did the best she could with what was available, which wasn't much. But Dr. McMillan scouted around and discovered somebody who had spring chickens for sale at a price, which must have been a good one, since spring chickens were about as scarce as ostriches in the Bitterroot Valley. (I should say parenthetically that in 1901 frying chickens were available only in the early summer and not the year round as they are today.)

McMillan had the chickens delivered to our restaurant in time to be prepared for our Fourth of July dinner. He spent an hour in the kitchen with the cook, giving instructions on how to cook the chickens Maryland style and what to serve with them—corn fritters, mashed potatoes, cream gravy, and hot biscuits. We showed up at the appointed time of 12:30 and found, as the editor of a local paper was fond of saying, that the table groaned under the weight of delicious viands.

Just as we sat down, an unexpected guest arrived in the form of the proprietor of the biggest general store in town. He'd given me the impression that he was sore about something or maybe he just didn't like strangers. Anyway, when I had spoken to him on the street, all he had done was glare at me. He was a regular boarder at our restaurant, and when he came in that day, he pulled a chair up to our table, apparently in the belief that our lady chef was serving the unusual dinner to all boarders in celebration of the Glorious Fourth.

"Please pass the chicken," he said, and McMillan picked up the platter and relayed it along to him. He looked it over carefully, selecting the most appealing pieces and then set the platter close by, where it would be readily available for an encore. The rest of us rose to the opportunity and pressed upon him the corn fritters, potatoes and gravy, and hot biscuits. I sat at one end of the table where I could see the door leading to the kitchen, where the staff took turns looking through the glass. They obviously knew the boner our guest was pulling, but he was too far from shore for them to rescue him.

There was ample supply of everything, and when we were sated, we left our guest picking over the remains. The cook must then have told him that he had horned in on a private dinner, for I have never seen anyone so embarrassed. He hunted us all up to apologize, and Dr. McMillan did his best to assure him that the pleasure of his company was all ours, which it was. I'm afraid, however, that our guest's experience impaired his appetite for chicken for some time afterward.

We went on to Missoula, where we fired two of our performers, who, besides being as funny as crutches, were troublemakers. Then we were lucky enough to locate Pat and Fanny Kelly in Portland, and they came on to Missoula.

We did a big business there in spite of a jam when I took a tapeworm from a man named William J. Hauk. While I was playing up the capture, I discovered that Missoula harbored another man who pronounced his name the same way but spelled it Hawk. He howled like a wolf at what he claimed was our deception, but I managed to get the real patient up on the platform, and that cleared the atmosphere.

When I announced the date of our closing, it turned out that we had put up our platform so that part of it was on a lot owned by somebody other than the owner of the lot I thought we had rented. It was a palpable hold-up, since the highbinder hadn't presented the bill until we had occupied the space for four weeks, and the amount was outrageous. We refused to be gypped and hired as our lawyer a former governor of Montana, who got us out of the jam.

We moved too soon, because I had yet to learn that when the take stayed at around eight hundred a week, as it did in Missoula, the town was nowhere near worked out. Anyway, we moved to Kalispell, another town in Montana, a hundred and some miles north of Missoula.

Chapter 7

*We Do Well in Kalispell—High Living in San Francisco—
Dr. Gregg and South Dakota—Back to Medical School*

To get to Kalispell, we took the Northern Pacific from Missoula to Ravalli, where we changed to a stage which hauled us to the southern end of Flathead Lake where the town of Polson is now located. There, we took a steamer which carried us the thirty-five-mile length of the lake and up the Flathead River to within a couple of miles of Kalispell.

The town opened well, and we took several tapeworms. Also, Dr. McMillan diagnosed a case of walking typhoid which the local doctors had muffed. As a result of these touchdowns, our business boomed.

We were introduced to McKnight's saloon, which was a sort of clubhouse of the dominant minority of Kalispell. In the saloon each evening, doctors, lawyers, merchants, chiefs, and a few judges and political officeholders sat in a poker game that had no rake-off except high-spading for drinks.

Dr. McMillan got acquainted with some of the players, who invited us to play. While McMillan had a good many other vices, he never played cards, but he offered to stand half my losses up to fifty dollars and split the winnings if I would sit in.

By midnight the first time I played, I had lost ninety dollars of our hundred dollar fund. When Dr. McMillan came in to rubberneck, I excused myself, and we went into the barroom, where I explained the situation. He wanted me to quit, but I refused because we still had some money in our common purse.

I offered to settle up right then and continue with my own money. McMillan hemmed and hawed but finally agreed to go all the way with me, win, lose, or draw. I went back to the game, and before it broke up, I had retrieved our ninety and won a hundred and fifty besides.

That experience was a lesson I resolved never to repeat. Suppose McMillan had not come to watch the game when he did? If he hadn't, I might have gone on until I lost the hundred and after that played with my own money. If I had ultimately won, as I did, I would have been over a barrel and would have had to split with him because I could never have explained that I lost with his money but won with my own.

We stopped at the American Hotel, where the food suited me but was not up to Dr. McMillan's standard. He nosed around Kalispell and found a modest little restaurant, run by John Listle, which was said to serve stall-fed beef shipped directly from a Chicago packinghouse.

One evening about eleven o'clock, when he had eaten nothing all day, McMillan proposed that we investigate Listle's restaurant. When we went in, the place was empty of diners. A waiter appeared and Dr. McMillan asked, "Could we get a steak cut about as thick as that brick?" He pointed to a brick on the counter on which cigar buyers struck their matches. The waiter said such a steak was possible but questioned whether McMillan really wanted it that thick. "Yes, I do," McMillan declared and added that he wanted it cooked rare and served with sliced tomatoes and hashed-brown potatoes. "We'll be back in half an hour," he said.

After we had hoisted a few in McKnight's saloon, we went back to the restaurant and found all in order. The steak, thick as the brick, taxed the capacity of the meat platter and was as rare as the one served a cowboy who protested that he had seen steers hurt worse than that get well.

I managed to down a small portion of the steak, and

McMillan ate the rest. Then I had to walk him around for a couple of hours before he dared risk going to bed. Thereafter, he became a regular boarder at Listle's.

Along with his gourmandizing and whiskey drinking, Dr. McMillan was a good office man, who often stepped out for a big fee and sometimes got it. One day an Indian came in, and McMillan set his fee at two hundred and fifty dollars, which was big money in those days. The patient didn't turn a feather, but he wasn't ready to ante and said he would be back the following Monday morning.

When McMillan told me about the fee he had asked, I hooted and offered to sell my share of it for ten dollars. Although he didn't go for that, he seemed certain that the patient would return. But when Monday came and no Indian, I gave McMillan the razz.

After office hours on Wednesday, however, he showed me a check drawn on a Missoula bank for two hundred and fifty dollars. The first thing the next morning, McMillan presented the check at the local bank, where the teller told him that the check was not only good but would have been good if it had been made out for five thousand. When McMillan came back from cashing the check, he said, "I felt in my bones that I was aiming too low, and that Siwash really got a bargain."

We hated to close in Kalispell, but we did and jumped to Dillon, a town on the Oregon Short Line about sixty miles south of Butte. There, the weather turned too bad for an outside show, so we sent the players to San Francisco, and Dr. McMillan and I turned around and headed back toward Kalispell.

While we were on the train from Dillon to Butte, it began to snow, which, since it was only September 6, 1901, was early even for that country. I am sure of the date because we heard as we arrived in Butte that President McKinley had been assassinated. We went on to Missoula and found all the saloons closed because of the tragedy, with the result that Dr. McMillan's schedule of a drink every eleven minutes was disrupted, and I had to depend on my watch to know what time it was.

We renewed acquaintances in Missoula and then went on to Sand Point, where we transferred from the Northern Pacific to a Great Northern train for Kalispell.

The lodestones that attracted us back there were, I fear, Listle's restaurant and the poker game in McKnight's saloon. But Dr. McMillan reopened his office, and I made several pitches on the street, each of us taking in enough to pay our board and room.

One afternoon when I dropped in at McKnight's, I found poker players present but not enough to start a game. Bob Ben, who owned the saloon, sent a message to a judge who was a regular player, telling him that I was there and that if he could get away, we could start a game. When the judge received the message, two lawyers were arguing a motion before him. He interrupted them, saying, "Now you fellows quit chewing the rag and get down to business. I've got to go up town."

As soon as the judge arrived at McKnight's the game started. I took out only twenty dollars' worth of checks; fortunately, as it turned out, since his honor beat a king full for me and wiped me out. That loss, however, left me ahead of the game over the whole period of our stay to the tune of about four hundred and fifty dollars.

The night we left, we went around to tell our cronies good-by. The poker game was going on as usual, and I offered to buy a drink. One of the players spoke up and declared, "We're drinking nothing but champagne tonight." That was fine with me, and they got their champagne. Another player said, "We're sorry to see all that money leaving town; but as long as it has to go, we're glad you got it." Although I returned to Kalispell almost a quarter of a century later, that was the last time I ever saw any of my friends at McKnight's.

McMillan and I went from Kalispell to San Francisco, where we immediately demonstrated that past adversity had taught us nothing. First, we engaged Wanskowski, a high-priced tailor on Montgomery Street, to outfit us with new wardrobes. I bought a couple of suits and an overcoat, and Dr. McMillan stayed with the Prince Albert, which he topped off with a silk hat. He offered to buy me one, but I declined because I knew I would look like the jackass I was. McMillan was the only man I ever knew who could wear a silk hat without looking as though he was going to a costume party.

All dressed up, we had plenty of places to go, which, with few exceptions, were expensive. We soon picked up several hangers-on, who were willing to go with us to any old French restaurant as long as we footed the bill.

The Techau Tavern was a favorite of ours, and there McMillan introduced me to the chateaubriand, which I had previously thought was a tenderloin beefsteak. McMillan also introduced me to a Mexican friend he had met in Bakersfield years before. The Mexican matched McMillan's appetite by regularly eating a dozen oysters as an appetizer, after which he was ready to have a little solid food.

Just as we were getting into our profligate stride, we ran into Jack Hern, another of McMillan's friends. Hern and his sister, Kittie, had been adopted by a wealthy land surveyor named John A. Benson, who had a ranch in Contra Costa County. Hern invited us to go quail shooting on the ranch, and we accepted.

A driver met our train with a horse-drawn station wagon, and took us to a fine ranch house in the middle of several hundred acres of mesquite, which teemed with valley quail.

Mrs. Benson and Kittie entertained us as though we amounted to something. Kittie was a marvellous cook and had all the markets of San Franciso at her beck and call. Every morning, Mrs. Benson would ask Dr. McMillan what kind of liquor he wanted that day, and a bottle of whatever he chose—bourbon, rye, Scotch, or Irish whiskey—would appear on his dresser.

Each afternoon, when Jack and I returned from hunting

quail, he would wait in the shade while I went into McMillan's room and handed McMillan's bottle out the window. When we had restored ourselves, I would return the bottle to McMillan's dresser.

One day, Mrs. Benson said to me, "I don't want to seem to criticize a guest, and I'm not criticizing Dr. McMillan now. But I must say that he can drink more whiskey than any man I ever knew." When I reported her comment to McMillan, he just smiled and didn't give us away.

The quail hunt was a wonderful interlude, for which I still feel indebted to the Bensons and Jack and Kittie Herr. I killed a lot of quail as well as one bobcat, which had the effrontery to pick up a quail I had just knocked down. I also picked up a case of poison oak which I thought would last forever.

San Francisco acquaintances recommended numerous remedies. I tried them all without avail and collected enough lotions and salves in my room at the Golden West to stock a drugstore. One day, I stopped at Dan Carter's cigar store in the front of the Davy Crockett Saloon, and when I reached for a cigar, the clerk saw the eruption on my hand. He asked me if I had poison oak, and when I said I did, he told me of somebody he knew from San Jose who got poison oak every year and cured it by going to the Hamam Turkish Baths and taking a sulphur bath without a rubdown.

I didn't have much faith in the recommended remedy, but almost anything seemed better than going on scratching; so I went around to the baths and told the attendant there what I wanted. He knew about it and put me into a dirty-looking tub filled with some kind of sulphur solution. It was plenty hot, and he let me soak there until I was so weak he had to drag me out. Then, without a rubdown, he wrapped me in a blanket and put me on a cot, where I stayed all night without scratching once.

The treatment relieved me from then on, but the sulphur reacted with the sugar-of-lead solution I had been using on my face and left me for a week or two looking as though I were painted for the warpath.

The bright lights began to pall, and in early January 1902 when I had recovered from New Year's Eve, I organized a show and opened in Susanville. Dr. McMillan was to follow, but he still had too much money and kept stalling. But when I wired him that if he didn't come, I would close the show, he came on.

It was a bad time of year, and we didn't do much in Susanville. I looked up the driver with whom I had made the drunken trip nearly a year before from Hayden Hill to Susanville, and we hired him to take us in his stage from Susanville to Alturas.

There, the city attorney insisted that we had to pay a license fee of five dollars a night for our free shows as well as for those for which we charged admission. I refused to pay and continued to work, whereupon the town marshal arrested me five times in succession and each time marched me to the town bastille. He always weakened, however, and never locked me up. In court, I always demanded a jury trial with the full statutory number of twelve jurors, which, of course, the locals weren't willing to undertake. In the course of the fight, the marshal and I got so well acquainted that he lent me his shotgun and a humdinger of a Chesapeake retriever, with whose cooperation I killed a small wagonload of ducks.

We went from Alturas to several other places, winding up in Klamath Falls, Oregon. We closed there and took the train back to San Francisco, having made a little money and having saved a good deal more by staying out of the city.

Dr. McMillan felt right at home in San Francisco, but I soon got itchy feet and wanted to get on the road again. He was unenthusiastic, so we parted amicably, and I cast around for a new office man. I found him in the person of Dr. Gregg, who had been with me the week I worked in Martinez, and we agreed to tackle Montana. He went on to Hel-

ena in order to get registered, while I went to Seattle hoping
to organize a show. There, I was lucky enough to find Pat
and Fanny Kelly and a soft-shoe dancer named Vic Cook
and jumped with them to Deer Lodge, which Dr. Gregg
had picked as our first town.

He couldn't have done worse if he had tried. Although
Deer Lodge was one of the oldest settlements in Montana,
nothing supported it but a few big sheep and cattle ranches
and the state penitentiary. All I can recall of the town, aside
from its deadness, was that the hotel had a stuttering bartender and dining tables with lazy-Susan centers, said to
have been invented by sheepmen so disinclined to conversation that they wanted to avoid asking fellow diners to pass
the potatoes.

In Deer Lodge I met a former Methodist preacher who
had quit working in the Vineyard of the Lord in order to
sell life insurance, at which he seemed to be prospering.
When I complained about Deer Lodge, he offered to bet
me a hat that we'd do a lot better if we moved to eastern
Montana. I took him up; we moved; and he won the hat,
which I still owe him, since I never saw him again.

We moved to Miles City, where we did a big business.
However, Dr. Gregg spilled a lot of beans by getting drunk
and invading one of the local seminaries.[1] It was two blocks
from our hotel, but far into the night I could hear him singing "Asleep in the Deep," and I surely wished he were there.

We jumped to Glendive and did nearly as well there as in
Miles City. After we closed in Glendive, we jumped to
Aberdeen, South Dakota, but before we could open our office in that state, Dr. Gregg had to get registered. He had
plenty of credentials, but when he got to Canton, where the
secretary of the board of examiners had his office, he found

[1] Since Miles City in 1902 was far from being a center of religious training,
my father must have used the term *seminary* facetiously, probably to mean
what in those days was called "a house of ill repute."—OSS.

he had been preceded by a libelous letter from an Aberdeen physician. The secretary issued the certificate and also gave Gregg the letter.

We engaged the most prominent firm of lawyers in Aberdeen and sued the letter-writing doctor for libel. We didn't expect to collect, but we surely led that doctor a dog's life for a time and made him spend some money.

We did all right in Aberdeen, but winter was approaching, and I decided to quit because the continuous grind had worn me to a frazzle. Dr. Gregg, however, continued alone in halls all that winter and made a barrel of money while I was going broke.

Back in my hometown in Illinois, I caved in. I had been working too hard and smoking too many Key West cigars, with the result that on several nights my heart woke me up by nearly knocking me out of bed. Then I came down with something like malaria that had my doctor puzzled. He gave me a course of calomel, which I survived, although it took me several weeks to get back enough strength to go to California.

When I arrived in San Francisco in early January of 1903, I found that Dr. McMillan had inherited a wad of money from his father's estate in Missouri and for the time being, at least, was not interested in the medicine business.

For several years, a sort of an arcade known as the Nickelodian had been operating near the corner of Market and Kearney streets. The admission was a nickel, and when you got inside, there were various boxes into which you could look through a peephole while you turned a crank and saw a primitive kind of movie, with well-clothed bathing beauties diving off diving boards and so on. Then some enterpriser opened a showhouse on Market Street above Powell, where he put on short movies interspersed with vaudeville and did six or eight shows daily. At ten cents a crack for admission, he seemed to be making money.

I had been hunting for a way to get out of the medicine

game, and the sight of the crowds milling in and out of that showhouse made me think there might be an opening for such a place in Portland. I asked Dr. McMillan to join me in the venture, and when he seemed enthusiastic, I left for Portland.

I didn't know how much money McMillan had, but I had about a thousand dollars and a three-carat diamond, all of which I was willing to bet. I had six years of experience in herding the kind of actors we needed, and I was sure we could make a go of it. But just as I found a building that looked as though it would do, I got a wire from McMillan, telling me to come back to San Francisco and talk it over. His feet had got so cold that he backed out, and down came my house of cards.

My memory of events in the next month or so is full of gaps, which I think resulted from my trying to keep up with Dr. McMillan's booze schedule without his ability to balance what I took aboard. I know that I made three sashays in the medicine game—one each in Washington, Nevada, and Los Angeles—all of them flops. The one in Los Angeles, I undertook with a character known as the Iron Gall Kid, and we advertised with banners held up by box kites flying over the city. When I was certain Los Angeles was a bloomer, Walton found an angel who bought me out. He and the Kid then went broke in Arizona.[2]

I kept slipping until I was down to the carpet. Then I went to Stockton where Berry and McMillan were working

[2] In a 1949 letter, my father wrote, "I knew a grafter known as the Iron Gall Kid who smoked opium. I have seen him doing it lying on a blanket on the floor, while another addict did the cooking. That was done by putting on the end of a long hatpin a ball of gum opium. The cooker held the opium in the flame of an alcohol lamp and, after it was lighted, transferred it to a small opening in the pipe. Then the smoker would take a long draw and inhale the fumes. When hopheads were under the influence, they wouldn't eat and could do four men's work. But when the charge wore off, they became bleary-eyed and not worth shooting."—OSS.

and borrowed a hundred dollars from McMillan. That was all he would let me have, claiming he had the rest of his money on time deposit in a bank.

In possession of that hundred, I didn't stall but took the next train for Aberdeen, South Dakota, where Dr. Gregg was still located. Before I left, the bartender in the Davey Crockett Saloon gave me a going-away present of a quart of Hunter Rye to put in my grip. On the train, I soon located another drunk, and we drank my bottle and all the booze he had before we landed in Denver. We arrived on a Sunday and had to wade through snow for about a mile before we found a saloon with a back door open. There, I took the last drink I drank for more than a year.

I arrived in Aberdeen in the midst of a blizzard on April Fool's Day, 1903. Dr. Gregg and I worked towns in the Dakotas and Minnesota that spring, summer, and fall. We went to Chicago for the holidays and while there, paid three hundred dollars for the outfit of a phrenologist, whom old age had compelled to retire. We threw away his cranial charts but hung onto several skeletons, many skulls, the mounted cadaver of a child, and a papier mache manikin made by a Frenchman named Azouizi. When new, the manikin must have cost a couple of thousand dollars, as one lateral half could be completely dissected. It surely paid its way until Dr. Gregg lost it in a freight shipment that went astray.

We organized a new show in Chicago and took off for South Dakota on December 30, 1903. We opened in Yankton in thirty below zero weather, which didn't seem to bother the natives who turned out in droves for our show.

During one of my spiels, a couple of drunks sat in the rear of the hall, perched on the back of a long bench. They were discussing some important matter and occasionally raised their voices until they could be heard all over the place. I admonished them two or three times, but after being quiet for awhile, they would forget and raise their voices again.

Then I noticed Gene Couch, our two-hundred-pound

tenor, working his way quietly along one wall toward the
rear. He took a stance behind the drunks and stood with his
arms folded until one of them raised his voice. Then Gene
stepped forward, pulled the drunk off the back of the bench,
and threw him through the swinging doors that led to the
outside. Some of the audience heard the impact, but when
they turned to look, Gene stood calmly with his arms
folded, leaning against the wall. The other drunk looked a
little bewildered at the sudden disappearance of his companion but soon tiptoed out to join him.

We did well, working several towns in South Dakota and,
in the spring, arrived in Lead, with a six-person show and
an overhead of more than fifty dollars a day. We built our
platform on a rented lot, and then it began to rain. It rained
and rained and poured and poured for a full week, dropping
enough water to wash out the railroad.

One day, while Gregg and I looked out the hotel window,
watching the water gush off our platform, he turned the
ring on his finger and wondered aloud, "How much do
you think we can raise on our diamonds?" Fortunately, we
weren't required to learn the answer to his question, for the
rain let up before we went broke.

After a bad two-dollar start with an all-male audience
standing in the mud, we got into the swing of things, took a
whole covey of tapeworms, and showed for eight weeks on
our lot to steadily increasing audiences. Then we left too
soon, as the people in Lead proved by following us down
the gulch to Deadwood City.

Deadwood City almost lived up to the vision I had formed
of it during the days when I read dime novels. The town
was certainly high and wide and a little bit handsome and
contained the only drugstore I have ever seen that had a bar
license.

From Deadwood, we went to Spearfish, where, during
the second week of our stay, I found my disposition deterio-
rating to the point where I was like a Malamute named Wolf
I had seen in Alaska. Somehow the dog had got his tail

chopped off, and he nursed the sore stump around the saloons and dancehalls in a frame of mind that made him ready to bite anybody who so much as looked at it. I had lost my finesse at handling crowds and once or twice nearly got into fights with smart-alecs in the audience. I knew that wouldn't do, so I left Gregg to work Spearfish alone and went to southeast South Dakota, looking for a town in which to make our next stand.

I picked Huron and when I applied for a license found that I had to go to the mayor, who turned out to be a physician. He was inclined to be insulting, and I felt like punching him in the nose. But I held myself in check and got the license.

When the performers arrived from Spearfish, we opened on a rented lot without Dr. Gregg. The performers knew nothing about where he was except that he had left them in Sioux City.

Although I made big sales the first week, I was handicapped without the doctor. I kept stalling the crowds and meeting every train, hoping for his arrival. I was sore at him and also worried because I knew that he sometimes got drunk and had a lot of money on him. That combination might spell anything.

At long last, one afternoon I saw Gregg get off a pullman and slowly walk toward where I stood on the station platform. He had a grin on his face, and when he came up to me, I handed him a four bit piece. "What's this for?" he asked.

"That's so that if you hang onto it, you'll always have enough money to wire me and let me know where the hell you are."

"Thanks," he said and put the half-dollar in his pocket. Four years later when he came to visit me, he still carried the same fifty cent piece.

Each night, I had played up Gregg's imminent arrival, and as the week went on with no sign of him, my crowds probably began to doubt his existence. But the delay seemed to have heightened their interest, for patients packed his waiting room every morning.

It was Gregg's and my custom to settle up each day by taking from the medicine sales and the office receipts what we had paid out on expenses and then dividing the remainder if there was any. I thought I must owe him a lot since he had paid the performers' expenses from Spearfish, and I was sure he hadn't taken in much there. But when I asked him how much I owed him, he said I didn't owe him anything and slowly counted out $800 as my share of the Spearfish profits. What a welcome windfall that was!

One evening after the show, we got to talking about the medicine game. "You know," Gregg said, "if I thought we were doing more harm than good in this business, I'd get right out of it."

That surprised me because not long before he had given me hell for being too truthful in one of my spiels and had said, "You talk to these people as though they had sense, when you ought to know they're nothing but a pack of damned fools. The bigger lies you tell them, the better. They expect to be humbugged, and they'll be disappointed if they aren't."

When I reminded him of what he had told me, Gregg shrugged and said, well, there was a lot of truth in it, but that was a side issue: he'd still get out of the medicine game if he thought he was doing more harm than good.

I said that that part of it didn't worry me because I figured that with the medicine sales, I was giving the buyers as much for their money as they'd get anyplace else. Then I said what I'd never put into words before: that I was sick to death of living like a nomad and having no home but a hotel room and being about as popular as a polecat with the home guards and having no friends and knowing that the medicine racket had no real future.

Listening to myself talk, I became convinced of what I ought to do and said, "I don't know what you're going to do about it, but, by God, this is my last town! I'm quitting!"

Gregg asked, "What are you going to do?"

"I don't know," I answered, "but it's going to be something different from this."

Gregg studied for a minute and then said, "You know what you ought to do? You ought to finish school."

That way out hadn't occurred to me, although I did have a start toward a medical degree. I had gone for two years to the St. Louis School of Pharmacy and learned more about drugs than most doctors knew. And a couple of years later, also in St. Louis, I had attended Barnes Medical College for one year.

I thought it over and wrote to the medical college, asking how long it would take me to complete the degree. The reply said that I could finish in two years if I passed the required examinations. That settled it, and I was on deck for the opening of the 1904–1905 session. My first year at the college, I'd given a note for my tuition, but this time, I laid the money on the barrelhead. I remember how lovingly Dr. Pinckney French fondled the hundred dollar bill which was part of my ante.

Just after the holidays when the World's Fair was over and rents had settled down, my wife and our seven-year-old son joined me in a rented flat on the corner of Compton and Franklin avenues.

Chapter 8

Family Matters—An Interlude:
Origins, Childhood and Youth, Marriage

In 1896, when I was twenty-eight, I had married Sarah Katherine Palmer (usually called Kate), the youngest daughter of Sarah Burnet Palmer and Winfield Scott Palmer. Kate was twenty-seven and lived with her family near Litchfield on a farm called Hilltop.

My wife's family on both sides was eminently respectable, whereas mine, although not disreputable, was considerably different.[1] I know almost nothing about my father's family, but I think he was born near Evansville, Indiana, about 1830. He had been a carpenter and a druggist in Louisville, Kentucky, before he entered a medical college in Keokuk, Iowa, from which he graduated in 1853. With a partner named Owen, after whom I was named, my father practiced in Litchfield until he moved to Newman, California, where he practiced with my half brother, who was thirteen years

---

[1] Kate's grandparents on her mother's side, the Burnets, were well-to-do Illinois prairie farmers who had come from New Jersey in the 1830s. Her father, Winfield Scott Palmer, had considerable local renown as an opponent of slavery and was a brother of John McAuley Palmer, a friend of Abraham Lincoln, who became a major general in the Union army, military governor of Kentucky, governor of Illinois, and United States senator before he ran for president in 1896 as a gold Democrat on what was called the Goldbug Ticket.—OSS.

older than I and a graduate of the University of Michigan medical school.[2]

My mother was born in Kentucky in 1838, the middle child in a family of nine children, eight of whom lived to maturity. My maternal grandmother, whose maiden name was Lucinda D'Arneil, was born near Lexington, Kentucky, in 1808 and could remember being afraid of Indians during the War of 1812. My maternal grandfather was a Virginian named Thomas Cave who died of cholera in the 1840s.

The Cave family moved every spring because, as my Uncle Singleton used to say, they wore the land out. According to him, they moved so often that when the wagon pulled up in front of the cabin, the chickens all ran out, lay down on their backs, and held up their feet to have them tied. The family migrated from Kentucky through Indiana and Illinois to Scotland County, Missouri, where they lit for awhile before moving to the American Bottom in Illinois across the Mississippi from St. Louis.

My parents' marriage lasted only three years before their divorce in 1870, a couple of years after I was born. After the divorce, my mother retained custody of me, and together with my grandmother we lived in Litchfield in a story-and-a-half house my mother had owned before her marriage to my father.

She sent me to school when I was six, and school was fine as long as the novelty lasted. When that wore out, I began to play hookey and sometimes got away with it for two or three weeks before I was detected. After each detection, my mother applied a rawhide whip with more vigor than judgment. After each hiding, I would retire to the privy where I

[2]I don't know what his relatives called my father, but the friends of his youth called him Tully or Tul. In later years friends called him Doc or Strat. I suspect that his first name, Owen, was infected with his mother's hostility to his father. At any rate, my maternal aunt, Elizabeth Palmer Tuttle, was the only person I ever heard call him Owen. Although I was given that name, my father soon nicknamed me Pete, a name that stuck.—OSS.

tearfully examined the welts on my legs while making dire resolutions.

A good many of my childhood memories are of scoldings, whippings, frustrations, and poverty. But I have other memories, too—of catching mudcats, crappies, and sunfish in Shoal Creek and of hunting pigeons and rabbits. I didn't own a gun, but I could borrow a Kentucky squirrel rifle that had an octagon barrel about five feet long, weighed twelve pounds, and had no trigger. I fired it by holding the hammer back with my thumb and letting it go at the right moment.

The rifle was a percussion cap muzzle-loader and would go off nearly every time when I could afford waterproof caps, which cost ten cents a box. But if financial stringency limited me to G. D. caps, which cost only five cents, the rifle was inclined to hang fire. When it did that, I had to keep it trained on the quarry until the cap made up its mind about whether it would fire or not. The rifle, loaded with shot instead of a bullet and poked through the fence smartweed and dog fennel along the Wabash tracks, was deadly on pigeons and doves picking up wheat spilled from freight cars.

The rifle was too ponderous for hunting cottontails, but occasionally I could borrow a Civil War musket. I loaded that with a charge of black powder, estimated in the palm of my hand, and on top of the powder rammed home a wadding of newspaper until the ramrod bounced out of the barrel. Then I poured in a load of number 4 shot and held it in place with more newspaper, gently applied. The musket was then Old Meat in the Pot when properly held on a cottontail running down a corn row, and there was nothing to beat a corn-fed cottontail with dumplings, cooked in an iron pot.

On one rabbit hunt, a boy named Louis Popplestone and I followed the three-prong tracks of a cottontail in the snow until they went into a culvert about a mile from town. When I knelt to look into the culvert, I saw a leather satchel which had been put there before the ground froze. I tugged on the satchel, but it wouldn't move, so we went back to Louis's house where we got a hand sled and a hatchet.

When we had chopped the satchel loose and opened it, we found some foreign-looking velvet clothing, some meerschaum pipes, and a bundle of deeds and mortgages. After we got the loot to my house, my mother remembered an advertisement in the paper offering a twenty-five dollar reward for a satchel which had been stolen from the Hofhine House. She notified the advertiser, but when he came for his property, he tried to renege on the reward on the ground that some articles were missing. He finally compromised on twenty dollars, half of which went to Louis. I wanted to buy a shotgun with my ten, but my mother wanted to buy a suit of clothes for me, and a suit of clothes was what I got.

My grandmother was sixty when I was born, and I never knew her when she had a tooth in her head. She was a tall, gaunt woman, and in my mind's eye, I can still see her squatting on her haunches, reading her New Testament without glasses, and smoking a clay pipe with a cane stem. She held opinions about almost everything and expressed them with all the cocksureness of an autocrat whose subjects could be persuaded only with a club. "Dog bite you!" was one of her favorite expressions. Her mind remained sharp as a tack to the day of her death in 1901 when she was ninety-three years old.

My mother had tough sledding, teaching the three Rs in country schools, peddling books or washing machines, taking in an occasional roomer or boarder. The only financial slack came from an occasional ten or twenty from Uncle Singleton, my mother's brother, who was two years older than she and a professional gambler.

In 1852, when he was sixteen, Singleton got into a fight with a younger brother. Singleton won, but when the battle was over, my grandmother accused him of always making trouble, and said she wished he'd pack up his duds and light out. He said he'd take her up on it if he had any money. She dug into the old cherry bureau where she kept her things and handed him a ten dollar gold piece. He took the money, gathered his few belongings, and lit out. They didn't see him again for thirteen years.

He headed for Scotland County in northeastern Missouri, where a sister and her husband lived on a farm that produced nothing much but boys. When Singleton arrived, he found a wagon train assembling in the nearby town of Memphis for the trek to California. He applied for a job, and somebody offered him board and transportation for driving an ox team hitched to a wagon. Armed with a goad, he walked beside his oxen all the way to California, where he arrived six months after leaving Memphis.

In California, he worked for wages in placer mines, waited on table in a restaurant, and did a variety of other things until he struck it rich playing faro in San Francisco, where he won sixty-five thousand dollars by making side bets with other players on each turn of a card. He decked himself out in the tallest hat and the longest tailed coat he could buy and basked in the encomiums of moochers who called him "the most dead-game sport in San Francisco." A few days later he was broke again and working for three dollars a day in the harvest fields near Suisun.

As the years went by, Uncle Singleton's fortunes alternated between chicken and feathers until the spring of 1865 when he made a killing at faro in Petaluma. Possibly because news of Lee's surrender to Grant had reached California, Singleton's thoughts turned toward home. He bought passage on a ship to Panama, crossed the Isthmus on the Panama Railroad, and took another ship to New York.

I don't know how much money he had by that time, but he had enough to stop at the Grand Central Hotel, where all went well until he took a walk, in the course of which he discovered that the hotel had become lost. Rather than expose himself as a hick by asking directions, he almost walked himself to death in search of the hotel. At last, he had the brilliant idea of hailing a cab and directing the driver to take him to the Grand Central. The driver closed the door on his passenger, mounted to his seat, and made a U-turn to the opposite sidewalk, where he stopped in front of the hotel. He charged two dollars for his services, and the passenger paid without a yip.

From New York he took the cars to St. Louis. He scouted around and located various relatives including his sister Lucinda, known as Lou, who became my mother and was then running a boarding house in Litchfield.

With family ties renewed and visits made, Uncle Singleton began plying the only trade he knew—poker playing. He had no trouble finding a game, since every town had one that went on almost continuously.

In those days, they played a lot of straight poker, in which every hand was pat with no discard or draw. Since there was no chance to improve a hand, even a small pair was valuable. Uncle Singleton told of one such game in which he made a big bet on a pair of fives. One opponent appeared willing to call, but as he began stacking his checks and adding some greenbacks that were required to size up to the bet, he was seized with an epileptic fit. He tossed his hand face up on the table and fell out of his chair onto the floor where he completed his gyrations. Somebody dragged him to one side while Singleton examined the discarded hand and found a pair of sixes.

In relating the story, Singleton asked, "Now, wouldn't anybody take it for a pass when he threw his hand in? That's what I did, anyway, and I raked in the pot. I was sorry the fellow had a fit, but as long as he had to have it, I'm glad he had it right then because if he hadn't, he'd have called me sure as hell."

When draw poker became popular, Singleton needed no help from epileptic fits. He had the patience of Job and would piddle along, sizing up the peculiarities of the other players, and after a while knew who would raise with two pairs, who would draw only one card to three of a kind, who would raise on a four flush and play it after the draw, who would stand pat on nothing, and who had enough curiosity to make him call every bet. Singleton could even deduce something from the way the other players hunched in their chairs and the way they would spit while playing a hand.

For a couple of years, he traveled around, playing poker in various Missouri and Illinois towns. Long afterward, a friend of mine recalled playing with him in Taylorville, Illinois. "He was a tough player," my friend said, "but his geniality offset his toughness. He once leaned over and whispered to me that if I'd take smaller drinks and make bigger bets, I'd do better."

In 1867, in Springfield, Uncle Singleton married a girl named Hattie Cooper, and about the time I was born they had a son they named Chauncey. From then on until age and the law shoved him to one side, Uncle Singleton ran cardrooms in St. Louis.

In the heyday of his prosperity, he was Santa Claus for everybody, and every day was Christmas. Not only his relatives but every bum could put the bee on him. Like so many other gamblers before and after him, he believed that his ability to make money would continue forever, which it never does. When you get old, you lose your nerve, and that happened to him. If he'd had the foresight to invest in Illinois prairie land when he could have bought it for $1.25 an acre it might have saved him from the sorrowful finish that is the fate of most gamblers.

Uncle Singleton was the nearest to a father I ever knew, and my earliest memories of him must go back to when I was eight or nine. Now and then, a telegram would come, announcing his arrival on that evening's Wabash accommodation from St. Louis. I would be sent to the store for unusual foods and then sent to the depot to meet the Wabash train and escort Uncle Singleton home.

He was about five feet ten and weighed nearly two hundred pounds. He had a reddish brown beard that came almost to the bottom of his vest and wore a fine black Stetson, a pleated white shirt with three gold studs, a made-to-measure gray suit and overcoat, and shiny black boots.

He always greeted me with a smile and stooped for a kiss through his parted beard. I then carried his grip and strutted by his side for the three blocks to our house. That stunt, coming and going, was always good for a quarter or a half, with others thrown in for keeping his boots shining like a mirror.

I was about ten when Uncle Singleton, Aunt Hattie, and my cousin Chauncey moved into the house in Litchfield and became part of the family. Then the curtains in the gloomy no-boy's land known as the "parlor" were raised and the horsehair sofa and chairs were shunted to one side to make room for a piano. Aunt Hattie could play, and Chauncey could sing. I couldn't carry a tune in a washtub, but when Chauncey got a new suit of clothes, so did I.

Periods of prosperity when Aunt Hattie wore silk dresses and diamonds alternated with periods when her dresses were cotton and her jewels had disappeared. More or less in time with these fluctuations of fortune, Uncle Singleton and his family moved back and forth, from Litchfield to St. Louis and from St. Louis to Litchfield.

From the time I was thirteen, I worked at various low-paid jobs until I was almost sixteen, when I got a job as clerk in a drugstore at four dollars a week. My second year in high school was approaching, and my mother and grandmother debated whether or not the certainty of my salary outweighed the uncertain benefits of higher education. The salary won out, and I continued in the drugstore, where after a year I got a raise to five dollars a week.

When I was seventeen, my mother began to suffer from ill health, which I am now sure was diabetes. They thought a change of climate might help her, so, accompanied by my cousin Chauncey, she set out for Goldendale, Washington Territory, where her sister and her sister's husband lived after emigrating from Missouri. The last I saw of my mother was her face as she peered out through the dirty window of a car on an Indianapolis and St. Louis train as it pulled away from the depot platform. She died in Goldendale a few months later, leaving me feeling like the captain of a ship who has lost his navigator.

Aunt Hattie and Chauncey moved in with my grandmother and me, and Uncle Singleton visited us when he could get away from his St. Louis cardroom.

Uncle Singleton wasn't much of a guide to a young man like me whose comb was beginning to turn red and who was prey to strange urges. He believed he had performed his duty when he furnished whatever money the boy asked for. He had an almost conscientious disinclination to give advice, and as far as I can recall, the only time he ever departed from that attitude was when I applied for the job as house man in his poker game.

"I would sooner follow you out to Calvary Cemetery," he replied, "than see you become a professional gambler. When I started, almost all men gambled, and it was no disgrace to be a gambler. But all that's changed, and people now put gamblers in the same class as whores, which is where most of them belong."

Nobody could have been kinder or more good-hearted than Uncle Singleton and Aunt Hattie, but through the prodigal misuse of money, they had raised Chauncey so that he was hardly worth shooting. He was four months younger than I and one of the most loveable characters I ever knew, but he wasn't worth a damn and never held a worthwhile job in his life. He would run any kind of errand for anybody, could sing all the popular songs, and would sing them anywhere, with or without accompaniment. He could work his mother for anything, and when it was money, I could take it away from him playing cards. Uncle Singleton once told somebody, "That son of mine is satisfied when he can just stay in a poker game, but that other one [meaning me] is out to kill."

With the example of Uncle Singleton constantly before me, it isn't surprising that I aspired to become a gambler. I could see that he didn't have to punch a time clock and could sleep in the morning as late as he wanted. He wore

Owen Tully Stratton, left, in about 1885 with his cousin Chauncey Cave.

finer suits and linen than any man in town, and when money
was needed, all he had to do was reach into the inside pocket
of his vest and come up with a roll big enough to choke
a bull.

I, in contrast, had to get up at five-thirty each morning,
sweep out the drugstore, clean the oil lamps, wash bottles,
polish the colored bottles in the window and the handle on
the big front door, and then wait on customers all day long.
After supper, while I was resting, I had to meet the Indianapolis and St. Louis train and deliver the St. Louis *Post
Dispatch* all over town. I did all that and more for five dollars
a week and the hope that I might become a pharmacist and
qualify for a job that paid fifty-five a month. When I
thought that over, I said, "To hell with it!" and quit.

Aping Uncle Singleton, I sent my stand-up collars to
Terre Haute, where they were laundered and starched stiff
as a board for thirty-five cents a dozen. I took his discarded
suits to William Dapper, the tailor, who cut them down to
size. I wore Uncle Singleton's cast-off Stetsons and learned
to swear with good clean oaths like a pirate. I tried to chew
fine-cut tobacco as Uncle Singleton did but couldn't handle
it. Nor could I learn to walk the way he did with his feet
turned out. I sharpened my claws by taking on other youthful Litchfield outlaws in any game of chance they wanted to
tackle.

Draw poker was my favorite, although there wasn't much
money on the table in any of the games where I played in
Litchfield. Sometimes I would win twenty or twenty-five
and sometimes I would lose about that much or a little
more. On the whole, I probably lost more than I won.

The Litchfield games were like playing for matches compared to the games in Uncle Singleton's rooms in the Hotel
Scott. That was a three-story brick building on the corner
of Olive and Pine in St. Louis. Uncle Singleton had a sepa-
rate entrance where a stairway led to a nail-studded door of
about the weight you would find in a calaboose. If you
pulled a handle in one of the doorjambs, a bell rang inside,

and shortly afterward, an eye would appear in a peephole in the top center of the door. If the inspection that followed was satisfactory, there would be a rattle of chains and bars, and the door would swing open, revealing Matt Lewis, the smiling Negro porter.

Going through a bedroom, the visitor entered the club-room, a room about twenty-five feet by forty, with three windows opening on Seventh Street and two on Olive. The floor was covered with a velvet carpet on which sat two round tables, each big enough to accommodate eight players with plenty of elbow room. Between each pair of comfortable walnut chairs there was a brass cuspidor. A linen crumb cloth under the table, chairs, and cuspidors prevented bad marksmanship from soiling the carpet. Matt and Luke, the two porters, changed the table covers every day and kept the room spotless.

Anybody who played there played in fast company, and that would usually have let me out even if Uncle Singleton had been willing to let me play. But on one occasion when he had gone to visit a friend in Indianapolis, the regular players were short one player and invited me to sit in. I had a little money, but what was more important, Lady Luck was on my side, and I came out winner.

After that, I kept horning in whenever Uncle Singleton was away, and Lady Luck stayed with me until I had a roll of about five hundred dollars with a fifty dollar bill for a wrapper. It wasn't long, however, until I was down to the rubber band which formerly enclosed my wealth.

One evening I was present when two detectives named Moberly and Kelly with a police escort raided the establishment. When they demanded admission, all they got was a Kerry Patch jeer through the peephole. Then the cops took turns swinging an axe on the calaboose door until they chopped a hole big enough for them to reach in and unbar the door. By the time they got into the clubroom, they found that all the evidence had been burned in the hard-coal heating stove.

The raiders looked the party over, and when Jimmy McLean said I was only there visiting, they motioned me to one side. But they took the others, and I stood at one of the Olive Street windows watching my friends, some wearing silk hats, go through the pouring rain and take their places in the patrol wagon.

Such raids were mainly nuisances. As soon as a new door could be hung, the games would go on as usual. The police reporter for the *Post Dispatch*, however, always wrote them up in stories accompanied by a cut of Uncle Singleton, whom the reporter called "the Patriarch Gambler." I thought the picture was a good one, but Uncle Singleton didn't agree; and if there was anybody he hated more than he hated a cop, it was a police reporter.

Along with my hankering to become a gambler, I retained some of my earlier urge to become a pharmacist, and in October 1887, I enrolled in the St. Louis School of Pharmacy with Uncle Singleton paying my tuition. I attended the night lectures and the afternoon laboratories, and when I took the final examinations in March of 1889, I passed them without trouble.

When I became twenty-one in October 1889, I came into possession of my mother's homestead, which was probably worth around $2,500. Uncle George Zinc and Uncle Singleton seemed to think I would quickly poop off my inheritance, so Uncle George, who was a lawyer, suggested that I accept $300 from Uncle Singleton and deed him a half-interest in the property. That was fine with me, as I would have given him a deed to the whole thing without any payment. I realized that I owed him that much and more, and I still do. One of my great regrets has been that I was never able to show my appreciation of him except in small dabs over the years. At that, I probably came closer to repaying him than any other beneficiary of his generosity.

I accepted Uncle George's proposal and went to St. Louis to receive the three hundred dollars. On my way back to Litchfield, I decided to take Horace Greeley's advice and go west to Yakima in Washington Territory where a cousin lived. I bought a hand-me-down suit and a second-class railroad ticket and was soon on my way to St. Paul, where I changed from the Minneapolis and St. Louis railroad to the Northern Pacific.

On the Northern Pacific, I rode in what was called an Emigrant Sleeper, in which the travelers furnished their own bedding and mattresses and slept in wooden berths that were about as comfortable as corncribs. A coal miner offered to share his blankets with me if I would buy a couple of shuck mattresses from the news butcher, and the arrangement worked out all right except that I picked up crabs from the miner's bedding and nearly scratched myself to death before my affliction was diagnosed and a cure applied.

At one end of the Emigrant Sleeper, the women cooked on a coal range and made the atmosphere thick with odors from frying pans and stew kettles. Those odors, combined with the smell of unwashed human bodies, made a stench that seemed to stick in my nose for days after I reached Yakima.

I stayed in and around Yakima for about five years, working at various jobs, only one of which amounted to much. That was a stint of a year and a half as a deputy United States marshal, engaged mostly in arresting bootleggers for selling liquor to Indians.

When I returned to Litchfield in December 1894, I had a fairly good bankroll and a hazy notion of going to medical school. I hung around Litchfield, loafing, playing poker, and getting rid of my bankroll until September 1895, when I entered Barnes Medical College in St. Louis, giving a note for the tuition.

The following winter was one of the toughest I ever went through. I paid two dollars and fifty cents a month for half of a double bed in a room containing another double bed occupied by two other students. For ten dollars a month I boarded in a boarding house run by a student and his wife, using provender shipped from the farm they had come from in Missouri. I could only occasionally buy a five-cent cigar, and my only amusement was to go to the Union Station and watch the humanity passing through its gates.

I stuck it out to the end of the session in the spring of 1896, when I returned to Litchfield and got a job in the post office at sixty dollars a month. I lasted long enough to pay off my note at the medical college, and then I either quit or got fired. I can't remember which, but I think I quit because I would probably remember it if they had fired me.

I lived with Uncle Singleton, Aunt Hattie, Chauncey, and my grandmother. Our finances reached such a low ebb that the butcher, the baker, and the candlestick maker, not to mention the grocer, began to look at us quizzically. We took the daily Chicago *Record*, which I read assiduously because I had nothing else to do. Each issue contained a chapter of a serial mystery story which would be published until the next to the last chapter was reached. At that point, the readers took over and competed for prizes to be awarded for the best solutions to the mystery. I sent in my solution to a mystery called "The Incendiary" and won a fifth prize of fifty dollars.

I offered to contribute the prize to the grub fund, but Uncle Singleton suggested that we use the money to start a poker game in the Litchfield Hotel. We did so, and when we had retrieved the family fortunes to a degree, Uncle Singleton, contrary to his attitude when I was younger, wanted me to continue in the business with him. But I had also changed and no longer thought much of gambling except as a makeshift. However, I continued with him until the fall of 1896 when I was irresponsible enough to talk Kate Palmer into marrying me.

After my marriage, I simply could not devise any way of steadily bringing in the sheaves. We finally reached such a low point that my wife insisted on taking in some of her relatives as boarders. That touched my pride as the end of the limit. I took on a job as city editor of *The Courier* in Jacksonville, a town forty or fifty miles north of Litchfield.

At the end of the first week I received seven dollars, which, with four and a half deducted for board and room, didn't leave much to send home. At the end of the second week, I got eight dollars, which encouraged me to stick for another week. But when at the end of the third week my wages remained stuck at eight dollars, I threw in the sponge and returned to Litchfield.

Not long after that, I heard of a job as pharmacist in a drugstore in Winona, Minnesota. I borrowed the money to get there, and when I arrived, found that the drugstore had gone broke. To bring the first part of my story full circle, that was when I met Jim Ferrell, who, after I helped him with "the give," staked me to enough money to get back to Yakima.

My wife remained with her family at Hilltop. There, in the same room where his mother was born, my first son, Paul, was born on the night of August 21, 1897, the same night I boarded the steamer *Queen* leaving Tacoma for Alaska.[3]

[3] I don't know how many visits my father paid to his family between his return to Yakima in the summer of 1897 and the fall of 1904 when they joined him in St. Louis. Without mentioning his family, he recorded one visit to Litchfield in the fall of 1899 and another in the fall of 1902. He may have made other visits, but if he did, they were neither frequent nor lengthy. When I knew him, he was generous with whatever money he had, so I assume that when he was on the road, he sent money to his family.—OSS.

Chapter 9

I Finish Medical School in St. Louis—I Open in Toppenish,
Washington—Toppenish is Too Wild West to Suit My Wife—
We Close in Toppenish and Move to Tacoma

In medical school, I found that my mind wasn't as retentive at age thirty-six as it had been when I was younger, and the dictionary became my most useful single book. I got up early, went to bed late, and burned barrels of midnight oil. Although it wasn't required of second- and third-year students, I took dissection both years and stayed at the College each day until they locked the doors.

It turned out that I didn't quit the medicine show game in 1904 as I had sworn I would. By the spring of 1905 when I finished my second year of medical school my bankroll was getting thin, so I spent the summer working towns in Iowa with Dr. Gregg. Things were tough for awhile, and Gregg was in two thousand dollars before we got going. But then we began to hit pay dirt, and I came back to St. Louis with fifteen hundred dollars more than I had when I started—enough to get me through the last year of school.

When I graduated in the spring of 1906, my diploma, attesting that I had the degree of Medical Doctor, might have made a patient think I knew something; but I was aware of a woeful shortage of practical knowledge and skill. Although packed to the gills with theory, I'd never had the advantage of practicing under a preceptor, never dressed a serious wound, had never given a hypodermic, had never been present when a baby was born. I had no bedside manner, since I had never attended a bedside in a professional capacity. High on the list of things I really needed besides money was an internship in a hospital; but I had a family to support, and interns in those days worked for nothing and boarded themselves.

Hoping I might learn something useful, I invested a good part of the little that was left from my valedictory swing as a medicine man and bought a ticket to Newman, California, where my half brother had practiced medicine for twenty-five years. He did his best to give me a postgraduate course in the rudiments of the game, but the time was too short to accomplish much.

As I was afraid to tackle the California board, which was said to be a tough one, I went on to Tacoma, where I passed the Washington board in July. That gave me another document to nail on the wall along with my diploma but did not do much to lessen my doubts about my ability to offer a patient an even break between being better or worse off for having consulted me.

I told myself that I wouldn't need to know much to practice in a small town, a boner many other doctors have pulled. I soon found out that a small town was just the place where a physician needed to know *all*. Toppenish, just emerging from the Yakima Indian Reservation in south-central Washington was the small town I elected to tackle. I recalled the place when it had been nothing but a flag station on the railroad and consisted of a post office and general store run by a squaw man named Vade Lilly. But now, in 1906, it had acquired a nondescript population of about 700 and was wild and wooly and full of fleas.

When I lit there, the town had no doctor, the last one having decamped in the middle of the night shortly before I arrived. The main street had the usual purveyors of goods and services found in a boomtown—a bank, a hotel, a livery stable, pool halls, barbershops, and two drugstores. The first drugstore I entered smelled like a distillery, and I soon discovered that both the drugstores were more interested in selling booze than drugs, a consequence of a law that permitted the sale of liquor on an Indian reservation only for medicinal purposes.

One of the druggists introduced my first prospective patient and provided a diagnosis. "This man's pretty sick," the druggist said. "What he needs is a prescription for some spiritus frumenti." The patient stood by his sponsor's side, gently weaving, with a silly grin on his face.

"Well," I replied, "if I'm to prescribe for this gentleman according to my best judgment, I'll prescribe a stomach pump to extract the booze that's already in him." That prescription instantly lost me a patient and a booster.

I hadn't been in Toppenish long before I found out why my predecessor had left town in such haste. I was called to attend what turned out to be his last patient and found a young woman in bed in the upper half story of an annex to the hotel. Under the July sun, the temperature in her room was hotter than the hinges of hell, but she was in the throes of a violent chill. I took her temperature and found it slightly over 105 degrees, the result, as I soon discovered, of an infected abortion.

My first impulse was to send for a doctor. Then I realized that I was the doctor, and it was up to me. After I examined her and cleared away as much of the debris as I dared, I gave her a course of treatment which consisted of watching and waiting and hoping for the best while I tried to make her as comfortable as possible with ice packs. To my great surprise, she made what I afterward learned to call an "uninterrupted recovery."

As I later came to expect in such cases, she was broke, the absconding medico having taken her for all she had as compensation for nearly killing her. I have often thought of the anxiety with which he must have scanned the newspaper for a scarehead item about his handiwork. Boy, was he lucky that a good doctor succeeded him!

The story had an almost unbelievable ending. After my patient recovered, she went to Canada, and I thought that was the last I would ever hear of her. But one day, some months later, I got a letter postmarked Calgary, and in the envelope was a money order from her made out for the amount of my fee.

My next call came by telegram from the conductor of a passenger train requesting me to be on hand at the station when the train arrived in order to attend a wounded brakeman. What happened was that the brakeman had dragged a young hobo off the rods of a pullman. When the train began moving, the hobo pulled out a pot-metal revolver and let the brakeman have it as he stood in the door of the car vestibule.

The train was a long one, and I had to hoof it under the broiling hot sun to a pullman where I found the brakeman lying in a berth attended by some excited lady passengers. His white shirt was bloody, and his face was as white as the rest of his shirt. I felt his pulse, which was as good as mine, so I judged that he was more scared than hurt.

When I suggested that he come to my office where I could make a complete examination and dress his wound, he asked in astonishment, "Do you mean I can walk?"

"Sure," I said. "Let's go."

Carrying his coat, I helped him off the car, and he walked to my office without trouble. There I found that he had a flesh wound, the bullet having passed out under his left mammary gland after glancing off a rib. If it had hit him two inches further to his right, he would have needed an undertaker instead of a doctor. As it was, all he needed was a sterile dressing. I applied one, and he returned to his train.

Other than the septisemic girl and the conductor, most of my practice involved minor ailments and accidents, none of which were too serious for my limited skill. One of my cases was a drunken Indian whom I saw being bucked off a horse. When I reached his side, he was as limber as a dish-rag, and I was afraid he had broken his neck. But a deputy sheriff who was another witness turned out to be a better doctor than I and cured the patient by squirting cold water on him from a hose. The Indian then departed under his own steam.

A good deal of my practice among the Indians was pulling aching teeth. I did it with cold steel, without anesthesia, keeping in mind the surgeon's maxim, "This won't hurt *me*." It helped a little, however, that I had some knowledge of Chinook jargon, which I had acquired when I served as a deputy United States marshal.

One Indian for whom I pulled a molar remembered me from those days, and when he told me his name was John Molisset, I remembered him. When I knew him, he was a big, young skookum buck. Now he wore a homemade artificial leg, which he required after tangling with a freight train.

Once, in Walla Walla after a session of the U.S. District Court, John entered the passenger coach where I was sitting and was even soberer than the judge before whom he had testified in a bootlegging case. Fifteen minutes later, after the train started, he showed up again, so drunk he couldn't feel his rear end with both hands. I searched him and found the remains of a pint of alcohol in his pocket. I took it away from him and also relieved him of a china cup bearing on its side the words "Forget me not," which he had tied to the backstrap of his overalls. The conductor and a brakeman threw him off when the train stopped at Hunt's Junction, and I last saw him sleeping peacefully on the platform. I'll bet that when he came to, he drank enough out of the Columbia to lower it a foot.

One day in Toppenish, in the company of a tough-looking white man, an Indian with his hair in long braids and wearing a big, high-crowned black hat and a blanket pinned around his shoulders passed me on the street. The white man, who seemed irritated by something, let loose a volley of obscenity. "Sh-h-h!" the Indian warned. "Don't use that kind of language. Some lady'll hear you."

When I described the incident to Will Crook, who clerked

in the largest of the two stores in Toppenish, he said, "Why, that Indian must have been Oscar Spencer. Oscar graduated from Carlisle and went wild again when he came back here."

Will then told a story about Oscar's father, who was one of the big tyhees of the Yakima tribe and owned the allotment on which the townsite of Toppenish was located. Old Spencer could neither read nor write, but he had a sharp mind, and everybody respected him.

Oscar started out his career as a booze hound by drinking whiskey he bought from local bootleggers; but when he got a little older, he branched out and extended his drinking range to include Spokane. On one of his binges there, the police had a tough time subduing him, and solved their problem by shooting him.

Back on the reservation, a messenger boy brought a telegram to old Spencer's wickiup. Spencer had the messenger boy read him the telegram, which was signed by the Spokane chief of police and read, "While arresting your son Oscar an officer shot him in the head with a Colt's forty-four. Oscar not expected to live. Come at once."

After old Spencer had the boy read the telegram again, he laughed and said, "Hell! They can't kill Oscar with no forty four." He turned out to be right, and Oscar was soon back, stamping around his old stamping ground.

After he told the story about the Spencers, Will Crook told another story about an incident in the big store where he clerked and sold everything from needles to threshing machines. The clerks had become so accustomed to waiting on Indians, half-breeds, and blanket stiffs that they were often careless with their language. One day, two ranchers had a fight in the store, and one of them badly worsted the other. A little while afterward, a lady customer, who had heard of the fight, asked one of the clerks, "Did Mr. Galloway hurt Mr. Jones very badly?"

"Did he?" the clerk replied. "Why he just naturally beat the shit out of him." He didn't realize what he had said, but all the other clerks were ducking under counters to hide their laughter. After the lady departed, they had a hard time convincing the offending clerk that he had said what they heard him say.

Toppenish was no place for a clergyman to bring up his son—or his daughter, either, for that matter. But I wanted my wife and son with me, and she was willing to try it out. So I floated a loan in Illinois and introduced my family to the far west.

We put up in the hotel, and the first night was normal, with the usual fights taking place in the street outside. They didn't bother me, but Kate was up half the night, barricading the door with all the furniture except the bed, which, with me in it, was too heavy for her to move. The next day, while she was inspecting a house I had rented, a bunch of Indians rode by, whooping and yelling. Then she plaintively asked, "Do we *have* to live in a place like this?"

That was a stumper, as I was the only doctor in Toppenish and doing better than I had expected. But I left the decision to her. It was thumbs down, so I shipped our dunnage to Tacoma, and we followed it on the train.

Chapter 10

*Puyallup—I Send My Wife and Boy Back to Illinois—I Take
the Idaho Board—Steamboating on the Columbia—The
Cowboy Doctor in Brewster—I Make Him a Promise and Open
in Bridgeport—Rattlesnake Tag and Bridgeport Characters—
I Begin to Learn to Set Bones and Deliver Babies*

Tacoma civilization was more advanced than that of Toppenish, but the Tacoma citizens stayed away from my rented office in hordes. With my bankroll rapidly dwindling, I decided to make another jump and took a chance on the suburban community of Puyallup.

Puyallup wasn't a town I would have picked to make a stand in during my medicine show days, but for some reason I thought such an appraisal of the place wouldn't apply now that I was practicing "legitimate" medicine. Most of the people in Puyallup scrounged their living, such as it was, out of an acre or two of pasture, a milk cow, and a berry patch. Their cash income came from selling strawberries and raspberries to a local cannery, and they had nothing to spare for a new doctor who was trying to buck two well-established competitors.

Both of those gentlemen were very friendly when I called on them, probably because I didn't look as though I could take anything away from them. In the course of our conversation, the first one I called upon asked me, "What in hell is pus-in-the-tubes?" When I told him what I thought it was, he continued, "Well, every case that other son of a bitch down the street gets, if it's a woman, he calls it pus-in-the-tubes."

When I visited the pus-in-the-tubes specialist, he said,

"Every case that other son of a bitch up the street gets is either pneumonia or the worms."

In the course of my visit to pus-in-the-tubes, a woman entered, carrying a sick baby. The physician diagnosed the illness as mumps and wrote the woman three prescriptions, for which he charged her fifty cents. I didn't know what the prescriptions could have contained, but when a local druggist offered to pay my office rent, I figured out why the doctor could afford to charge the woman the kind of fee he did.

We stayed in Puyallup all that winter, during which rain fell almost incessantly. The rain tried my wife severely, partly because of the gloomy weather, but mostly because she could not bring herself to let her washing flap on the line until the weather broke long enough to dry it. As a result, she dried it in the house. My son, Paul, didn't seem to mind the rain, though, even though he often came home from school as wet as though he had fallen in the ocean.

My practice consisted mainly of listening to the stories of a saloonkeeper named Mont Shepardson, who called me in to look at a sore throat he had, explaining that the reason why he had called me was that he had noticed I didn't drink. "A doctor knows little enough when he's sober," Shepardson said, "but when he's drunk the way those two others mostly are, he doesn't know a God-damned thing."

What saved me from a bad case of cabin fever was a letter from one of my medical school classmates who had been practicing in Brewster, a small Washington town on the Columbia River above Wenatchee. He had been doing pretty well in Brewster, but when his father struck oil in Sapulpa, Oklahoma, my classmate abandoned his practice and speedily returned home to take care of the old man. My classmate recommended Brewster as a good location for me.

Almost any location looked better than Puyallup. It might snow in Brewster, but at least it didn't rain all winter. I thought I'd give the place a try, but I was afraid to drag my

family along on such a dubious venture with my frazzled
financial shoestring. I folded up things in Puyallup and sent
the family back to Illinois while I went to Portland on my
way to Brewster.

From Puyallup, Portland was almost in the opposite direction from Brewster, but Dr. Gregg had located in Portland, and I thought I'd pay him a visit. When I got there,
he was about to leave for Boise to take the Idaho board and
suggested that I go along with him and do the same. I
couldn't imagine what use I'd have for certification in Idaho,
but, once I was in Portland, Boise didn't seem all that far
out of the way, and Gregg was a good traveling companion.
So I agreed, and we went to Boise, where both of us passed
the board.

I went on east to Pocatello, where I took the Oregon
Short Line to Butte. In Butte, I boarded a Northern Pacific
train and after changing to the Great Northern in Spokane,
arrived in due course on the Columbia in Wenatchee. There,
I transferred to a steamboat for the rest of the journey to
Brewster.

Maybe somebody in those days had thought about dam-
ming the Columbia, but if so, it was only a thought, for the
river ran free and fast with not a dam in its entire length.
Now, of course, it's almost a series of still lakes.

Approaching a rapid, the pilot of the steamboat would
work it into a cove along the shore. Deckhands then dragged
a wire cable upstream and attached it to a tree or rock. The
boat end of the cable was wound on a windlass, turned by a
stationary steam engine called a donkey. When all was
ready, somebody started the donkey, which wound up the
cable, dragging the boat along as close as it could get to
where the cable was attached ashore.

With a head of steam in the boiler that looked as though
it would blow the top, the pilot held the boat stationary in
the current while a man left ashore for the purpose detached
the cable. Then the steamer would make a diagonal dash
across the rapids into another cove on the other side of the

river. If the boat made it, everything was jake, and the lining process would be repeated. If the boat didn't make it, the pilot would drop back down to the foot of the rapids and try again.

The process looked mighty dangerous to me, but it must not have been as dangerous as it looked, for I never heard of a boat wreck. I could have walked the eighty miles from Wenatchee to Brewster in the twenty-four hours the boat usually took to make the trip, but I wouldn't have been able to sit and smoke cigars while I did it. So I figured the price of my boat ticket was well spent.

Brewster, at the junction of the Okanogan and Columbia rivers, then had about three hundred people in it. It had one doctor, a pioneer named C. R. McKinley, who was somewhere in his sixties when I met him. He was known as the "Cowboy Doctor" and covered his extensive territory on horseback, carrying instruments and medicines in saddlebags. McKinley smoked a corncob pipe, chewed tobacco, drank whiskey, and played poker. His rough-and-ready personality made a hit with most of his patients. No distance was too great to cover when he decided to respond to a call, but he might sock the patient with a fee big enough to cover his losses in a poker game. On the side, he was developing a peach orchard on the bank of the Columbia above Brewster.

When I introduced myself and explained that I was looking for a place to light, McKinley thought I had money and offered to sell me his drugstore in Bridgeport, a town about like Brewster, on the other side of the Columbia and twelve miles upstream.

When I told McKinley that my bankroll would go just about far enough to pay the first month's rent on an office, I must have sounded apologetic because he said, "Hell! That's all right. I've been so broke myself that I could smell bacon frying for five miles. I'm sick of sitting in the office; so let's go over and I'll show you what Bridgeport looks like."

We went out back to his barn, where he harnessed a horse

and hitched it up to a buggy. He must have liked my company because after we got to Bridgeport and looked things over, he offered to let me have my office in his drugstore rent-free. McKinley's kindness prompted me to make a fool promise to the effect that if another doctor came along with money and wanted to buy the drugstore, I would move on. That promise had a big effect on my life.

Bridgeport was the product of a pipe dream of some speculators from Bridgeport, Connecticut, who operated a mine at a place in Okanogan County called Ruby, which is now a ghost town. In 1891, the year Jim Hill pushed his Great Northern Railway across the Columbia at Wenatchee, the Ruby speculators thought up a scheme for pumping water up onto a bar a mile or so down the Columbia below the site they'd picked for Bridgeport. The water would irrigate orchards, and everybody would get rich raising fruit.

Trying to create a boom and sell stock in their enterprise, the speculators built a two-story brick hotel in Bridgeport and prevailed upon a man named Thomas Hopp to bring in a printing plant and start a weekly paper. When I arrived in Bridgeport, the hotel and Hopp were the only remaining evidences of the speculators' dream, other than a few scraggly, drought-stunted trees on the bar where orchards were supposed to flourish.

More than forty years later, I find it hard to account for the fascination Bridgeport exerted on me. As a town it didn't amount to much—the brick hotel rising above a string of frame houses and one-story wooden buildings, some with false fronts, on each side of a quarter-mile length of main street, backed by a little scattering of shacks in the sagebrush. The centers of assembly were two gin mills, one run by Charley Goldberg, with Al Sawtelle as bartender, and the other by Pete Miller, assisted by Jack Carter.

One day, coming back from a call and headed up Main Street to Delafield's livery stable, I saw a bunch of barnyard savages playing what looked like a game of tag in front of Pete Miller's saloon. One, holding a tin can, chased the others and tried to cast something out of the can onto the back of one of his playmates. Another took the can and used his foot to scrape what had been flung back into the can. Then he raced after the rest and cast the object out again.

Whatever was going on seemed to frighten my team, so I swung them to the other side of the street and tied them to a hitching rack. When I crossed back over the street on foot, I saw what had been causing such laughter and producing such frantic footwork: it was a live rattlesnake that sounded plenty sore about being made "it" in a game of tag. I persuaded the playmates to kill the snake, although they couldn't have been in much danger, so well fortified were they with snakebite medicine.

During another arrival in Bridgeport after I had been away for awhile, Charley Goldberg followed me to the livery stable. While I unharnessed my team, Charlie told me that something had interrupted the delivery of freight by the river steamboats, leaving his emporium almost high and dry. Then Charlie enumerated the things he was out of.

I went to the saloon, where Al Sawtelle stood behind the bar. Al was a Frenchman in his early fifties and equipped with a hair-trigger temper. When I entered, he greeted me with a smile and asked, "Well, what'll it be, Doc?"

"Oh, give me a little Hunter Rye," I answered.

Al paused in his mopping of the bar. "Sorry, Doc, but we're out of Hunter Rye."

"All right, then. I'll take a shot of Three Star Hennessey."

Again he stopped mopping. "We're out of that, too."

I pretended to think it over and asked for White Rock Mineral Water. That drew another blank, so I decided I'd have a General Arthur cigar.

Al slammed his towel down on the bar and roared, "This is the God damnedest saloon I ever tended bar in! We're out of every God damned thing!" Then he peered at me across the bar. "By God, Doc, I believe you knew we were out of all those things." He joined me in laughter.

For awhile, a saloon fighter named Archie McCloud hung

around town. I thought I remembered him as a bootlegger, selling alcohol to Indians, whom I had arrested fifteen or so years before when I was a deputy U.S. marshal in Yakima. I refrained from recalling that to him in Bridgeport as he was a tough baby and a rough-and-tumble fighter, especially good among drunks.

One day, Al Sawtelle had stood as much as he could from McCloud and came around the bar to throw him out. McCloud objected with his fists, but Al drove him out the door and into the street, where he got McCloud down. When Al picked up a rock and drew back his arm, a bystander grabbed his wrist.

"Let me loose!" Al protested.

"No, Al. You'll kill him if you hit him with that."

"Let me go, God damn it! I'll have to kill this son of a bitch sometime, and I might as well do it now."

Another time, I was visiting with Al, and a drunk kept interrupting our conversation. Finally, Al came around the end of the bar and gave the drunk the bum's rush out through the swinging doors. When Al came back in, red in the face and breathing hard, I asked, "How do you know when to throw a guy like that out?"

"How do I know when to throw him out?" Al replied. "I throw the son of a bitch out when I can't stand him any longer."

Cal Warner was another one like Archie McCloud who only thought he was a fighter. Cal weighed about a hundred and ten pounds soaking wet, and after he took on a load of Dutch courage, which he did every payday, he would challenge everybody in sight with the dire warning, "I can lick you on a sheepskin and give you the tail to run back on!" Even Archie McCloud was enough of a sportsman not to take Cal up on his offer because it was well known that his wife, who cooked at the hotel, whaled the hell out of him when he came home drunk.

Mont Rawson who drove the stage between Bridgeport and Coulee City told a story about Cal Warner. Mrs. Warner was sitting up in front alongside Mont while Cal sat on the seat behind, listening to the conversation. Mrs. Warner went on at some length about her fifteen-year-old daughter and concluded by saying, "I don't know why, but she just don't seem to develop like she ought to."

The stage went on for a little piece, and then Cal leaned forward and entered the conversation for the first time. "What do you mean, she don't develop?" he asked. "You mean she ain't got no tits?"

One man I always enjoyed in Bridgeport was a big, jovial German named Hank Klaas, who, with his partner, Sam Brown, ran the flour mill and sawmill. Hank always had a smile, which was transformed into a booming laugh whenever he stoked himself up on beer. That laugh could make the glassware on the backbar of Goldberg's saloon jingle and make cayuses tied out in front try to pull loose.

Among the many stories Hank told was one about his trip from Canada in a rowboat. He and his partner bought their sawlogs in Canada, where the logging company branded them and then dumped them into the Columbia. Although some of the logs passed Bridgeport in the night and were written off as a loss, a boom caught most of them, and Hank and his men towed them to shore with rowboats.

One spring, a sudden drop in the water level stranded a good many of Hank's logs, and he went to Canada to see what he could do about getting them afloat again. He bought a skiff and hired a lumberjack, and they worked their way down the river, rolling the stranded logs into the river with canthooks.

The lumberjack, who had held himself out to be an expert river runner and familiar with the Columbia, kept talking about the drinking place. When Hank asked what the drinking place was, the lumberjack said, "Never mind. You'll know it when we get there."

After awhile, they reached the head of a canyon, probably about where Grand Coulee Dam was constructed many years later. The speed of the river increased, and they could see white water ahead. The lumberjack said, "Well, we're almost to the drinking place."

"And, by God, I *did* recognize it all right when we got there," Hank said in relating the story. "It was a place where you could stand up in the boat and take a drink out of the river without bending over."

I established my office in the back of McKinley's drugstore in Bridgeport, and soon patients had me going day and night. In my hotel room, I had no need for an alarm clock because I became so sensitized that the soft sound of a saddlehorse's hooves in the sand surrounding the hotel would bring me out of a sound sleep, knowing that a messenger was arriving in search of the doctor.

Fortunately for my patients, my practice presented no problems too great for my limited knowledge and skill. The obstetrical cases all fell into the happy category that required only the patience to sit and watch the hole. At first, fractures gave me a good deal of trouble as I had to learn everything from scratch, but I was armed with *Scudder on Fractures* and was a diligent student. I soon learned to recognize deformity and compare an injured limb with its mate. Then when I got the broken limb yanked out until the measurements were the same, I knew I was jake.

My first serious fracture case was that of a rancher who had both bones of his lower leg broken by the kick of a stallion in a horse parade. I didn't see the accident and never did know how he managed to get kicked, but it created much excitement among the rancher's friends who carried him into the drugstore. In the crowd was an itinerant preacher who posed among his parishioners as a sort of doctor, but he must have confined his practice to laying on of hands because he shied away like a skittish colt when I asked him to administer chloroform.

With the help of the bystanders, I got my patient across the street and into a room at the hotel. There, I administered the anesthetic myself and set the leg in a fracture box with a pull of attached weights for extension. That was the recommended treatment at the time, but I soon found I could do better by applying a plaster cast at once, swelling or no swelling, then splitting the cast along the top to allow for the swelling which might follow. Anyway, crude as my attempt was with my first case of the kind, the rancher's bones united, although I'm afraid he always walked with a limp afterward.

Early one morning as I came out of the drugstore, I saw a little Irishman I knew coming toward me, supporting one wrist and walking as carefully as if he trod on eggs. He related that he had drunk too much the day before and on his way home had fallen off his wagon, which had run over his arm. He had spent the night on the porch of a vacant house and in the morning caught a ride on a load of wheat coming to town.

He had plenty of nerve and only grimaced a little as I examined his arm. When I felt along the humerus, the bone of his upper arm, it felt like a bag filled with small bones. I knew it was a serious injury and tried to persuade him to go to Spokane, where he could get someone who knew what he was doing to attend to the arm. Although the Irishman had plenty of money, going to Spokane was a long trip, and he refused to consider it. So it was up to me to treat him.

He declined an anesthetic while I molded the pieces of bone into position and attached a bag containing about three pounds of birdshot to his elbow to provide a weight that would extend the arm. With the birdshot hanging from his elbow, he couldn't lie down and slept as best he could in a chair for more than two weeks. The method of treatment was not in my book, but it did the job, and I obtained union in a bone that is notorious for its refusal to unite. I have done the same thing many times since with good results.

Elbow fractures were the ones I most dreaded. In an elbow fracture, one or all of three bones may be involved. Since I had no X-ray, I had to remember my anatomy and how to recognize three bony points even through enormous swelling.

As my experience increased, so did my confidence. I soon overcame the desire to crawl under the barn when a fracture case approached and became a fairly capable bonesetter. I learned that nature would do the job if it had a little assistance applied gently with care and judgment. In fact, after almost fifty years of general practice without much help, I would say that the greatest aids to a physician (and his patient) are two female deities: Lady Luck and Mother Nature. Maybe the man at the Mayo Clinic doesn't need their help as much as his distant colleague at the forks of the creek, but the Mayo Clinic man needs it, too. And so does his patient.

Chapter 11

I Keep My Promise to the Cowboy Doctor and Move On—Conconully—Preacher Thomas—Back to Yakima—The Houseboat on the St. Joe—I Move On

When September came it found me in velvet. I had a dandy team of bay mares, a mountain buggy, and around a thousand dollars in cash. I had about forgotten my promise to McKinley to move out of Bridgeport if another doctor came along with enough money to buy the drugstore, but one day McKinley reminded me of my promise by showing up in the company of a stranger. The stranger turned out to be a doctor who had sized up Bridgeport and had stayed for one night in the hotel. During that night I had responded to three calls. Concluding from that and other things he had seen and heard that the location was a gold mine, he was raring to buy the drugstore. There was no way to head him except to renege on my promise to McKinley, but I believed that promises should be kept; so, before the end of the month, with my traps in my buggy, I was on my way again.

With no particular objective except to see the country, I drove to Okanogan, a town up the Okanogan River from Brewster, where I found one doctor on the job. He looked pretty seedy and almost cried when I told him I was thinking of locating in Okanogan. I decided to have mercy on him and take a look at Omak about four miles further on. I found no doctor there, but somebody told me that one was about to light. Since Omak looked like a good place for a doctor to starve to death, I was easily discouraged and went on to Conconully, a town on Conconully Lake.

Conconully, with about a thousand people in it, was the oldest settlement in Okanokan County and was the county seat—the metropolis, you might say—and it had no doctor. During the several days I spent there trying to size the place up, just about every property owner in town tried to sell me his property. Their willingness to part with what they claimed to be valuable real estate at far below its true worth indicated an itch to leave town that didn't strike me very favorably.

I learned that their last doctor had been a dope fiend and had recently departed for places unknown. Several of his former patients told me what a wonder he was or could have been, anyway, if he had left dope alone. For some reason, that is a common layman's assessment of hophead and drunken doctors.

In a general store, I found the departed doctor's stock of drugs, sans dope, which the store proprietor offered to give me if I would locate in Conconully. The stock was worth about fifteen dollars, so that wasn't much of an inducement to stick.

One night, somebody routed me out of bed to attend a confinement case, which turned out to be remarkable only in that the baby was born with a caul, which meant that he would be lucky or that he would have second sight, depending on which superstition you believe. Come to think of it, I suppose he could be both lucky *and* vested with second sight. The father of the fortunate infant paid me a twenty dollar gold piece for my services, and my guess was that I took all the money the family had.

Somebody told me a story about a political character called Preacher Thomas who used to wander around Okanogan County. If I ever knew his real name, I have forgotten it. Maybe he had actually been a preacher at some time because he was a formidable windjammer. Anyway, he was running for sheriff and making a house-to-house canvass, which was a considerable job because the houses were several miles apart. Late one afternoon, hoping to get a vote or

two and also to find a place to spend the night, he rode up
to a ranch house.

As he was getting down from his horse, a woman came
out and asked what she could do for him. He explained his
situation, and she said, "Fine. I'll get supper on, and it'll be
ready by the time you put your horse in the barn and get
washed up." She paused and added, "My husband's away
riding for cattle, and he won't be back for several days."

She set out an excellent meal, which Preacher Thomas
ate, plugging his candidacy between forkfuls. After he dried
the dishes for her and she put them away, he said he guessed
he'd better hit the hay, which was literally true, since he'd
spread his blankets in the haymow. She said yes, morning
came early and also said that she slept in the bedroom just
off the kitchen. "There ain't any locks on the doors," she
went on, "and sometimes I get real scared that somebody'll
slip in and get in bed with me."

"My goodness!" Preacher Thomas responded. "That
would be a terrible thing!"

"Yes, wouldn't it?"

He went out to the barn and slept soundly until the
woman woke him up in the morning by banging milk pails
around below him and swearing at a cow she was trying to
milk. The cow was bawling, a sign that she was in heat,
which ranchers called bulling. Preacher Thomas got up in
his long underwear and looked down out of the big door at
the end of the haymow. The bull, which was the object of
the cow's attentions, lay by the corral fence, chewing his cud
and paying no more attention to the cow than if the cow
had been a badger. The woman came out of the barn, irritated by the antics of the cow she was trying to milk, and
banged the lazy bull over the head with her milk bucket.
"What do you think you're doing, you lazy son of a bitch?"
she shouted. "Running for sheriff of Okanogan County?"

In spite of the bucolic humor in Okanogan County, with
winter coming on, the place didn't look good enough to me
to take a chance on it. So I turned my rig around and headed

south, down the Columbia through Wenatchee and over Colockum summit to Yakima, where my horses started eating their heads off in the livery stable. With my capital dwindling, I looked for somebody to buy my team and found an Indian to whom I sold the horses and the buggy, with harness, for two hundred dollars. The mares alone were worth more than that, but I wasn't in any position to try to do better. I wore a diamond ring for which I had paid $400 in palmier days (it would be worth $2,000 today), and I sold it for what I had paid for it to a wheat buyer by the name of Ed Olwell. I had to wait eight days before getting paid completely because the panic of 1907 was on, and the bank where Ed had his money limited withdrawals to fifty dollars a day.

From a traveling salesman I heard of an opening in the Idaho panhandle for a doctor in a hospital serving construction workers building the Milwaukee Railroad. Although I congratulated myself that Dr. Gregg had persuaded me to take the Idaho board so that I was licensed to practice in Idaho, I was not very hopeful; but, anyway, I wrote Dr. John Busby of Harrison, Idaho, who held the medical contract. Back came a reply asking me to come for an interview. I countered with a proposal that he stand half the expense of the trip, and he accepted by return mail.

Harrison is on Lake Coeur d'Alene, not far from where the St. Joe River runs into the lake, and I learned from my conversation there with Dr. Busby that his hospital was on a houseboat that could be moved with a tug as necessary along the St. Joe, which was said to be the highest navigable stream in the world. My duties would be to take care of the workers constructing the railroad and of loggers in several logging camps. One of my predecessors on the houseboat had been a drunk and the other, to judge from stories I heard, had been a sadist. So the men were in open rebellion. Busby asked if I thought I could bring order out of chaos, and I declared I could do so if allowed to treat the patients like human beings. Busby needed somebody too badly to hem or haw and offered me the position, with my salary open.

The boat hospital consisted of a ward with about ten beds, an office, a kitchen, and bedrooms for doctor, nurse, and cook. It was well equipped, being part of a setup that included the main hospital in Harrison and a receiving ward at Marble Creek near the Montana line. A line doctor, really a druggist, traveled the line on horseback, visiting the construction camps, and making preliminary examinations of workers presenting symptoms that might need medical attention.

The patients, all male, had a dollar a month deducted from their pay to cover all services—hospital, surgical, and medical—for everything except chronic and venereal diseases.

Besides my duties on board the hospital, I had to visit the lumber camps once a month. They were on mountain ridges and I had to climb on foot to reach them.

Although the nurse and I had no blood transfusions or intravenous salines or glucose to administer, no vitamins, no antibiotics, and no biologicals except smallpox vaccine and diphtheria antitoxin, I had to sign but one death certificate while I was on the St. Joe, and that was for a drunk who choked to death on a piece of meat he tried to eat at the free lunch counter in a saloon. I don't suppose it had anything to do with his death, but he was a holdout who had no hospital ticket.

What made up for the shortcomings in my medical skill was the natural resistance of my patients. When they could wade fifteen miles through deep snow with an attack of lobar pneumonia, appear with a head so badly swollen with erysipelas that it couldn't be put in a half-bushel basket, battle for weeks with relapsing typhoid, present infected wounds that would chill the blood of any doctor, be brought in with face and eyes peppered with gravel from powder explosions, have compound fractures exposed to every type of contamination, submit to emergency surgery in surroundings that were anything but aseptic—when they could do all those things and still get well, they were using resources not contained in any *materia medica*.

When I came on duty every morning at 8:00, I first attended the hospital patients. Then I would see the ambulatory patients who always thronged my office. After that, I put on shoes equipped with lumberjack caulks and climbed to the logging camps, seeking holders of hospital tickets who needed attention.

The beds were usually filled, with the more serious patients being transferred to Harrison where there was a better setup. My one nurse was a marvel of efficiency and endurance, who, in spite of her sunny disposition, occasionally approached the breaking point.

One of those occasions was brought on by a Swede named Johnson, who had several relapses in an extended attack of typhoid. I believe he relapsed mainly because he wouldn't adhere to a diet, and, when watched, he got hungrier than a wolf and twice as mean.

One day when I entered the ward, I found the nurse, Hazel Oury, in tears. When I asked her what the trouble was, she said, "Oh, it's that . . . that . . . that Johnson! I just wish he'd die!"

"Oh, no, you don't. Not really."

"Oh, yes I do because that's the only way we'll ever get rid of him!"

Johnson refused to accommodate her and finally recovered.

On another occasion, I found a drunk in the trail-boat that served as a woodshed. As the weather was very cold, I roused him and took him into the ward. While Miss Oury prepared his bed, he kept interfering with her work by trying to lie down on it. Finally, she picked him up and slammed him into a chair with such violence that his head vibrated on his neck like the cracker on a whip. That made a good dog out of him.

How she stood duties both day and night that would tax the equanimity of a saint I did not understand. I will never forget her telephone voice, which sounded as though she were singing. She did all that for sixty dollars a month and board and room.

My stay on the St. Joe was my only experience with contract medicine. It was condemned by many in the medical profession because it compelled the patients to patronize certain doctors. But it was the only way in which patients like those on the Milwaukee and in the logging camps could be assured of medical attention when they needed it.

Some loggers bought tickets good for a year, for which they paid ten dollars, two dollars under the monthly price. The more sensible ones considered the tickets as insurance and counted themselves lucky if they required no services. Others, however, thought themselves gypped if they didn't get some sort of service during each month for which they had paid. Therein, I suppose, lies the weakness of governmental attempts to provide medical and hospital services. Too many people are anxious to abuse their right to be hogs by trying to lie down in the trough.

On the St. Joe, patients would appear with minor ailments like a cold who would never have gone to a doctor if they had had to pay for it. Occasionally, after I prepared the medicine I thought indicated, the patient would say as he fondled the container, "Doc, I feel pretty sick. I think I should go in the hospital."

"Oh, you feel that bad, do you? Well, I'll call the nurse." In the patient's presence, I would tell Miss Oury, "This man is pretty ill and should be in bed. Put him there, take his clothes away from him, give him a light diet, and don't let him smoke. In a few days, if we're lucky, he ought to whip out of this."

If his entry occurred in the morning and if my diagnosis that there was nothing much the matter with him turned out to be correct, I could count on him sending for me along toward the middle of the afternoon and saying, "Doc, I'm feeling a lot better, and I think if you'll let me have my clothes, I'll go on uptown and then head back to camp."

With his clothing restored, away he would go to where he could drink and smoke if he had the money, a well-satisfied ticket holder. If I had let him sit around the ward, loaf and smoke and chew the rag, we'd have had him as a boarder all winter. And to tell the truth, I couldn't really blame him because back on the job, he would have to bow his back in the snow and cold, putting and taking on a shovel handle, and drawing down $1.80 a day for it, which was the standard wage for a laborer during the panic of 1907. Even without pay, the hospital, transformed into a clubhouse, beat that all hollow.

Occasionally, a foxy one would hook me. I remember an Irishman who complained of pain in his ribs for which I could find no cause. I thought he was spoofing me, but I wasn't sure; so I gave him the benefit of the doubt and put him to bed. Before long, however, he overplayed his hand by getting drunk on some booze a friend of his smuggled in, and I threw him out.

The St. Joe was snow country, and a foot of the stuff often fell overnight. As my transportation was mostly on shank's mare, I found the needle-sharp caulks in my shoes to be lifesavers on slick logs and ice and snow. Once, however, stepping from a barge into a skiff, I caught the heel caulks on my left shoe in the hem of my overcoat. For what seemed five minutes, I did a fancy one-foot balancing act on the seat of the skiff, trying to keep out of thirty feet of icy water.

Somebody must have seen my act because afterward people would ask solicitously, "Well, Doc, cut your throat on your caulks yet?" I never got them that high, fortunately, because I could see what they did to saloon floors and toilet seats upon which finicky loggers declined to sit. In the interest of the linoleum, I always took my shoes off before going into the hospital.

The railroad had rigged a telephone line along the right-of-way and connected the hospital to it. One day, I got a call from one of the Gleason brothers, who were subcontractors on the railroad. Gleason reported a serious accident that had injured several men. I told him to get the line doctor, but Gleason said he couldn't find him. "Hell, Doc," Gleason said, "you can walk here in half an hour."

With that assurance, I set out along the railroad grade, taking many detours around unfinished cuts and bridges. The half hour's walk produced no sign of Gleason's camp. Expecting to see the camp around each curve, I walked for an hour more and then for another hour, getting madder by the minute. After ten miles or so, I arrived and was greeted with a lot of laughter about my half hour's walk, which Gleason seemed to think was a huge joke. I soon calmed down, however, while attending the injured. After I got them patched up to the best of my ability, the cook set out an excellent supper, and Gleason gave me his own bed, which he said was the best in camp.

Next morning I retraced my steps, and wherever work was going forward on a rock cut, I passed a small fire where a powderman was thawing dynamite. Although I had been told that dynamite would burn without exploding, I didn't delay when I came to one of those fires.

One day at the hospital there appeared a Montenegrin as big as a moose, accompanied by a group that included an interpreter who didn't speak much more English than his principal. When I unwrapped a foot about the size of a suitcase, I found it badly infected from an untreated abrasion. I explained to the interpreter that it needed an incision. When English failed, I tried sign language. The patient and his interpreter got the message at about the same time, and there ensued a lengthy conversation. At last, the interpreter turned to me and shook his head and said, "No."

"All right, then," I answered. "Get the hell out of here."

After a good deal more conversation with the patient, the interpreter said, "Hokay, Doc, but jus' a leetle bit," indicating with a finger on his thumb the distance I might cut.

When I got the foot cleaned up and the instruments laid out, I made a sizeable incision. The patient didn't flinch, but the interpreter did a highland fling around the ward, shouting, "Not so much, Doc! Not so much!"

When I had calmed the interpreter and was dressing the foot, I explained to my audience of other patients the reason for the interpreter's distress and the patient's phlegm. "You see," I said, "I was cutting in English which the interpreter could understand, but the patient could not." Anyway, the incision was all right in any language, and the patient soon recovered.

As I review my practice as a contract physician, I believe it was about as satisfactory as any in my experience. Among the reasons was that I seldom had to win an argument in order to apply the right treatment. Few of my patients had a book of any kind, and none was exposed to the misinformation inserted in present-day news magazines in order to fill space. No grandmothers or neighbors tendered advice on treatment. Most of the surgery consisted of the repair of trauma, and most of the diseases were acute. I was a prophet honored in his own bailiwick, and, to cap it all, I could make as many visits as I thought indicated without being accused of running up a doctor bill.

All good things must end (and bad ones, too, as far as that goes): the railroad was nearing completion, and my employer thought I was making too much money and could be replaced by someone who would work for less. So, when the geese were flying high on their way to their Canadian nesting grounds, I was on the move again.

Chapter 12

*I Debate Between Twin Falls and Mansfield—I Light in
Mansfield—I Lose my First Patient—Dry Farm
Country—My Cayuses, Sam and Copper Bottom—My Family
Comes to Mansfield—How We Lived—Babies and More
Babies—Sanitary Problems and Typhoid—Winter Travel*

One day in April 1908, maybe a month after I left the St.
Joe, I sat in a room in the Palmerston Hotel in Spokane,
counting my potatoes. That did not take long. I had looked
up train fares and had enough to get me to Twin Falls,
Idaho, where I would arrive dead broke. Why Twin Falls?
Well, forty years later, I'm not sure. I think I'd heard that
the place looked like an up-and-coming town—which it
turned out to be—but I think the main attraction was that
Twin Falls was as far as my money would take me. Actually,
if I had gone to Twin Falls then I would probably have a
good many more potatoes in my old potato sack than I now
have, but I would have missed out on a lot of good hunting
and fishing.

I had also heard of a place in the Big Bend called Mansfield where there was no doctor. (If you wonder what the
Big Bend is, look at a map of central Washington, where
you will see that the Columbia interrupts its journey south
from Canada to turn north at Grand Coulee, then west,
then south again, thus forming the Big Bend, which frames
an area of about thirty-five by thirty-five miles as the crow
flies.) Mansfield was close enough to Spokane that I could
make the trip and arrive with a few dollars in my pocket,
retaining a degree of dignity of sorts.

I got off the train at Coulee City, the stop closest to
Mansfield, and took the horse-drawn stage to my new lo-

cation. I'll never forget my depression when I first saw it. It was just a wide place in one of two intersecting roads, around which clustered a general store, a harness shop, and three small frame houses, one of which accommodated the post office and telephone exchange. None of the upper Columbia country was exactly verdant until you got back into the yellow pine country on the eastern slope of the Cascades, and that went for Bridgeport and surroundings. But that area was an oasis with date palms and glittering fountains compared to the Mansfield country, where only ribs of black lava broke the monotony of sagebrush flats. Tough as Mansfield looked, however, I knew there was a homesteader on each quarter section of the extensive surrounding territory, and, best of all, Mansfield was only twenty miles from Bridgeport, where I had left many friends.

I climbed down from the stage and carried my bags into the general store, where I introduced myself to Frank Hamilton, who owned the emporium. He received me almost with open arms, showed me a room off his store that I could use for an office, invited me to board with him, and put a team and buggy at my disposal. Then he put in a fire alarm call over the telephone line, announcing that a doctor had arrived.

My first call was to see an old man named Buntin who lived on a dry farm twenty miles away. I diagnosed pneumonia and made several visits, but Doctor God was out when I called, and Buntin went over the Great Divide. That wasn't the best beginning for my practice. Maybe I could have saved him if I had had sulphas and penicillin, but I think the old fellow had run up too much mileage even for "wonder drugs."

Not much time passed before I was as busy as I had been at Bridgeport, although my clientele was not as prosperous. They were wheat dry farmers, and dry farming is always an uncertain business. Most of the precipitation in that part of the world falls as snow during the winter, and if the snow, plus the fall and spring rains, was sufficient, the dry farmer could make a crop that would equal the value of the land, assuming a reasonable price for his grain. But if the moisture fell short, then the dry farmer had to depend on local merchants to carry him over for a year, paying 12 percent interest on advances. The dry farmers were like gamblers— one year, chicken; the next year, feathers.

E. A. Freeman, who lived in one of the houses at the crossroads and had given Mansfield its name after his hometown of Mansfield, Ohio, decided to move to Bridgeport. He rented his house to me and accepted my note for a team, harness, and dilapidated buggy.

The team consisted of two cayuses weighing about a thousand pounds apiece named Sam and Jack. Sam was a gray and Jack a sorrel. After I got acquainted with him, I renamed Jack, giving him the name of Copper Bottom on account of his durability. They were good horses and on one trip covered fifty-four miles in a day. I treated them the best I knew, feeding them wheat hay and stuffing them with oats. In the winter I had them shod at Bridgeport with never-slip shoes, which carried sharp caulks that prevented the horses from slipping on snow and ice. I always carried horse blankets with me and took time to blanket them when I stopped. I retain a deep sympathy and affection for those enduring friends, and if they are not in Horse Heaven, it will be all right with me if St. Peter slams the door in my face when I come for my reward, if any.

My only amusement was shooting ground squirrels, which infested the fields and were the bane of the ranchers. I bought a .22 caliber Stevens single-shot rifle with an octagon barrel and once killed ten squirrels without moving from my tracks. By shooting about a wagonload of cartridges, I became as good as Deadeye Dick. One day I walked a mile along a section line and killed eighty squirrels with one hundred cartridges. Shooting squirrels was the only outlet for a Nimrod except for an occasional shot at a coyote with a .32 automatic pistol I carried in my buggy. I always missed and blamed Copper Bottom for it since he was gun-shy and always tried to turn around in his harness to see what I was doing, thus disturbing my aim.

I continually ploughed any surplus from my practice back into my anchorage. On credit, I bought material with which to build a story-and-a-half office and did the unskilled labor, helping a carpenter put it up. The office was about completed when my wife wrote that she, the boy, and her mother were on their way to Mansfield.

That was a fairly desperate venture for a lady who had always seen better days, but she may have seen something in her fiddle-footed, addlepated husband of which he was unaware.[1] Anyway, there they came in a few days, riding the Coulee City stage. My wife reported that when Mansfield came in sight, the driver pointed with his whip and said, "Well, Paul, there's your town," to which the boy replied with a prolonged "Ah-h" of disgust and disbelief. My wife and her mother were more restrained, but the place must have looked even more dismal to them than it did to me when I first saw it.

They arrived to find me up a tree—metaphorically, since no tree grew within twenty miles of Mansfield—in an effort to diagnose a malady that afflicted a two-year-old boy in the house next to the one I had rented. I had become fond of the youngster, who was generally under foot while I did my chores. He had become desperately ill—I knew that; but I couldn't make a diagnosis. I read every book I had that might bear on the problem and went over the child several times a day without the glimmer of an answer. I acknowledged my bewilderment and asked that another doctor be called.

When the doctor from Coulee City arrived, I gave him the history of the case, suggesting that he make his examination without the possible embarrassment of my presence, and said that I would await his conclusions in my office next

[1]People who moved frequently were said to be afflicted with fiddle foot.—
OSS.

door. He spent considerable time with the patient before he came to the office. "Doctor," he said, "I don't like to express my opinion." Well, that really astonished me, and I told him that if I had pulled a boner not to hesitate about telling me. He hemmed and hawed and then said, "Well, the fact is, I don't believe there's anything the matter with the boy."

In spite of his optimism and my awareness of my own ignorance, I knew better, and so did the parents. As a result, before the Coulee City man got home, we had another doctor on his way from Reardon, a town on the other side of Coulee City.

When the second doctor arrived, I stood by while he made his examination. He gave me another shock when he said, "This child has diphtheria." I had examined the child's throat many times for the possible presence of that disease and had ruled it out. But the Reardon man insisted that he could see a membrane, and I shot the child with the indicated antitoxin.

I asked my colleague to go with me to look at another patient a couple of miles away, and when we returned to Mansfield, we found the boy in convulsions that any doctor could have diagnosed as caused by tubercular meningitis. The boy lived only a few days.

Forty years later I am certain of that diagnosis, which, like many other medical puzzles, was easy once you had thought of it. I learned something from the case that I will pass along. A mile east of Mansfield there lived a young woman with active pulmonary tuberculosis, who was a friend of the child's family. She made frequent visits, during which she played with the boy, and, although I can't prove it, I am certain that it was from her that the child got his infection. True, the young woman had other contacts that were unaffected, but they were older.

Tuberculosis was fairly common in those days, and people, through both ignorance and carelessness, were not as assiduous in their hygiene as they should have been. I always insisted that children, particularly, should be protected from

contact with active cases; and that is just as important today
as it was then because prognosis with meningeal tuberculosis remains as dismal as ever, despite the addition of strep-
tomycin to our armament.

My boy and his grandmother moved into the house I had
rented, and my wife and I occupied a room over the office
next door. Our water supply reached the office and house in
buckets carried from a well seventy-five yards downhill. A
galvanized washtub did double duty for both laundry and
baths, using water heated in a copper washboiler on top of
the kitchen stove. The horses had to be led to the well twice
a day and given as many buckets of water as they felt like
drinking.

For light, we depended on kerosene lamps. (Most people
in those days called kerosene coal oil.) We heated the house
and office with coal hauled from Coulee City thirty miles
away and were regarded as effete easterners for doing so,
since most of the dry farmers burned sagebrush, a fuel that
lasts only a little longer than straw and produces a fine, pun-
gent odor that made a room full of dry farmers smell as
though it were full of Indian smoke-tanned buckskin.

I do not believe there is anywhere in the world a more
aggravating climate to try men's and especially women's
souls than the climate of the Big Bend upland. Most of the
time, the wind blew, in summer toting volcanic ash; in the
winter, snow—this last sometimes with the thermometer
registering twenty-five or more degrees below zero.

One day when my wife had hung an entire week's washing on the line, a gust of wind blew one of the clothesline
moorings loose and dumped the laundry into the dust. That
was the only time I ever knew her to become hysterical, and
for five minutes she alternately laughed and cried.

The nearest school was five miles away and taught by a
rancher named Ezra Darling. My son got there and back by
riding double with Hamilton's daughter on a cayuse named
Chub. Chub was an original with a glassy eye, meaner than

hell, and would run away at the drop of a hat. His young riders avoided the danger of getting caught in stirrups by omitting the saddle and riding bareback, which enabled them to slide off onto the ground when Chub took a notion to go places not on the schedule.

One day while I was unhitching my team, Chub boiled out of the stable with Paul half on and half off him. Just as they got opposite me, the boy let loose and hit the ground full length. When he got up, he hopped around on one leg, yelling, "My leg's broke! My leg's broke!"

"Well," I said, "you're doing pretty good for a fellow with a broken leg." Paul stopped crying just like that.

As the summer followed its normal course with no rain, the dust got deeper and deeper. The wind kept it moving, and I recall one three-day period when we could see across the road only during lulls. During some trips with the wind at my back I could hardly see my team. The wind scoured potholes in the road, and when a buggy wheel dropped into one of those, the top of my head seemed to rise and slam like a cellar door. When I reached the house of a patient after one of those trips, I took the dust off my skin with a dry towel before washing up, because water was a valuable commodity and the preliminary dusting reduced the amount of it necessary to get clean.

In those days, most parents tried to avoid starting their children in life branded with an IOU and did their best to pay for confinements, which were my principal source of revenue. There was no prenatal care, and the doctor seldom advised the expectant mother until the stork was circling the house. Sometimes the baby arrived before I did, which could result in argument about the size of my fee.

Once when a baby had been born before the arrival of the messenger summoning me, the mother was in a snarly mood when I got there. "Well," she said, "the baby probably wouldn't have been born yet if you'd been here."

"Maybe not," I agreed, "but if I'd been here you wouldn't

have the tear in your behind that you've got now." I met the fundamental requirement of a good obstetrician and left her in better shape than I found her.

I recall one twenty-four-hour period during which I delivered four babies from as many mothers. Whatever the size of the wheat crop, there was never a shortage of babies.

Every homestead had a well, the sole source of water for household and livestock. More often than not, the homesteader had located the well with an eye more to convenience than sanitation, with the result that it received drainage from barn, hogpen, and chicken house, with an outdoor toilet not too far away. Frequently the well was insufficiently curbed, leaving openings for everything that walked, crawled, or flew. I have scrubbed up in water that was so offensive to my nostrils that I made them boil it first, yet the family was using it for domestic purposes. The many horses provided manure piles, which, in turn, provided incubators for millions of flies. Since few houses had screen doors and window screens, I was run ragged in the late summer and early fall, attending children with bowel complaints.

I carried with me an irrigating outfit consisting of douche can, colon tube, Kelly pad, and a rubber apron. Sometimes I stayed on the job a day or two, trying to control a child's diarrhea. Too often I failed and slunk away like a hound pup with his tail between his legs.

I have seen malted milk traverse the alimentary tract of a baby and come out unchanged, hiked along by peristalsis with no chance for digestion. When I discarded the dictum of the authorities that children cannot stand opiates, I and my patients did better. If castor oil and subnitrate of bismuth with a dash of sulphur had no effect, I gave paregoric after each bowel movement. The little patients would take anything that was liquid, and the clink of a spoon in a glass would arouse them from profound stupor.

I soon learned that if there was the slightest chance for my directions to be misunderstood, they would be misunderstood. Even with a graduate nurse on the job, I have stayed to supervise the dosage.

In one case of a desperately ill baby, the untrained attendants decided it was too much trouble to change diapers. Upon discovering their neglect, I blew my top in a manner that would have shocked Dale Carnegie. When I got ready to leave, a woman neighbor who had listened silently to my tirade, asked for a ride to her ranch a couple of miles away. She remained silent all the way, but after she got out of the buggy in front of her house, she said, "Doctor, if you ever talked to me like you did to those women back there, I would never again let you set your foot in my house."

"Well, by God, Madam," I answered, "if you ever neglected a baby like they have done and I was responsible for its recovery, I sure as hell would tell you just what I told them. As for your house, if I never set foot in it, that will be too soon."

She grunted, and I drove off. At home, when I told the story, I made a guess that I would never be called to attend a member of that family. A few months later, however, I was passing and stopped to pass the time of day with her husband, who was fixing the fence in front of the house. The woman saw me and came out. "Doctor," she said, "I owe you an apology." I had forgotten the incident and asked her what she was apologizing for. "Well, I thought over the way you talked to those women about not changing the diapers, and the more I thought about it, the more I thought you didn't put it strong enough."

No cases were more harrowing to me than typhoid fever. Every fall I would have a few, and they would hang on and hang on with little change until I was worn to a frazzle. In none of the cases did I succeed in tracing the source of the infection. But I lacked both the equipment and knowledge for that task.

Once I had three cases simultaneously in Bridgeport. Hank Klaas turned over a fine house to me to serve as a hospital, and I put my typhoid patients there in charge of a graduate nurse who had been brought in from Spokane. The patients were a man and two women. The nurse became careless and gave the man a whole orange which he ate without chewing it, with the result that he died from an intestinal perforation. One of the women became violently delirious and had to be watched day and night. The nurse kept asking for more morphine to keep the delirious patient quiet until her demands aroused my suspicion. I asked her to let me see her left arm, and when she refused I fired her. Later I checked with people who had known her in Spokane and learned that she was a dope fiend with a big habit. I made many twenty-mile trips to attend my typhoid ward, but all I got out of them was the ride.

When winter came, I replaced the buggy with a small wagon box mounted on two sets of sled runners, what were called "commonsense bobs," the front set being steered by the wagon tongue. In the buggy, the driver sat high enough to see over the horses, but the sled was so much lower that the driver had a view mainly of the horses' rear ends. In order to see ahead, I had an especially long neck yoke made as well as an extra long doubletree, which kept the horses far enough apart that I could see ahead between them. (Since few of my readers, if I have any readers, will have ever seen a harnessed team, I should explain that a neck yoke is a wooden pole that supports the front end of the tongue and is attached at each end to a snap on one of the horse's collars. A doubletree is a wooden bar attached to the tongue behind the horses and carries two swingletrees to which the tugs or traces are hooked.) For awhile I used a charcoal foot warmer but abandoned it after I thought it caused me to catch cold. The heat was fine, but the perspiration it created was not so good when I had to get out of the sleigh to adjust the harness or open a gate.

The wind blew mostly from the north, and the wire fences along the roads that followed section lines running east and west acted like snow fences and created drifts that made the roads impassable. I carried wire clippers, and when I came to a drifted section of road, I would cut one of the fences and take to the fields to get around the drifts. That was hard on the ranchers' fences, but there was no help for it.

Since the roads followed section lines, when I traveled an east-west road, every mile I crossed a road of sorts running north and south. And when I traveled a north-south road, every mile I crossed an east-west road. So when I traveled north in the face of a brisk wind with the thermometer twenty or thirty below, I would whip the team up to a gallop and exercise them for a mile. Then I turned either east or west and trotted them for a mile. These zigzag manoeuvers helped keep the horses warm, but I remember the conclusion of one sixteen-mile trip northwest toward Dyer, as I pulled up on the leeside of a barn at my destination where some men waited to take my horses. As I walked away, I looked back and saw icicles hanging from the horses' nostrils that made the cayuses look like walruses.

I discovered that lines on a harness are about the coldest things in the world. Gloves were useless, but mittens with wool gloves inside them did the trick. I also wore woolen underwear, although I had hated it since the days when my mother would stitch me into red flannels that were itchy beyond imagination. (She put the stitch at the top to prevent me from going into an outhouse and taking the underwear off until time to put them on before going home.) In spite of my insulation, when I got in the house after a long drive, I would shiver like a dog on a brush pile with a rabbit in it. I found, however, that a shot of Pennsylvania rye would stop that if I didn't have to go outdoors again.

Altogether, it was a great life if I didn't weaken, and I can recall only one occasion when I did weaken. That was on a Sunday with the kind of blizzard raging from the north that explained why ranchers in winter ran guidelines from the back doors of their houses to their outdoor toilets. A rancher who lived about fifteen miles north of Mansfield had engaged me to attend his wife, who was not far from giving birth. Knowing the genius of the stork for picking an inopportune time, I told my wife, "This is just the night when Mrs. Sanders will have her baby, and I'll be damned if I'll let anybody, backed up to a hot stove, call me out in that storm. If they come for me, I'll go; but otherwise, not."

The telephone was equipped with a small gadget that was supposed to protect it from lightning if anybody was there during a lightning storm with enough sense to pull the gadget out. When it was out, neither lightning nor a call could get through. So I pulled out the gadget and went to bed. No messengers disturbed my sleep, and the next morning I replaced the gadget.

A few days later, on another call in his neighborhood, I met Sanders. "We tried to get you the other night," he said, "but the line was out of commission. Anyway, we got along all right with help from a neighbor woman, and the baby arrived without any trouble."

I damned the telephone line and said it was always going out just when you needed it and said I was glad everything had gone all right without me. Which indeed I was.

The advocates of state medicine say that it will provide better medical service for the poor. Like hell it will. There I was in Mansfield, responding to calls day and night (with the single exception I have recounted above) to Tom, Dick, and Harry and their wives and children, many of whom didn't have a cent and wouldn't have paid me if they'd had a barrel of money buried in the backyard. Before I went, I never asked them if they had money but responded as promptly as I could at all times of the day and night in all kinds of weather. I am now nearly eighty years old, and I believe that if I hadn't made some of those trips, I'd be close to a hundred.

Although many of my toughest trips were fruitless in the sense that they produced neither money nor gratitude, when someone sold something to me, he wanted cash on the barrelhead. One year, for instance, there was a shortage of oats, and the price of them went to forty dollars a ton. I was nearly broke, but I had to have oats if I was to go on driving. I found a farmer who had oats and told him that I wanted to buy some but needed a little time for payment. Now this fellow had owed me several fees for varying periods, but he said, "God, Doc, I'd like to accommodate you, but I've got to have the cash."

My pockets were filled with uncollectable promissory notes from clients who owed me money, but I frequently had to scratch to get enough cash to feed the family.

Chapter 13

The Railroad Comes to Mansfield—The New Town—I Lose a
Quart of Whiskey—The Engineer Borrows his Wife's
Horse—Euthanasia—I Take a New Doctor More Seriously
than I Should Have—I Buy and Sell a Drugstore—
Postgraduate Work in Chicago—and a Visit to the Mayo Clinic

In 1909, the Great Northern started building a branch line toward our metropolis, but they stopped short two miles away in order to give a railroad-owned townsite company a chance to scoop up a little gravy. That was a common manoeuver of the railroads, an outstanding example of which was the Northern Pacific caper of 1884 when the N.P. went beyond Yakima City and laid out a new town they named North Yakima. The old residents had little choice but to move and buy lots in the new town after the railroad bribed and otherwise persuaded the state legislature to designate North Yakima as the county seat, and the courthouse went there.

After the new Mansfield townsite was surveyed, Frank Hamilton, the storekeeper in the old town, Theo Radke, the harnessmaker, and I bought lots in the new town and moved our buildings. We hated the expense but had no choice. With my office building on the new site, I added an ell, making a residence and office combined.

As with all mushroom towns, get-rich-quick hopefuls soon showed up from all points of the compass, and it wasn't long before we had two of everything: two grain elevators, two banks, two lumberyards, two hotels, and two livery stables, when one of each would have crowded sufficiency in a town that had fewer than five hundred people in it.

When the railroad construction gang was nearing the

townsite, the engineer in charge and the contract doctor were frequent visitors to the old town. They were sociable men and carried their liquor fairly well.

The engineer's wife accompanied him on the job, and they occupied a tent in the construction camp as it moved along. She was a peppery little woman with plenty of woman's "ignition," which she seemed to need, given some of her husband's characteristics.

One day, while lit up like a church, the engineer accompanied his wife on a shopping tour to Hamilton's store. He passed the time while he waited for her by visiting with me on the steps of my office. After a little, she came out of the store, looked in our direction, and energetically beckoned with her arm. The engineer lumbered to his feet, cut a few pigeonwings in the dust until he got equilibrated, then turned to me and said, "Doc, did you ever have a bumble bee after you?"

During one visit with the engineer, I asked him when the railroad would reach the townsite. He set a date which I thought too early, and I bet him a quart of whiskey he wouldn't make it. I would have won the whiskey if he hadn't laid ties and rails across the prairie with no roadbed under them so he could run a locomotive onto the townsite before the deadline. He won the whiskey, all right, but I wonder how much it cost the railroad company for him to do it.

The engineer's wife owned a good saddle horse and rode it astride, wearing a divided skirt. One time while she was away somewhere, the engineer and two of his friends hitched the saddle horse to a two-seat buckboard, along with another horse they borrowed from somebody, and went to Bridgeport, where two saloons welcomed them with open doors.

When the engineer's wife returned to camp, she noted her husband's absence and also the absence of her saddle horse. She borrowed another saddle horse and went hunting for the missing, making an accurate guess that her spouse had headed for the gin mills in Bridgeport.

Going down Foster Creek, she met the convivial trio, who were headed back for the construction camp. They had bought a gallon of ice cream in Bridgeport and after eating all of it they could hold as they went along, they had taken to throwing handfuls of it at each other. They were sticky and the targets of a million delighted flies that had showed up from every direction. The engineer's wife stopped the happy group at the foot of the long hill up out of Foster Creek canyon, unhooked her saddle horse, unharnessed it, and departed, leaving the merrymakers stranded with a buckboard, two sets of harness, and one horse. They pulled the buckboard off to the side of the road, loaded the extra harness on their remaining horse, and walked the fifteen miles to town under a broiling sun.

One day a serious powder accident occurred on the rail-road job. The contract doctor couldn't be found, so they called me. When I arrived, the injured man had been moved into a tent that was hot as a bakeoven, and his fellow work-men were doing what they could to relieve him, which didn't amount to much.

He had been tamping sixteen sticks of giant powder, which had exploded. Why, I don't know. Maybe he had been tamping the powder with a steel bar, which powdermen who didn't know better sometimes did, often with disas-trous results. Anyway, when I looked at the man, I didn't know where to begin. His eyes were gone, the bone in his upper arm stuck out through the flesh, and he had a big hole in his chest. His right hand looked all right from the back, but when I turned it over, I found nothing but a shell. The palm had been sheared away as though it had been done with a knife.

The first thing I did was to give him a shot of morphine, not worrying about the size of the dose. Then I began what I felt was nothing better than a bluff, dressing his wounds, aided by his comrades between their vomiting spells. The injured man became wildly delirious, continuously talking about his boyhood in West Virginia. I kept repeating the morphine shots until he quieted down and passed over the Great Divide.

No doubt the Celestial Keeper of Records and Seals has me debited with an act of euthanasia, to which I plead guilty. The worst thing that could have happened to the man once the powder went off would have been to live afterward.

After the new town got going, the managers of one of the banks vacated their building for a larger one, and I rented the old building for my office. Then, sight unseen, from an old doctor in Davenport I bought the stock and fixtures of a drugstore, had them moved to Mansfield, and housed them there in a store building I talked the Wright Brothers lumberyard into putting up.

I knew something about running a drugstore and intended to open one. But before I could do so, a rancher who wanted to get in on the new urban prosperity made me an offer I couldn't refuse. I sold out at a considerable profit, even though I had to split it with a banker.

Somehow, I got credit for having known the railroad was coming and for having put myself in a position to benefit from it. That was crediting me with more savvy than I deserved, but maybe people did it because I had proved that a doctor could make a precarious living in Mansfield. I heard afterward that there was some gossip in Tacoma and Seattle that I was the most prosperous doctor in the sagebrush and was simply wallowing in money. My circumstances, however, were as I have described them, with little or no financial elbowroom until I sold the drugstore.

In those days, there was no shortage of doctors, and I had been expecting one to light in Mansfield. Sure enough, it wasn't long before one moved in, a young fellow, stillborn from college but not averse to advertising in a Wenatchee paper, where he ran an ad claiming he had graduated at the head of his class in a postgraduate school and had all the answers known to medical science. Although every doctor knew that his claims were strictly bunkum, the public didn't know it, and his advertising impressed many of them. That was my introduction to the wiles of alleged "ethical" practitioners, too many of whom are about as ethical as an alley tomcat.

Looking back at it, I think I took the new doctor's tactics more seriously than I should have when I told him off one day after meeting him in the street. I then heard that he had bought a revolver and had begun carrying it to protect himself from me. When I heard that, I sent word by my informant that the new doctor would be well advised to file the sight off his new six-shooter so that it wouldn't hurt him so much when somebody shoved the barrel up his ass.

I suppose I was on the prod because I was suffering from battle fatigue, fed up principally with delivering babies all over the Big Bend country. I had delivered a baby in every house on my street, including my own, and had named the street Stork Alley.[1] I wanted a vacation someplace where I wouldn't even hear of a woman having a baby.

I suppose, too, that I was restless. Although I hadn't really made much money from selling the drugstore, it was more money than I had seen in a long time, and the possession of an unusual amount of money has always made me restless,

[1] I was the baby he delivered in his own house on September 25, 1910, when he was just a few days short of his forty-second birthday and my mother was a little over a month past her forty-first. My brother was thirteen. My mother used to tell a story about a neighbor woman who came to call the day I was born and said that she had thought the baby had arrived when she saw Doc Stratton out at the well that morning pumping a bucket of water for the house. Apparently my mother had performed the chore until the time of her confinement.

My mother used to tell another story in somewhat the same vein about the night when another frame house not far from ours caught fire and burned down. Several men came with a ladder and climbed up onto our roof, where they used wet sacks to put out burning embers that flew from the other house. My father got up, looked out the window, and then went back to bed. When my mother asked him if he wasn't going up on the roof to help the neighbors save our house, he said that it sounded as though there were already enough men up there.—OSS.

which is one of the reasons why I shall shortly die broke or nearly so.

Anyway, a postgraduate course seemed to provide an answer for my battle fatigue and my prosperity-induced restlessness. I decided to go to Chicago and see what I could learn in the course of a couple of weeks.

That decision made, I hunted for a doctor to take over my practice while I was gone. One man who had heard of my search called me on the telephone from Wenatchee. I stated my proposal, which was that he could use my office, equipment, and driving outfit and keep all he took in during my absence. When I returned, I would help with his collections.

It seemed to me a fair proposal, and I still think so, but he hemmed and hawed, backed and filled, then postponed his decision, saying he would let me know. I couldn't see his hand nor observe how he spit, but he didn't fool me. I told my wife, "This is one of those cunning birds. If I don't go to Chicago, we'll never hear from him again. If I do go, I still won't hear from him, but he'll slide in and try to get established while I'm away. But to hell with him. I'm going anyway." Sure enough, when I returned, I found him on the job.

I must say it was a pleasure to get on the pullman in Wenatchee, repair to the observation car when I felt like a cigar, eat at leisure in the diner when I felt hungry, and not stir off the train for days except to stretch my legs until we pulled into Dearborn Station in Chicago.

My arrival coincided with the first meeting of the American College of Surgeons, and I found Chicago teeming with surgeons from all over the map. I signed up for the entire curriculum at the Chicago Polyclinic Postgraduate School.

One evening in the lobby of the Sherman Hotel where I stayed, I heard a loud, braying, familiar voice. I went around some potted palms and on the other side, found my old friend Jim Ferrell, who had broken me into the medicine game. He was as glad to see me as I was to see him. He introduced me to his companion, saying, "Stratton, here, is one of our old gang, but he quit us to join up with them ethical guys. But I'll bet he ain't making the dough he made with us." Jim occasionally lapsed into the truth, and that was one of the times. In spades.

Jim didn't wait long to tell me that he had a date with some classy dames. He invited me to come along, declaring that the evening was on him. I declined with thanks, and although we corresponded afterward, that was the last time I saw him. Two years ago, he dropped dead in a Baltimore hotel, and his son wrote me that he was able to put his father's entire estate in an overnight bag. So maybe, after all, I didn't do too badly when I switched to the so-called ethical side of the medicine game.

I soon picked my way to the various clinics, which I found going in high gear for the edification of the visitors. I spent as much of my time as I could in watching and listening to John B. Murphy at Mercy Hospital and to A. J. Ochsner at Augustana Hospital. I observed that Murphy used rubber gloves when doing surgery while Ochsner disdained them, as did Joseph Price of Philadelphia. That appealed to me, as I found the gloves cumbersome. I have always believed that asepsis is determined not only by the knowledge but also by the conscience of the surgeon. He should know when he is clean, and if he doesn't or isn't willing to take the time to get that way, he should abandon surgery. Incidentally, researchers at Barnes Hospital in St. Louis have recently discovered that the talcum powder commonly used on rubber gloves creates adhesions in abdominal surgery.

Murphy was the best teacher of surgery under whom I have ever sat or, rather, above whom I have ever sat, since I observed him from a seat in an operating theater. He continually spoke practical wisdom, and I found in the years afterward that his *Surgical Clinics*, all of which I have in my library, were reliable guides.

He could on occasion, however, be a little fast off the mark. One morning after he had opened up a patient, he pointed with his scalpel at the incision as he turned his head to address his audience. "Just as I suspected," Murphy said, "This patient's peritoneal cavity is studded with tubercles." He had no more than delivered himself of this snap diagnosis when the referring doctor lumbered to his feet and said, "Doctor Murphy, some time ago we injected some vaseline in this patient's abdomen in the hope of preventing adhesions."

Murphy took another look and crushed one of his tubercles between thumb and forefinger. "That's exactly what they are," he said. "Encysted vaseline." Then he was off again, hitting his stride and cocksure as ever.

In one clinic Sir Arbuthnot Lane, the English surgeon, demonstrated bone surgery. He was a fanatic about asepsis, at least in words. "Not even the gloved finger should enter the wound," he declared. While this utter refinement may have been worthwhile, to untutored Americans Lane's English sounded as though he had his mouth filled with porridge. One spectator demonstrated his difficulty in understanding by calling out, "Louder, please." Lane obligingly raised his mask with his gloved hand and repeated his remarks. Then, leaping over this break in asepsis, he reentered his field.

I heard Dr. Karl J. Weiss of Germany deliver a long lecture in German on childbirth sleep. He spoke in Orchestra Hall, and when he finished, I applauded like the others as though I knew what he had said. Then we waited for the translation, which took much less time. Weiss's method did not prove popular with the medical profession, which soon abandoned it, partly because its virtue in making the mother forget her travail had a counterbalancing effect in being bad for her offspring.

In those days, we had no news magazines playing up the bizarre and sensational in medicine, but we did have supplements to the daily newspapers, which did much the same thing. In 1910 Dr. Paul Ehrlich's "606" was announced as a cure for syphilis, and the supplements played it to the skies.

When I attended a symposium on syphilis staged by the North Chicago Medical Society, I learned that Ehrlich's cure was not yet accepted by the assembled syphilologists. I must confess that most of their debate went over my head, but I did hear one of those present say, "I challenge anyone to name one well-authenticated case of syphilis which has been contracted from contact with an inanimate object." No one volunteered, and that challenge, which I pasted in my hat, makes me dubious about the sense of state laws requiring Wasserman tests from all food vendors. I'll add that it makes me suspicious of the bona fides of the politicians and public officials who insist on such a test.

From Dr. Paul Gronnerud's class in operative surgery and anatomy I learned the desirability of making the incision as far to the right as possible when operating for a possibly ruptured appendix. That approach avoided the danger of entering the general peritoneal cavity, and I know it was a lifesaver in many hazardous operations.

From Chicago, I went to Rochester, Minnesota, where Will and Charles Mayo were just getting into their stride. The Mayos sponsored an organization at their clinic which they called the Surgeons' Club. It was made up of whatever medical visitors happened to be there from all over the world and met every evening as a sort of town meeting in which the events of that day were discussed. Reporters for the following day were then appointed, their responsibility being to report to the next evening's meeting what they had observed during the day.

Each reporter received a badge which entitled him to a position in a little runway next to the operating table, which gave him a fine view of what was going on, so good a view, in fact, that once when I was serving as a reporter, I was so close to the operative field that an artery spurted in my face.

The friendliness of the Mayo staff was remarkable. They

would listen to the most foolish questions without a sign of irritation and answer the questions plainly and civilly. The exchanges were not all one way, however one-sided they may have been, for Dr. Will Mayo once said that the staff acquired many kernels of wisdom by listening to the bush leaguers. Several times in my practice when stuck for an answer I have written to Mayo's for help and they never turned me down. I can't speak too highly of the contribution they made to the improvement of medical practice.

Chapter 14

Cold Feet About Surgery—A Drunken Surgeon—A Hot Cake
Cook Charges for Accommodation—A Fly in My Cocoa—A
Patient with Broken Arms and Concussion—Close Calls

When I finished at Rochester, I headed back to the sticks, not looking forward a hell of a lot to my arrival. I had learned a little, but my bankroll was shot full of holes, and I was sure I faced a tough winter. To make it worse, the flesh-pots of Egypt had softened me up considerably.

The stork was still leaving babies all over the sagebrush; ranchers' cayuses were still running away, kicking hell out of things, and producing fractures; the wells continued to provide typhoids and "intestinal flu"; and vermiform appendices persisted in abscessing.

My feet were not yet warm enough to tackle an appendectomy, but I did, with fear and trembling, undertake my first tonsillectomy. During my visit to Chicago, I had seen several tonsillectomies, which had seemed pretty haphazard, with a lot of groping in the dark in a very bloody field. No operator seemed sure of anything except that tonsils should come out while leaving the pillars and uvulae intact. I have performed a good many tonsillectomies since then and removed only one uvula, but I regard a tonsillectomy as a major operation and have never removed tonsils just because they were there. I have never seen any use in a vermiform appendix, but I believe that tonsils serve some function in health and that they should not be taken out unless they are badly infected.

Taking out an appendix was something else, a no-man's-land for me, and I backed away from it. I knew the symptoms all right because I had suffered them myself and had also memorized Dr. John B. Murphy's description of them. They were, "First, a generalized belly-ache around the navel; second, nausea and vomiting; third, development of a tender spot in the region of McBurney's point; fourth, a little fever, which might be overlooked. These symptoms should always occur in proper sequence, or the diagnosis remains in doubt."

Two additional symptoms that occurred in my own case were that if gas in my intestines could get by an obstruction, I would be relieved, and, second, using one finger, I could locate what must have been the base of my appendix. In my practice, I have had many young patients without much stomach fat do the latter for me, and it has been an infallible sign.

The first patient I had whose symptoms were in order was a rancher named McDowell. He had driven a freight wagon with no springs from Coulee City, a distance of thirty miles, arriving home late in the night. He had then taken on a load of meat and potatoes and gone to bed. About daylight, he had been awakened by a bellyache so severe that he called me. I checked him and double-checked him until I was sure that he needed surgery and then sent him to a surgeon in Spokane.

All I knew about the surgeon was what I had read in the papers, and he seemed to be doing a lot of surgery. He removed McDowell's appendix and in due time sent the patient home. A few days later, I received a letter from the surgeon enclosing a check for 40 percent of the fee and stating that if I had accompanied the patient and assumed half the responsibility, my share would have been 50 percent.

That was my introduction to feesplitting. I mulled it over for a few days and concluded that refusing the split wouldn't help my patient, so I cashed the check. I said nothing but did not refer any more patients to that surgeon. Since then, I have wondered if I did not make a mistake by wiping him from my list, for he was probably just as good a surgeon as some of those who kept the whole fee.

I had yet to learn that referring a patient to supposedly greater authority, whatever other effects it had, often lost the patient to me. Thereafter, the patient was likely to go elsewhere when he thought he had something serious the matter with him.

My next appendicitis case was a young woman in Bridgeport. When I had made my diagnosis, she asked me to call a young surgeon practicing in Wenatchee. To get to Bridgeport, he had to travel eighty miles in a buggy, and when he arrived, he was drunker than a lord.

I hardly knew what to do. But since I knew my patient needed surgery, I decided to let him make the incision while I served as assistant. We gave the patient a shot of HMC (hyoscine, morphine, and codeine) and an hour and a half later repeated it. Thirty minutes after that, with the surgeon's driver handling the chloroform mask under my supervision, we went after the appendix. It was what I have heard Dr. Ochsner call "a darling" because it hopped right up in the incision and was removed with no difficulty.

My surgeon, in his drunken enthusiasm, discarded contaminated instruments by throwing them against the wall. The patient knew nothing of that, and her convalescence was uneventful. With that experience, my surgical feet warmed up a trifle.

My next appendicitis patient was a rancher named Fritts, who afterward was elected auditor of Douglas County. I called the same surgeon, who arrived sober and driving a Winton Six. That was the first automobile to enter the Mansfield community, and I still wonder how he managed to get it there, given the unreliability of automobiles in those days and the state of the roads. Certainly he could not have done it if he had fortified himself as he had done before, since automobiles go where you point them, something horses usually have better sense than to do.

We propped our patient up in bed so that he could sign a

note, which must not have greatly increased his confidence in our estimate of the outcome of our treatment. Then we operated under a local anesthetic.

We operated on a Saturday. Overlooking the fact that the next day was Sunday, I didn't warn the family concerning visitors. Well, they came in flocks and entertained the patient with all the surgical horror stories they had ever heard.

When I arrived that evening, I found the patient wildly delirious and difficult to keep in bed. He waved me to one side, shouting, "I'm all right, doctor! We don't need you anymore! I'm doing fine!" While I hoped he was telling the truth, I wasn't so sure about it. Finally, I edged my way in among the bystanders and got him quieted down. After that, he recovered without trouble.

His note was gilt-edged, and my surgeon cashed it at a local bank. Then he gave me 40 percent of the proceeds. This time, I had no scruples about accepting the split, as I had earned it with worry, if nothing more. I also began to figure that the only thing the surgeon had on me was a little more nerve.

I especially dreaded lobar pneumonia. In those days, we had no better treatment for the malady than prayer. If the patient, with what little help we could provide, tided himself or herself over until Mother Nature stepped in with what we called the crisis on the fifth, seventh, or ninth day (it seemed always an odd number) the patient usually made it.

Once, I had a patient in her forties, desperately ill with the disease on a homestead fifteen miles from Mansfield. I made daily visits, and I would look ahead on each visit when I came in sight of the house to see whether the bedclothes were hanging on the line. If they were not, I would whip up with hope in my heart that she might make it.

One day I had a driver named Shorty Robbins, who not only understood horses but was good and welcome company on those long trips. By the time I had checked over my patient and we were ready to leave, a blizzard had come up, and the thermometer had dropped below zero. (Blizzards and, indeed, most weather other than the changes of seasons surprised people because there existed no better weather forecasts than rings around the moon and jingles about red in the morning, sailor's warning.) The wind howled from the direction in which we had to go, and Shorty was not keen to tackle it. Nor was I. He went out and put the horses in the barn, and we got set to spend the night.

The patient's husband whipped up a batch of hot cakes for supper, and after we ate, Shorty and I occupied a makeshift bed. Next morning the husband repeated the supper menu for breakfast, and I did what I could for the patient. The wind had shifted around and was blowing in the direction we had to go; so we set out and fought our way through the drifts back to Mansfield. A day or two later, the patient hit crisis, muddled through, and before long completely recovered.

A year later, when I had gone to a new location and put my accounts in the hands of the bank for collection, the husband of my lobar pneumonia patient offered to pay his bill, but with an offset of $7.50 for accommodation furnished my horses, my driver, and me. My wife, who had stayed behind until I got settled, wrote and asked whether she should accept the payment. I wrote back, "For God's sake, yes! They must need the money worse than we do."

I will say, however, that the hot cake cook was an exception. Most of my patients were tickled pink when I stayed over and never so much as thought of charging me for it. Well, you never can tell what a homo sapiens will do to you when he thinks he's got you.

On another occasion, when I had remained all night at the bedside of a hopeless patient, injecting normal saline in a forlorn hope that a miracle might happen, the patient's granddaughter served breakfast to my driver and me. While we ate, a fly gave up the ghost in midair and dropped into my cocoa. The sharp eye of the hostess noted it, and she exclaimed, "Oh, doctor! There's a fly in your cocoa! Let me strain it for you."

I couldn't see that straining the cocoa would improve it, so I just picked the insect out between thumb and forefinger and dropped it on the floor. I doubt that I could do it now, but then I had a strong stomach and downed the flyless cocoa because I knew I would need it during the thirty-mile drag back to Mansfield. The last I heard, Shorty Robbins is still alive, and I know that if we should meet again, after our first greeting, he would cry in a falsetto voice, "Oh, doctor! There's a fly in your cocoa! Let me strain it for you."

One night in Mansfield about eleven o'clock, while an unusual rain fell in a steady drizzle, the telephone rang. I answered and found that the call came from a ranch twenty miles away in the Columbia River breaks. The caller said, "Jimmie Pattie has fallen off the barn, and we think he's dead. Will you come to see him?"

"Well, if he's dead," I answered, "what the hell do you want with me?"

"Well, we're not sure," the caller said, "and we'd like you to come look at him."

Shorty Robbins thought he knew the road, but the night was darker than the inside of a cow, and the rain didn't help. Even in daylight the road was no cinch to travel, and the last mile wound in a narrow grade along the side of a canyon wall. The horses could see better than we could, however, and got us there safely.

The patient, a stranger to me, turned out to be a Scotsman, who had persuaded a schoolteacher to marry him when he was not as young as he had once been. They had a daughter about three years old. He had been building a barn, working by himself, and had apparently leaned on a rafter which had snapped off, precipitating him headfirst to the ground thirty feet below. He had broken his fall a little with extended arms, but had lain out in the rain for an hour or so before they found him. Then they packed him into the house and called me.

When I took inventory, I found him with a brain concussion and both arms broken above the wrists. I thought that in his dazed condition I could reduce his fractures without an anesthetic, but when I touched one of his wrists he put up a battle, though only semiconscious. With assistance from the hired man, I chloroformed the patient, reduced the fractures, and put the arms in splints. I wasn't sure, however, whether he had a fracture of the skull.

I stayed all night, serving as both doctor and nurse. His restlessness suggested that he needed to urinate, but I couldn't get him to use an improvised urinal. So we carried him outside and held him up on his feet, in which position his reflexes took over and his drainage system functioned all right.

The next morning his daze seemed to have improved, so I left for home and telephoned Spokane from there to engage a graduate nurse. She arrived that day, and I took her along on my visit the next day.

Even with the nurse on the job, I had to make many visits, on one of which I found the patient's wife using a shovel handle to kill a big rattlesnake in front of the woodshed. She said there were so many rattlenakes around that they never let the little girl out of the house unless someone was with her. A great place to raise a family!

After Jimmie Pattie had recovered from his concussion, he came to town and asked me to remove the splints from his right arm so that he could write a check. I had learned that he was pretty well off, and when he asked what he owed me, I suggested that he write me a check big enough to pay for an automobile. He nearly fainted, as a car at that time cost two or three grand, not counting another couple of hundred for a team to tow the car back to town after it had broken down on the road. I was kidding Pattie, of course, and quickly brought him out of his shock by telling him that I would settle for $300. That was fine and dandy, and he seemed to take pleasure in writing the check. During the remainder of my stay in Mansfield, Jimmie came in every time he visited the place to show me his wrists and always made the same remark. "Doc, I can pitch as much hay as I ever could." I wish all my patients had been equally satisfied with what I was able to do for them.

Playing a lone hand in the practice of medicine has its drawbacks, but it does compel the practitioner to assume responsibility while keeping his mind on the race. Any misstep, and he is in trouble.

One day a rancher stopped me and asked me to come to see his father-in-law, who had injured his leg while riding the running gear of a wagon. Since the trip was twelve miles, and it was late in the evening, I asked, "How long has he been hurt?"

"Oh, about a week."

"Well, if he's stood it that long," I said, "he ought to be able to stand it until tomorrow."

The rancher agreed, and the next morning on my way to his place, I tried to guess the nature of the father-in-law's injury. I guessed that it was a Pott's fracture—both bones of the leg broken above the ankle. When I arrived, I found that I was right.

They had been trying to cure the old man with home remedies, and the leg was badly swollen and very painful. I could see no choice but to chloroform him, which was not the best thing that could happen to a man of his age. I checked him over, and he seemed sound enough, so I took a chance.

When I got him under, I turned the mask over to a volunteer neighbor and began applying a plaster of paris cast to the leg. I became too interested in what I was doing, and when I looked up, the patient had stopped breathing.

I abandoned the leg and began to apply artificial respiration while fighting off the family, who saw that something had gone wrong with Grandpa and tried to keep him from taking off for the Golden Shore by hugging him. Through loud talk and some profanity, I got them out of the way and got the old man breathing again. Then I finished putting on the cast.

This was before the day when the Rotary Club or the

Elks Lodge presented the fire department with a pulmotor. When I see a picture of the donors and the recipients sitting up like picket-pin gophers at the presentation, I always wonder how many helpless victims will have their lungs overextended by the machine. When you need a pulmotor, time is of the essence, and the Shaefer method of artificial respiration will do everything that a machine can do if anything at all can be done.

Three weeks after I resuscitated the old man, his son-in-law brought him to town to have a new cast put on. The son-in-law served as my assistant by holding the leg while I worked on it. I was washing the leg and looked up to find my helper on the verge of fainting and trying to keep from falling by hanging onto the injured limb. I pried his fingers loose, and he fell like a log onto the floor. Since he had assumed a position with his head low, he needed no further assistance, and I finished the new cast while he got himself back together.

Fainting is hard to predict. There was nothing particularly repulsive about the old man's leg, and there was no pain or blood, which affects some observers. On another occasion, I had put a patient on the kitchen table in her ranch house and had her daughter holding a kerosene lamp while I performed a curettement. The patient cried, "Look, doctor!" and I turned around just in time to take the lighted lamp out of the girl's hands before she fell. A narrow escape!

Another narrow escape came when I had delivered a baby at a ranch without much trouble and was hurrying to get away because a blizzard was coming up. I got into my fur coat and went into the bedroom before I left to say good-by to the patient.

"I don't feel very good, doctor," she said. I thought she was complaining unnecessarily until I felt of her abdomen, which was ballooned out as though she were about to have another baby.

Believe me, I shucked out of my fur coat like a quick change artist. I forgot all about the blizzard and spent the next few hours trying to save my patient from a postpartum hemorrhage. Fortunately, I succeeded, but I still flinch when I think what would have happened if I had moved a little faster and got away.

Another time, a rancher came to my office to get some medicine for his wife. I asked him what he wanted it for, and after I asked him a few more questions and he answered, I said, "You don't need any medicine. What you need is a doctor, and you need him damned quick!"

He was in a Model T Ford, and I followed him with Shorty Robbins driving in another. I got there just in time to find the rancher's wife *in extremis* from the lodgement of the placenta of an abortion. The time was too short to scrub up properly before I removed it. After I did so, I elevated the foot of the bed so that she was nearly standing on her head, and she recovered after a long convalescence, in the process eating all the salt in the neighborhood to replace what she had lost with her hemorrhage.

I have delivered many babies, some of which were difficult instrument deliveries, in every type of surroundings, but I always tried to keep my mind on my chain of asepsis. The only case I lost was one in which the patient had septemia from an infected induced abortion and was having chills that shook the house when I first saw her. We gave her about a million units of penicillin, but it was no more effective in her case than so much rainwater would have been.

My experience makes me agree with what Dr. Will Mayo once said. "People acquire a resistance to their own germs. If no aliens are introduced, they will have little trouble." That is why an aseptic conscience in a surgeon is so valuable.

Chapter 15

I Offend Mrs. Carter—Her Tapeworm Treatment—A Breech
Presentation and Profanity—Paul Spends His First Night
Away From His Mother—Jasper the Game Rooster

In 1910 the role of the country doctor was so unenviable that I have sometimes wondered why I stayed with it. Maybe I was like the Irishman on a bucking horse to whom a bystander shouted, "Why don't you get off?"

"Get off, hell!" the Irishman replied. "It's all I can do to stay on."

Tough as it was, however, there were other doctors who thought I had a cinch, and two of them lit in Mansfield, anxious to divide the spoils. One was better trained than I, having served an internship at Massachusetts General Hospital in Boston. The other had plenty of gall and a talent for four-flushing, which favorably impressed a number of people. Three doctors in a town that had four hundred people in it when the chickens were all home, didn't leave much surplus for any of us.

Besides the competition, getting adequate nursing was often a problem. When the patient had enough money to pay for her, I could get a graduate nurse from Spokane in a day, and some of them were excellent, especially the women who had trained in Catholic hospitals and were as disciplined as soldiers are supposed to be. They would stand at attention for their orders, and I never had one suggest a better way. Occasionally I tried one of them out by asking whether the treatment I prescribed was the way they did it in Spokane. Invariably, the nurse replied, "It looks all right to me, doctor," leaving me wondering if it truly did.

Most nursing, however, was done by practical nurses, who were all right when they recognized their limits. But a little knowledge was a dangerous thing, and those who had it often thought they knew more than the doctor. They were happy to prescribe. If their remedy had a bad effect, they would not report its use; if it had a good effect, they told the cockeyed world about it. Fortunately, most of their remedies were as harmless as they were useless.

Several women in the community practiced as midwives as well as nurses. They got along all right in OB cases that required nothing more complicated than standing by and receiving the new arrival, but greater demands got them beyond their depth.

One morning about daylight, old Mrs. Carter, one of the midwives, called me to see a patient. Mrs. Carter had been up all night with the case and decided at last that she needed a doctor. She was like the medical student who found his roommate studying a book on obstetrics. The roommate had come to a plate which showed the arm of a baby sticking out of a vagina. "Bill, what would you do in a case like this?" the roommate asked.

Bill bent over to look at the plate and said, "Why I'd shake hands with the little son of a bitch, and then I'd send for a doctor."

When I arrived at the house to which she had called me, Mrs. Carter met me at the door and briskly ordered, "Give me your forceps, doctor, so I can sterilize them. This is an instrument case." I said to wait a minute, that I'd like to see the patient first. "No need to do that," Mrs. Carter replied. "I've been here all night, and the baby hasn't budged an inch."

I insisted on seeing the patient, and much against her better judgment, Mrs. Carter led me into the bedroom, where I found a young woman in her fifth labor and almost exhausted. She had never had a doctor for any of her previous deliveries, and although she was young, she had a pendulous abdomen from so many pregnancies.

I watched her when she had a pain and found her exerting her propulsive powers, not in the axis of the uterus but, instead, pushing the uterus with the baby in it over the rim of her pelvis. I supported her abdomen during the next pain and felt the baby move. A few more pains with the same support, and I had the baby. I doubt that old lady Carter ever forgave me for not using forceps.

Another time, Mrs. Carter was nursing a patient who had lobar pneumonia. He was a pioneer preacher named Barrows, who had a tough time making ends meet while he labored in the Vineyard of the Lord. I was doing what I could to keep him out of Heaven, but I didn't like the prospect. I had called in two other doctors, but they were as helpless as I.

Barrows sensed my distress at his impending end, which didn't scare him at all, an attitude testifying to the solidity of his faith. He even kidded me with a quotation from the Bible, which I am sorry to have forgotten.

The night he died was a beautiful moonlit night, and Mrs. Carter and I were sitting on the veranda, I hoping against hope that a miracle might save my patient and she recollecting some of her experiences. She told one story about a woman who had a tapeworm which had baffled the medical science brought to bear against it in efforts to expel it. Mrs. Carter took charge. "I just fed her a whole passel of sugar, giving her one spoonful after another until the tapeworm got so sick he just stuck his head right out of her mouth. Then I took the shears and whacked his head off. You bet that settled him!"

I registered proper astonishment, but didn't tell Mrs. Carter that in my medicine show days, I had been a tapeworm specialist and a good one, with many a notch in my tapeworm coupstick. I was better with tapeworms then than with pneumonia later.

With our ordeal over and my patient gone to his reward, which should have been a good one, I got permission from his widow to do an autopsy. Because the patient had seemed a little jaundiced, one of the men I had called in as a consultant had questioned my diagnosis of pneumonia. I invited him to attend the autopsy, and we found the right lung completely consolidated. That helped my confidence in myself as a diagnostician.

In relating my experiences, I am not trying to pass myself off as somebody who knows all the answers. On the contrary, I have been just an ordinary run-of-the-mill doctor, on duty around the clock. I didn't know enough to hurt me and still don't, but I ploughed back any surplus, trying to become a better doctor. Although I don't think I was ever inhumane, I was not a professional humanitarian with a soft heart and softer head, expecting monuments to be erected to me.

There were times when I was all in, physically and mentally, but I can recall going to sleep in a chair only once. That occurred following an all-night session, and when my wife shook me awake, the telephone was ringing its bells off a foot away from my ear.

The call came from someone at Lahey, a stage station twenty miles away. He said there was a man there who wanted me to come to a confinement case over on the Columbia, about ten miles from Lahey. I suggested they get somebody from Coulee City, which was closer than Mansfield, but the man on the phone said they had tried that, and the line was down. I told the caller I couldn't start before one o'clock, and after a conference at his end, he reported that that would be OK and that the messenger would wait for me to show me where to go.

I started at the time I promised and hazed my horses through. At Lahey, the messenger got into my buggy and led his saddle horse behind. Although I have never been in the neighborhood since, I believe that the ranch to which

Owen Tully Stratton, M.D., about 1945

my guide directed me was near the site of the present Grand Coulee Dam.

When we came in sight of the house, I could see a woman run out, waving frantically at us with her apron. Pretty soon, another woman joined her and did the same thing. I whipped up the horses and made a Garrison finish at the rear of a two-story house, where a man waited to take my team. Jumping out of the buggy, I grabbed my grips and hustled through the back door, into the kitchen.

Since I knew I had been called to a confinement case and that the behavior of the apron wavers indicated that all was not yet over, I stopped in the kitchen, shucked off my shirt, and took the dust off me with a dry towel. Then I began to scrub up to a tune furnished by an excited woman, who begged, "Oh, please hurry up, doctor! Hurry up! Oh, God, she's dying!" I continued scrubbing until I was sure I was clean.

One lady afterward told me, "I thought you were the slowest man I had ever seen in all my life."

When I was ready, I found the patient to be a young, buxom woman, who had been pounding her firstborn-to-be against her pelvic bone for hours and was a long way from dead.

It took me awhile to determine that the baby was trying to enter this world of trouble and tears backward, for which I could hardly blame him. Alongside his butt, there was a foot that looked almost as big as mine and was as black as the ace of spades. I untangled him and delivered him and got him into a dishpan of warm water on the floor. Down on my knees, I slapped him and folded him and dashed him with cold water. Before long, he was demonstrating a powerful set of vocal cords and telling the cockeyed world that he didn't like me, not even a little bit.

When I was sure the baby was all right, I attended to his mother. When I had done everything for her that I could and given instructions to the women in attendance, I was ready to go home. The father, whose name was George Judson, had my team hooked up, and when I appeared, he asked how much he owed me. When I told him seventy-five dollars, he staggered as though I had hit him on the jaw.

"Hell! I'm no millionaire!" he exclaimed.

"Well, neither am I," I answered, "and I don't ever expect to be." Then, thinking of the thirty-mile trip in the dark still to come, I added, "And if I had to do it over again, damned if I know whether I'd do it for that fee."

That cooled Judson down a bit, and he said, "Well, I haven't got the money now, but as soon as I sell my wheat, I'll send it to you." He turned out to be as good as his word.

A few days after I'd made the call, a neighbor of the Judson family met me on the street and said, "Doc, I've got a good one on you." I said I didn't doubt it and asked what one it was that he had on me. "Well, my mother was one of those women over at the Judsons' when you delivered their baby. My mother's a straightlaced Presbyterian from Indiana, and she's been out here only for a month or so. When you were down on your knees working on the baby, she leaned over your shoulder and asked, 'The baby's dead, isn't it, doctor?'

"You never looked up but said, 'Yes, I think it's deader than hell.' She was pretty shocked, but I think she'll get over it."

I didn't remember the incident, but I could believe it happened and sent his mother my apologies.

Profanity in such circumstances was the product of thoughtlessness, plus irritation and worry. They used to tell a story in Bridgeport about C. R. McKinley, the so-called Cowboy Doctor, who had been called to deliver a baby for the wife of the Bridgeport postmaster. It was one of those drawn-out, tedious affairs, which exhausted the patience of the mother, the attendants, and the doctor. Maybe even the baby. Nothing much was the matter except that the force behind the passenger was inadequate to overcome the resistance in front of him.

Just when everybody was about ready to give up, the baby emerged. Dr. McKinley straightened up, pressing his hands on his aching back, and exclaimed, "Well, there's the God damned little bastard at last!"

I used to go over to Bridgeport occasionally for no reason except to visit with Al Sawtelle, Hank Klaas, and the others around town. On one such trip, I took Paul with me and discovered that what amused me bored him. When I was about ready for the return trip, I got a call to go way up the Columbia to see a man who had always come to me when I practiced in Bridgeport, and I thought I should respond.

I told Paul about it and suggested that he go to bed in the hotel, where Mrs. Barney, the motherly landlady, would take good care of him. The boy was eleven years old then, had never spent a night away from his mother, and was not happy about spending the first one by himself in the Bridgeport hotel.

He couldn't eat his supper and kept swallowing lumps that must have felt as big as golf balls, to judge from the way he gulped. I called up his mother, and he talked to her over the telephone; but that only made him feel worse.

I had to go, however, and took him to the hotel, where I turned him over to Mrs. Barney. I didn't get back until three in the morning and found the boy wide-awake. I don't believe he had slept a wink, but by the time I got undressed, he had turned over and gone sound asleep. I think that was the time of times when he was most glad to see his dad.

In 1908, the first year we were in Mansfield, many of the Bridgeport citizens went in for raising game chickens. I never heard of any cockpit battles or that anyone ever made any money out of the fad, which is what it was, one of those things that occasionally strikes a small town and breaks the monotony for awhile. Anyway, there were many game roosters of high and low degree around Bridgeport.

In the course of buying chickens for the market, Hamilton, whose store was next to my office, acquired a Leghorn rooster that was a fighter of such capacity that he soon licked all the Plymouth Rock and dunghill roosters in Hamilton's flock.

One day in Bridgeport, I happened to mention the Leghorn's prowess, and one of my listeners brightened up and offered to lend me a gamecock, which he assured me could lick any Leghorn in the world. When I went to get my rig for the return trip to Mansfield, I found in my buggy a box containing a game rooster.

I conveyed him to Mansfield and the following morning turned him loose among Hamilton's chickens. The Leghorn immediately knocked the socks off the game rooster. So on my next trip to Bridgeport, with the defeated battler as a passenger, I related what had happened.

When I was ready to go back, I found another gladiator in my buggy. This one did better with the Leghorn until, while trying to deliver an uppercut, he tore the web between two toes and nearly bled to death before I could catch him and stop the bleeding. When he had recovered from his wound, I returned him to his Bridgeport sponsor and heard nothing more for awhile.

Then a stage driver delivered a box containing a game rooster to my office. The rooster had been on the road for several days, spending a lot of time outside stage stations, waiting for connections and receiving little care. He was a sorry-looking bird, who had evidently amused himself during layovers by taking on local battlers through the slats of his box. Most of his plumage and tail feathers were missing, but his head, although bloody, was unbowed. I let him recuperate in his box for several days until I got tired of feeding and watering him and turned him loose.

To me, he didn't even look like a rooster, but all the other roosters seemed certain of his sex and surrounded him, taking turns bowing their backs and calling him dirty names. He paid them no mind and just walked away, pecking aimlessly at gravel and an occasional grain of wheat. Finally, one of his challengers advanced to the distance the stranger had apparently been waiting for. He shot through the air as though delivered by a catapult and knocked his challenger fully ten feet. When the latter recovered from the shock of the impact, he looked for an opening and discovered one in the form of a hole in the fence.

From then on, Jasper, which I named him for no particular reason, was the head cock of the walk. His knockout punch was so impressive that I caught him and weighed him and found that he tipped the scales at seven and a half pounds.

By the time Jasper had grown a new suit of plumage, he had corralled all the Leghorn hens into his harem. He required no shots of the testosterone recommended by Paul De Kruiff in order to qualify as the sultan who, when he blew the light out at his harem said, "Well, that's thirty for tonight."

Jasper's progeny testified to his virility. When no bigger than pigeons and without a red feather on them, the little roosters would fight like bulldogs. They didn't have enough secondary sex characteristics to enable me to tell them from the girls, but I had to keep a pole handy to rake out contending gladiators who carried their quarrels to the space under my office. Out in the open again, heads bloodied, they would go at it once more even though they weren't yet old enough to crow.

When the new town arose from the volcanic ash, I gave Jasper to Shorty Robbins, who had opened a livery stable. Jasper picked up a living from wheat shattered from the hay Shorty fed his horses and extended his territory. When he heard a rooster crow, even on the other side of town, he would be on his way. Jasper met his end before long from a shotgun in the hands of an irate chicken grower who had got tired of seeing his aristocratic roosters beaten up by a professional thug. I believe that Jasper died happy.

Chapter 16

I Look Salmon Over and Decide to Move—The Other Doctors—Two Ectopic Pregnancies—An Appendectomy at Hughes Creek Ranger Station

I must have been a glutton for punishment between my thirty-eighth and forty-second years because I stuck with Mansfield during that time. But in 1911, I got sick enough of it that I decided to find a decent place to live.

With that in mind, I took a trip to the upper Snake River Valley in Idaho, but didn't find what looked like an opening. That was not as disappointing as it might have been, for the wind, which was high on my list of things to avoid, seemed as bad in the Snake River Valley as in Mansfield.

After I returned home, I saw an article in the Spokane *Spokesman Review* about a town named Salmon on the eastern edge of the central Idaho wilderness. The story said the citizens had recently completed a $40,000 courthouse and a $45,000 high school. Those sums don't sound like much today, but they were substantial in 1911 and suggested a degree of prosperity in the town. A little later, I read another story in the *Spokesman Review* saying that a disgruntled patient had shot and killed a physician in Salmon. The latter story indicated that an opening had opened up, and the first story indicated that the opening might be worth filling.

I took a jump in the dark and sold my office equipment to a competitor in Mansfield and told my wife that if the climate and living conditions in Salmon appeared endurable, I would stick there, no matter what the competition.

To get to Salmon, I had to take the train to Butte, transfer there to the Oregon Short Line, and travel south on that to Armstead, Montana, the junction point of the Oregon Short Line and the Gilmore and Pittsburgh, a one-hundred-mile line over the continental divide, completed only the year before.

A mixed train, consisting of a dozen or so assorted freight cars with a passenger coach on the end, went over one day and came back the next, making three trips each way in the course of a week if the weather or a mishap did not interfere.

Most of my fellow passengers seemed to be old-timers, returning from what they called "the outside," which meant anyplace in the world outside the Salmon and Lemhi river valleys. They evidently liked the train, rattletrap though it was, and I'm sure it was a considerable improvement over the stagecoaches that until 1910 had provided the only pub-lic transportation between Salmon and Red Rock, a station on the Oregon Short Line.

The time passed pleasantly between Armstead and Salmon. I was interested in the scenery, although it was mostly sagebrush-covered hills until we got over the con-tinental divide and came down into the Lemhi River Val-ley at Leadore, a new town fifty miles from Salmon. From there on, the railroad ran mostly through ranch country, with the high peaks of the Bitterroot Range on the right, and brought us to Salmon along in the afternoon, where a Virginian named Joe Cockerell met the train with a horse-drawn bus. The bus was a wagon, entered from the rear by climbing two or three steps, and had a seat running length-wise along each side, on which passengers sat facing each other, with their baggage piled in between. Later on, I be-came very well acquainted with Joe and learned that he had been a long-line skinner, driving six horses ahead of a freight wagon. Now, with his bus, he whirled me and the other passengers into town and to the Shenon Hotel, a two-story brick building erected in 1895, according to a granite slab set in its front. Fifty-four years later, the hotel is still doing business, although under another name.

Among the guests at the hotel were two mining men, who were trying to develop a placer mine on Yellow Jacket Creek in the mountains to the west of Salmon, about fifty miles away. The mining men were strangers like me and were very friendly, as is usually the case when strangers in a small town are thrown together.

They accompanied me as I surveyed the town, but all they provided was company and not much information. For that, I relied on Percy Anderson, another guest at the hotel, who was made to order for my purpose. He had been born near the gold rush mining camp of Leesburg to the west of Salmon and had been brought up in Gibbonsville, another gold camp, thirty-five miles from Salmon on the North Fork of the Salmon River. Percy, who was then in his middle thirties, liked the sound of his own voice and seemed to know everything that had happened in those parts since Lewis and Clark came through.

Percy explained that Salmon had originated as a river crossing and supply point for the Leesburg diggings, which were discovered in the 1860s during the Civil War. Most of the several thousand men who joined the rush to Leesburg were draft dodgers, coming from both North and South, but the southerners were most numerous and named the camp after General Robert E. Lee. In 1911, about all that was left of Leesburg was a post office and boarding house run by Mrs. Mahoney, a stage station, and some tumble-down cabins, one of which was occupied by an ancient Chinese named Bu Kee, who had been there since the gold rush. The more canny miners had gone long before into ranching and business in the Salmon and Lemhi valleys.

Lemhi County was about the size of Rhode Island and, if flattened out, would have been about the size of Massachusetts, since most of the county stood on end. The ranches were in the valleys, irrigated by water from mountain streams. The main crop was hay, marketed in the form of horses, cattle, and sheep. The ranchers raised enough grain, beans, peas, and potatoes for local needs. They raised some fruit, mostly apples, but the altitude was too great and the area too far from a market to make fruit growing profitable.

A few people had made money from mines, but probably a good deal more money had been put into the ground than was ever taken out. Mainly, Lemhi County was good stock country, and that was about it. The population of Salmon, the county seat, was about fifteen hundred, with maybe three thousand people in the entire county.

The winters, at an altitude of about 4,500 feet, were long and cold, with considerable below-zero weather. But, as the natives always pointed out, the air was dry, and there was so little wind that the smoke rose straight up. That sounded good to me.

A gravity system supplied domestic water from Jesse Creek, a stream that came down from the mountains to the west of town. Jesse Creek water was always clear, cold, and soft, qualities I have never seen equalled in any other municipal water supply. Electricity came from a small hydroelectric plant powered by water from the Lemhi River, which flowed into the Salmon River just below town.

According to Percy Anderson, the many mountain streams teemed with trout, and the main Salmon and the Lemhi supported runs of chinook salmon, steelhead, and whitefish. The ranchers' fields produced sage hens, the spring gulches were alive with blue grouse, the duck hunting was excellent, and the mountains were filled with elk, deer, goats, and mountain sheep. All that sounded as though I had arrived where I wanted to be, but it left unanswered the main question—could I make a living in the place?

With Percy as my guide, I walked all over town, viewed the high school and courthouse, and found them as described in the Spokane paper. Along Main Street stood several two-story brick buildings called "blocks" and named after their builders—the McNutt block, the Anderson block, the Shoup block, and so on. It looked as though at least a few people had made some money, although whether they still had it or not remained a question.

Through all my walking and listening, I remained silent about my mission in Salmon. But I learned as I went along that there were four doctors in town, one of them nearly on the sidelines from age. Two dentists practiced there, and three drugstores operated along Main Street.

Two doctors practiced in partnership, and the third was the survivor of another partnership, which had been disrupted by an automatic pistol. The oldest doctor, who was away when I arrived, had been a nurse in the Union Army during the Civil War and had practiced as a veterinarian when he first came to the Salmon River country.

The location was a long way from a cinch for an additional healer, but the factors of schools, climate, and hunting and fishing were just what I would have ordered; so I rented a furnished house and an office and wired my family to come on.

My first step had to be introducing myself to my prospective colleagues. I dreaded it, but in those days, doing so was regarded as common courtesy. Nowadays, however, such courtesy is passé.

I thought I would call first on the partners and found the senior man, Dr. Whitwell, in his office. He gave me the big hello, but sagged back in his chair when I explained why I had come. When he got over the shock, however, he emerged as a doctor of the old school, a gentleman and a scholar. He had graduated from the University of Tennessee, and first came to Lemhi County as a doctor for the Indians at the Fort Lemhi Indian Agency, thirty-five miles up the Lemhi Valley from Salmon.

I had to return to meet Dr. Wright, Whitwell's partner, who turned out to be a native of Canada and a graduate of the University of Oregon. He had practiced for a short time in eastern Oregon and then in Rocky Bar, a mining camp in southern Idaho, before receiving an appointment like that of his partner at the Fort Lemhi Agency. Wright was philosophical about my invasion, saying that he knew some doctor would come, and it might as well be me.

Dr. Hanmer, the third doctor, was busy when I called, and when I offered to return at a more convenient time, he suggested that I come back at seven-thirty in the evening. I have spent a lot of my life waiting for other people, so I was right on time for the appointment, but found Hanmer's office closed and dark. I returned several times later that evening and found it the same. That was the end of my effort to call on him, and, as he offered no apology, I considered myself snubbed.

When I look back, I am astonished at the nerve I had. Or maybe it was just stupidity. Anyway, the possibility of failure didn't seem worth worrying about. My situation was a little like one I had got into a number of years before in Reno, Nevada. When a solo game broke up, Blackjack Wallace, then a political fixer for the Southern Pacific, challenged me to a game of cutthroat poker. I took him on and soon found out that I was up against the real thing. He had plenty of money and tapped me every time I stuck my nose in a pot. All I needed to do was to make one mistake, and he would have had me landed. But I ducked and dodged until I was about ninety dollars winner, when I remembered an important engagement and never came back. Of course, an important difference between setting up a practice in Salmon and playing poker in Reno was that in Salmon, no previous engagement would enable me to duck out.

One thing I had overlooked was that a local bank had gone broke only a year before. Then I found the natives considerably set in their ways, inclined to be suspicious of strangers, and intermarried to beat hell.

As far as I could tell, none of the doctors in town had made much money from the practice of medicine. One had hit it lucky in a mining deal but had sunk his profits back into the ground in search of another lead. All were afraid to charge a respectable fee, and if a patient paid within ten or fifteen years, he became one of Nature's noblemen. My trouble was that my shoestring would run out if I was confronted with much delay.

No one in the community had ever owned a real operating table or a sterilizer. The partners had the only X-ray, and it was a thing to behold. In operation, a spark about a foot long leaped between the ends of two horizontal lightning rods on the top of the machine, crackling like fury and supercharging the atmosphere with ozone. Even so, however, the machine would take useful pictures of bones if you weren't in a hurry.

One doctor recommended himself very highly as a diagnostician and another as an obstetrician, though he had acquired most of his experience among Indians and in mining camps where the only women were hookers. The third had considerable to say about his practical knowledge obtained as a nurse before he went to medical school.

One of my first obstetrical cases was a breech presentation in the wife of a lawyer. I tried to play it safe by calling the alleged obstetrician in as a consultant. He quickly demonstrated how much he knew when he pulled one leg of the baby down, with the result that we lost it because we could not get the head out in time. Then I heard that he was telling around town that the undertaker did not have to take care of *his* babies. I never called him again in his professed specialty.

Mainly because I just happened to think of it, I made a lucky diagnosis in an impending rupture of an ectopic pregnancy, one outside the uterus. I impressed the patient's husband with the need for immediate surgery, which I was afraid to tackle. He was a preacher and took his wife to a hospital of his faith in Boise, a long trip and a hazardous one in the circumstances. The Lord was with them, however, and they made it just in time.

Not long after, a similar problem confronted me, another ectopic pregnancy, with the difference that this one had ruptured. I was up against it with no chance to pass the buck, and kitchen surgery offered the only hope of saving the woman. I called in both partners, and they agreed with my diagnosis but left the responsibility to me.

The patient's husband was out of town on a homestead across a mountain range. The barbed wire telephone line was working, and I told him what we were up against. He said to do whatever I thought best, so I began to move.

Across the street from my patient there lived in a log cabin an old lady, who was a practical nurse. I persuaded her to take my patient and set up an operating room of sorts, using a long kitchen table. Then with the aid of two other doctors, I set out to perform what I thought would be a miracle if I got away with it.

The case wasn't one I would have picked for my first invasion of the peritoneal cavity, but it wasn't for me to choose. I made one of my assistants scrub up as he had never scrubbed up before and let him make the incision. The blood in the patient's abdomen was under such pressure that when my colleague cut through the peritoneum, a red fountain spurted three feet in the air. I ducked the deluge, dived in, caught the spurter with my fingers, and held on until we got it tied. I added a pitcher of normal saline solution to the blood in her abdomen and closed the wound. I believe the conservation of that blood and the salt solution were what saved our patient.

Of course, none of us had ever made a blood transfusion, so that was out. We elevated the foot of her bed, and the woman rallied promptly. When her husband arrived, she was able to talk, but I thought the problem was not yet solved.

Although she took nourishment in increasing amounts, she had a persistent fever which slowly increased. One of my colleagues said it was nothing but what he called "surgical fever," which didn't reassure me. I recalled an argument about the sponge count when we operated on the patient, and I had thought we were one sponge short. In my pessimism, I believed that the missing sponge was the cause of her fever, so I put her back on the table and examined her.

If we had left a sponge in her, I was in a hell of a mess, along with her, but, again, I had no choice. Nor, unfortunately, did she. With our patient prepared for an incision into the cul-de-sac, my assistant whispered, "When you get ready to cut, I'll send the old lady to the kitchen for a pitcher of water. If it's the sponge, then you can get it out before she gets back, and she'll never know it was there." But the nurse, probably thinking the same way I was thinking, set the world's speed record for getting out to the kitchen and back.

Fortunately, I didn't hurry and found that the mass I had felt in the patient's abdomen wasn't a sponge but was made up of disintegrating blood clots, the absorbtion of which caused the fever. All that was needed was draining, and from then on she got well without a bobble.

I collected $250 as a fee and divided it evenly with the two other doctors. There was nothing secretive about the fee-splitting, and it became an unwritten law with us that in all major surgery, the man in charge assumed the after-treatment and collection of the fee, which, when and if he got it, he divided evenly. That practice continued until all of us but me were gathered unto Abraham's bosom. Occasionally, one of my colleagues suffered a short lapse of memory, but on the whole, everybody toted fair. When the modern wolves moved in, however, they repealed the unwritten law. From five assists in major surgery in recent times, I have never received one cent, even though I shared the responsibility.

Although I got away with my first venture in major surgery, my success created no stampede in my direction. We still had a hard time making ends meet and, to save ten dollars a month in house rent, moved to a little cottage on what was called the Bar across the Salmon River from the business section. That added half a mile to the walk between home and office, but poor folks have to have poor ways.

There was little elective surgery, and what there was consisted of minor operations. Collections were tough, and the aphorism of deadbeats, that a doctor never expects to collect more than half his fees, was working overtime. My competitors were timid about asking respectable fees and often left that important matter to me, saying, "You make the fee. You've got more nerve than we have." And then more than once I heard that they had been telling around town what a hell of a robber I was.

As my competitors felt more animosity toward each other than toward me, they generally called me in as the consultant when they wanted to consult. In most cases, I had an opinion and expressed it freely, but they usually hunted for an opening through which to dodge in case anything went wrong. It was like the old frontier saw of "*We* killed the bear!" unless the purported bear turned out to be a calf, in which case the cry became, "*He* killed the calf!"

I knew that I wasn't much of a surgeon, but I'd had a little better training than the others and was the only one who had done any postgraduate work. I had done three years of dissection with my mind on surgical anatomy, performing the usual operations on cadavers and dogs and had practiced on pig guts until I could do a Conell suture standing on my head.

I read everything I could lay my hands on and could gut a book or an article as quickly as Robert A. Taft is said to do; but I had found out that operative surgery can't be learned from books: you have to get your hands right smack in the middle of it before you can learn your way around. Anybody in my position, of course, was liable to be branded as an "occasional operator" or even a quack unless he referred his patients. As I've said, however, nearly all my surgery was emergency surgery and couldn't be referred even when I wanted to refer it because the nearest hospital was too far away. Remember, there were no airplanes in those days.

At that time, doctors often diagnosed appendicitis as inflammation of the bowels and administered a drastic purge. If that didn't either kill or cure the patient, the next course was to try to freeze the ailment out by packing the patient with ice bags. Most country doctors regarded an appendectomy as major surgery, to be undertaken only as a last resort, with the result that it was often delayed too long to be of any help to the patient.

The first appendectomy in which I bore the responsibility I performed in the Hughes Creek Ranger Station, thirty miles from Salmon. The ranger had been in town not long before and had consulted me about a disgestive disturbance, but I didn't indict his appendix. Later, however, his symptoms, as described by his wife over the phone, made me think his appendix was guilty. I gave the usual advice: absolutely no food, not even a little, and no cathartics.

That afternoon, the ranger's wife called again and asked me to come to see him. Since I had to make the trip with a team and buggy, it took me awhile to get there. When I arrived, I found the patient in much pain and with all his symptoms in proper order. I advised immediate surgery, but I didn't have with me the equipment necessary to perform it. The forest ranger suggested that I use an axe, but instead, I gave him a shot of morphine and called one of my colleagues in town, asking him to get what I needed from my office and bring it to the ranger station.

He owned an automobile, which occasionally worked, but since there were two bridges out, he made most of the trip the way I had traveled. The wait seemed to go on interminably because when I have to do anything I dread doing, I want to do it right now. I kept from blowing my top by pacing the floor of the house and most of the immediately surrounding territory.

The word had gone out, and before long the neighbors began to assemble. I could see that they doubted my diagnosis and my ability as a surgeon, doubts that I was inclined to share. One lady followed me out into the yard, where she offered advice, saying, "I know what's the matter with Ora. He and my son ate a lot of ice cream, and my son was sick just like Ora. But I made him take a big dose of sal hepatica, and he's all right now."

I mulled that over, wondering, in my willingness if not in my eagerness to duck, if she might not be right. But then I figuratively took myself by the back of the neck and said to me, "Now look. Your judgment says he's got appendicitis, that he needs surgery at once, that you are the only one who can perform it, and you'd better start acting like you've got brains instead of liver inside your skull."

When, at long last, the other doctor came dragging in, we improvised an operating room. The ranger's family fortunately had an extension dining table, which made a dandy operating table after we extended it to its full length and bridged the gap with two leaves laid parallel. By that time, it was about eleven o'clock, and we had to depend on kerosene lamps for our light. A rancher named Lee Jones held one lamp, and after we got the patient under, his mother served as anesthetist.

While I made my incision, Mr. Jones favored us with some of his stored knowledge and wisdom. He owned and had read a book on osteopathy, and, to go with that accomplishment, he had the amount of knowledge which Pope said was a dangerous thing. "I've read," Jones said, "that lots of doctors only pretend to operate for appendicitis and charge a big fee for just cutting through the skin and sewing the patient up again."

By that time, I was in the general peritoneal cavity, where I swept my finger around in the best Dr. Paul Gronnerud manner until I felt an object which I knew sure as hell shouldn't be there. I didn't know what it was until I swept it into view, and it turned out to be an appendix as big as my thumb, black as the ace of spades, dry as a cork, and gangrenous to its base. It wouldn't have been long before it sloughed and produced general peritonitis with its usual outcome.

I was afraid to try to invert the stump; so I did a simple

ligation (that is, tied it) and whacked it off. After I had done that, I asked my torch bearer to hold out his hand. I dropped the appendix into it and said,, "Well, there's one that's really come out, hasn't it?"

He looked at it and exclaimed, "Well, by God, it sure as hell has! Look at that son-of-a-bitch!"

After applying the regulation carbolic acid and alcohol to the stump, I dropped it and the gut back into the abdomen. Then I made what I later decided was a mistake by inserting drainage tubes. That was the day of the maxim, "When in doubt, drain." Later, the maxim changed to "When in doubt, don't drain." Draining or not draining always bothered me. It was like a town with only two hotels, both bad. No matter which one you stayed in, you soon wished you'd stayed in the other.

I can't remember how many dressings I made, trying to heal the tract. It was slow work, but the patient finally recovered and is alive today.

Chapter 17

I Open a Hospital in 1917—Paul's Illness—We Move to
Montana—The Medical Corps—How to Educate a Boy

In 1913 I found I had a little surplus cash, and to keep it
from burning a hole in my pocket, I repeated my 1910 trip
to Chicago and Rochester. Arriving in Chicago during the
third annual meeting of the American College of Surgeons,
I repeated my 1910 rounds of the clinics. In addition, I took
a course on surgical anatomy at the policlinic, which this
time included practice in surgical technique, using dogs as
subjects.

I soon learned that the surgical anatomy of a dog differs
from that of homo sapiens, even when the latter is a son of
a bitch. The intestinal musculature of a dog is so great that
a divided gut will contract until it is difficult to recognize
the opening. That's why a gut-shot animal can live so long.
Pigs would have served the course better than dogs, as the
intestinal anatomy of pigs is almost human.

In 1916 I was assailed by an urge that too often affects
kitchen surgeons. I decided that I needed a hospital, knowing that if I got one, I would have to get it myself. In those
days there was no paternalistic government buying votes
with taxpayers' money, and if I had asked the community to
provide a hospital, they would have thought I was crazy.

By advancing many months of high rent, I induced a
property owner to remodel a residence to my specifications.
I installed six hospital beds, an operating table, a coil X-ray,
and a large preserving kettle as an autoclave. Then, with a

graduate nurse and a cook, I had the nearest thing to a hospital that had ever been in the community before.

When I look back, I can see that about all I had achieved was to move my surgery from the kitchen into the dining room. I had also thrown myself wide open for every deadbeat in the community. It was duck soup for the do-gooders, who could curry favor with the Lord by dumping the sick and indigent on me. Had I been practical and hard-boiled enough to insist upon cash on the line for hospital services, I might have made it pay.

In April 1917 we declared war on Germany, and there was a drive for medical officers for the armed forces. I tried to volunteer but was informed that they had enough all-around doctors and were taking only specialists. I found out later that they were talking through their brass hats.

That fall, my oldest son, Paul, who had completed two years of premedic work at the University of Idaho, matriculated in the medical department of Washington University in St. Louis. But he didn't stay long because the sound of martial music got too much for him, and he enlisted in the aviation corps.

His mother was much concerned until I assured her that when he appeared for his final physical examination they would reject him. I based my assurance on knowledge that he was breathing through a trachea the size of that in an eight-year-old boy. At the age of two he had developed a papilloma in his windpipe and underwent sixteen operations before it was finally removed. As a result he had worn a tracheotomy tube for six years, and any unusual exertion made him breathe like a wind-broken horse. But when he came up for his final physical, they were so hard pressed for pilots in the air corps that they accepted him without a quibble.

I stayed with my hospital grind until March 1918, when one of my competitors decided I had a cinch and bought me out. Intending to move to Montana, in which state I had held a certificate since 1914, I sold my equity in my home.

As we were packing for our move, we began receiving telegrams concerning Paul. While waiting in our hometown of Litchfield for the Army to call him up, he had decided to have his tonsils taken out by the old doctor who had saved his bacon when he had the papilloma. Then in what looked like an irony of fate, he developed a secondary hemorrhage. Although the telegrams assured us that everything was all right, they didn't make sense; so I loaded my wife and younger son on the train, and we pulled out for Paul's bedside. When we arrived, the bleeding had checked more from lack of supply than anything else. When Paul is dead, he will not be any whiter than he was then, but his blood-making apparatus appeared to be functioning, and we stayed until we were sure he was on the mend. Then we headed back to take up our ravelled skein of care.

I chose Great Falls, Montana, as my new location, but our arrival did not create much excitement.[1] As my bankroll became thinner, I was offered a chance to take on the practice of a doctor in Cascade, a place about fifteen miles from Great Falls. I found Cascade to be a town of about five hundred people, with a hospital over the drugstore in charge of a graduate nurse. Although the town was smaller than the one I had left in Idaho, it looked as though I might make a living there. So I moved into a rented house and set up my office in the drugstore. The people accepted me at face value, and I soon had all I could do.

While still in Great Falls in the spring of 1918 with the war news going from bad to worse, it looked as though there would be a call for men up to age forty-five. So I had wired Governor Alexander of Idaho, volunteering my services. I hadn't been in Cascade very long when I was told to go to Helena, Montana, for a physical exam. I had no trouble passing it, and a few weeks later I was tendered a captaincy in the Medical Corps and ordered to Camp Greenleaf in Chicamauga Park, Georgia, for induction. I

[1] In 1899 he had done well in Great Falls with a medicine show.—OSS.

applied for a week's delay, which was granted, and then I was on my way.[2]

Following my physical at Camp Greenleaf, I was given a quiz on medical subjects. One question was, "How would you treat a punctured wound?" I answered that I would open the wound and swab it with iodine, then apply hot packs of epsom salts solution. If that didn't do the trick, I would open the wound widely and continue my hot packs. "What else?" the examiner asked.

I knew I was overlooking something, and finally I thought of it. "Oh. Give him a shot of antitoxin."

That answer satisfied the examiner, but I still believe it to be the bunk in civilian practice. Although the worry about tetanus is profitable for the medicine men, in more than forty years of practice I haven't seen a case of lockjaw. I have, however, seen a number of people who might have been better off had they contracted it.

In my civilian clothing at Camp Greenleaf, I stood out like a member of B'nai Brith at a Knights of Columbus picnic. As soon as I was assigned quarters in a barracks, I changed into martial raiment and discovered that the horsehide puttees I was required to wear were about as comfortable as a hair shirt. Then they put me in the awkward squad and gave me the works for six weeks.

Except for swamping latrines, we were handed everything given to buck privates. Every morning before daylight we went through setting-up exercises. Then we policed the grounds, picking up litter such as cigarette and cigar butts. We filled fire buckets and had fire drills. We oiled the barracks' floors. We drilled until our tongues hung out. And we always had to keep our cots ready for inspection by our commander, a martinet of a first lieutenant who enjoyed rubbing it in.

One day after litter drill, my squad was marched to the stables. When we arrived, we heard the command, "All

[2]My mother and I spent the remaining months of the war in Litchfield. —OSS.

those who haven't had saddle drill, fall out!" I fell out as ordered and found myself with several others alongside a saddle horse in charge of a sergeant.

He showed us how to put the bit in the horse's mouth instead of under its tail, how to arrange a saddle blanket, and how to cinch a McClellan saddle in place.

Following our lesson, I took a look around the stables, where I found some wall-eyed cayuses with ribbons in their tails. I learned that the ribbons were intended to warn new recruits of danger at the rear ends of the steeds, any one of which might kick a recruit's head off.

Then I found out that we were expected to jump the critters over hurdles while trying to stay in the saddles. Next, I saw a doctor right off the sidewalks of New York, trying to mount a steed with his right foot in the left stirrup. If he had made it, he would have found himself facing the rear.

The whole business looked dangerous to me, and I was no prospect for the horse marines. So each time I was marched to the stables, I fell out for saddle drill and let that serve as my training in equitation.

Each evening except Sunday, we had to march in what was called retreat. Trying to keep step with music provided by two bands, we provided a spectacle which must have made old Mars weep. Our performances highly amused rejects who held surgeon's certificates of disability and stood on the sidelines. Occasionally they almost had hysterics while watching us try to obey commands.

After some weeks of attending a course in anatomy at the medical college in Chattanooga, I was ordered to Rockefeller Institute in New York City, where I became a member of a class taking instruction in the Carrel-Dakin treatment of infected wounds. One day as we neared the end of the course and a French lieutenant was addressing us in broken English, all the whistles and sirens in New York City began to cut loose. Our lecturer paused and then remarked, "Well, that sounds as though the war is over. Anyway, I'll finish this lecture." He did so and then dismissed us.

On my way to the Imperial Hotel, I got off a streetcar at Thirty-Second and Lexington, intending to walk the rest of the way. But when I reached Fifth Avenue, I found two processions going in opposite directions. Wading in ticker tape and ducking hugs from hysterical women, attracted not by my sex appeal but by my uniform, it took me two hours to get across Fifth. By the time I reached my hotel, I was fed up with what turned out to be the so-called False Armistice.

A few days later, I was ordered to Camp Dix in New Jersey, where I spent several weeks at the general hospital before being ordered to proceed to Colgate University in Hamilton, New York, to superintend the examination for discharge of enrollees in a Student Officers' Training Camp.

That was my first experience in a small town east of Illinois, and I aroused no visible enthusiasm among the natives. The clerk at the hotel seemed reluctant to let me register, and a barber shaved me without conversation. The next morning, the clerk thawed enough to direct me to the training camp, where I met the first semblance of a welcome by the commander, Major Louis B. Lawton. He had graduated from West Point and had served in the Philippines, Santiago, and Boxer campaigns. He had retired and had then been recalled to the position in which I found him.

He was also a stranger in Hamilton, and each evening we conducted a gabfest as we tried to keep warm by a dinky fire in a grate in his quarters. We talked over every problem confronting the nation and then, perhaps because of the environment of Colgate University, we discussed the proper method of educating a boy.

We didn't think much of the method of the Joneses, who took their son Davy right out of high school and sent him to college just because they could afford it. We agreed that it might be better to matriculate Davy in the University of Hard Knocks rather than provide him with a raccoon coat and cigarettes and let him rah-rah around a college for four years.

At the time of my conversation with Major Lawton, I had

an eight-year-old son on whom our theory would be tried. To leap ahead with my story, when my son, Pete, graduated from high school in 1927, I would probably have sent him to Colgate if I had had the money. But since I didn't have it, I let him drift. He was an average boy who had no trouble landing jobs at wages which would have been beyond my dreams at his age. But his employment was seasonal, and his outgo kept step with his income.

When he reached the age of twenty-four in the depth of the depression, I suggested that he might do better if he got something in his head instead of continuing to harden the muscles in his back. Surprisingly, he accepted my suggestion, even though I warned him that it would be a long, long trail with many hardships, perhaps dotted with missed meals. But he was game, and for the next six years he really hit the collar.

Although I helped him all I could, he had to perform menial tasks such as sweeping floors and washing dishes, and he had to work every vacation. I believe that his maturity helped him a lot in college, as he had no trouble in qualifying for a BA with a Phi Beta Kappa key at Reed College and picking up an MA en route to his PhD at Stanford.

Was his acquisition of academic knowledge and degrees worth enough to offset his effort and time? His older brother entered the commercial field instead of returning to college after World War I, and he made high honors in his business career.[3] Which son has been the most successful in the broadest sense of the word? As nearly as I can tell, they are equally happy with their lot. There are many roads to Heaven. And, of course, to the other place, too.

[3] See the following chapter.—OSS.

Chapter 18

Back to Salmon After the Armistice—Paul Enters the Grocery
Business—The Flu Epidemic—Dr. Tilden—The Obstetrician's
Story—I Visit the Tilden Health School and Decide to Move
From Salmon to Kalispell

After the Armistice, my son Paul and I were discharged
from the army at about the same time, and in December we
had a family reunion in my hometown of Litchfield, Illinois, where my wife and younger son had lived while I was
in the Army.

In Litchfield, I was debating the question of whether to
locate in Montana or return to Salmon when Dr. Frank
Wright settled it by sending me a telegram, asking me to
come to Salmon and help in the battle against influenza,
which he had been fighting alone. Shortly after that, Paul
and I set out for Salmon over railroads that were still badly
disorganized from the war.

When we boarded the Gilmore and Pittsburgh mixed
train in Armstead, Montana, the temperature at five o'clock
in the morning was thirty-five below, a harbinger of what
the rest of the winter was to be like. The news we heard was
mostly bad, largely about various people who had died in
the epidemic, and there were plenty of them, including Dr.
W. C. Whitwell, Dr. Wright's former partner.

The day after we arrived in Salmon, Paul rustled a job as
a clerk in Greene's grocery store. That proved to be destiny
shaping Paul's ends. In partnership at different times with
two Salmon grocers, he operated grocery stores in Dillon,
Great Falls, and Deer Lodge, Montana. In 1923 in Deer
Lodge, Paul and his partner sold out to Safeway Stores, and

Paul took a job as a clerk in a Safeway store in Butte. He soon became manager of a Safeway in Livingston, Montana. Then he became district manager successively in La Grande, Oregon; Boise, Idaho; and Cheyenne, Wyoming. He continued in increasingly responsible positions with Safeway until 1942, when he resigned to become a cofounder of the OSCO Drug Company with headquarters in Chicago. Paul never again mentioned resuming his medical career, which is probably just as well, or better. Now he pays more in income tax each year than I ever grossed as a doctor.[1]

To go back to January 1919, I had not much more than registered at the Shenon Hotel in Salmon when Dr. Wright appeared, asking me to see a patient at the Johnson Rooming House who was ill with empyema. When I examined the patient, he didn't look good. Wright had already decided that an operation was necessary and said he had everything ready for resection of a rib. We put the patient on a table in the kitchen and proceeded until we reached the stage of encircling the rib with a Giglii saw. Then we discovered that the director for passing the saw around the rib was missing. Fortunately, we were operating with a local anesthetic, so I rushed back to the hotel, dumped a trunk on the floor, and found the instrument we needed. Then we finished the operation. That was really "kitchen surgery," but our patient wasn't finicky and made an uninterrupted recovery.

Then began week after week of calls on every road a Model T could cover, traveling in weather that would have made a reindeer's teeth chatter. One night along Wimpy Creek, I found sick folks in every cabin, hovering over airtight stoves stoked with cottonwood that refused to burn. The trouble was that they had closed and sealed every window and door so that no air would circulate. "No air, no

[1] Paul was president and manager of OSCO until 1961 when he and his associates sold OSCO to the Jewel Tea Company. He served as chairman of the OSCO board of directors until 1965. He died in 1971, leaving his wife, two children, and six grandchildren.—OSS.

fire," I told them and opened things up so they could get warm. In one cabin, sealed with plaster until it was as tight as a cistern, I found two old sourdoughs who bellyached to high heaven when I kicked open doors and raised windows. They then got well without any medication—not that there was any medication that would do much good, and that is still true in this day of "miracle drugs."

In a ranch house up the Salmon River, I found eleven people all ill with the flu. They ranged in age from an old man and an old woman to a bottle-fed infant. Some of them lay on pallets made up on the floor and others were two and three in a bed. The main thing I could do for them was to provide fresh air, and they all finally got well.

While attending my grind, I surrendered my savings in Liberty bonds in order to buy the furniture in a cottage and to rent it. Then, with my family assembled, I reestablished my practice and began to scratch out a living.

A couple of years went by, all pretty much like the ones I have described. Then one day in 1923, there appeared a patient whose mind, such as it was, dwelt continuously on the state of his health. He had ceased worrying about his gonads, which left him free to concentrate on the rest of his anatomy. He knew that his pulse rate should be seventy-two, he should breathe eighteen times a minute while at rest, he should drink six glasses of water daily, and his bowels should act once a day or there would be hell to pay. He also displayed a wonderful fund of knowledge concerning calories, proteins, fats, and carbohydrates and the proper proportions of each in the human diet.

When I asked him how he happened to know so much, he produced a sheaf of printed diet lists and a set of books that told how to live forever and extolled the virtues of a miracle doctor who operated what he called a health school in Denver.

At first, the name of Tilden rang no bells in my memory. Then a day or two later in another connection I was recalling my apprenticeship in a drugstore in Litchfield, which brought to mind a Dr. Tilden who had practiced there and had disappeared into the West. I remembered him as a dapper individual wearing a plug hat and a long-tailed coat, carrying a gold headed cane as he tripped through the town square on his way to the drugstore.

Out of curiosity, I wrote the health-school Tilden, asking if he was the man I recalled in Litchfield. He answered my letter, saying that he was one and the same. He didn't remember me, but he did remember my father, Dr. Francis M. Stratton, and my father's partner, Dr. Richard Owen, for whom I was named.

Tilden also mentioned seven other doctors who practiced in Litchfield in his time there, a considerable number for a town of not more than five thousand people. I doubt that any of them made much money, although they probably made more than they were worth to the patients they treated.

Those were the days when a young fellow aspiring to become a physician usually served a term under a preceptor before attending a medical college. Then, following two terms of five months each, he was assumed to know all the answers concerning the healing art.

The obstetrician who taught obstetrics at Barnes Medical College when I went there always told a story in his opening lecture about the apprenticeship he had served under an uncle who practiced somewhere in southern Missouri. As the professor told the story:

"Shortly after I enlisted, my uncle, wanting to get away on a trip, assured all his expectant mothers that I was really a bear cat in obstetrics, even better than he. This, in spite of the fact that I had never attended a case. So, I dressed myself up in my best bib and tucker and took charge of my uncle's practice.

"It was not long before I was called to see a patient in the country. When I arrived at the house, I found a woman seated in a chair and apparently in much pain, which seemed to strike her in spasms. While I was trying to size up the situation, an elderly woman who was serving as a nurse kept flipping the patient's skirts and then asked, "Aren't you going to examine her, doctor?"

"Thinking there might be something wrong with the patient's legs, I got down on my knees in order to get a better view. Just then, the woman's bag of waters burst, and the contents drenched the front of my best Sunday suit. While I was trying to mop myself off with a towel, the nurse hustled the patient into bed, where, in spite of everything I could do, the baby was born.

"The nurse tied the umbilical cord, cut it, and carried the baby out to the kitchen, leaving me seated in a chair at the patient's bedside. As I sat there, the patient had another pain and out popped the placenta, which slithered off the bed and onto the floor.

"I took a good look at the placenta. Then, assuming what I thought was a professional manner, I went to the kitchen where the woman was attending to the baby. There, I rendered a hopeless prognosis. 'We've done all we can,' I declared, throwing up my hands, 'but the woman is a goner. She is bound to die.'

"'My God!' the nurse exclaimed. 'What's the matter? She was all right just a few minutes ago.'

"A good deal peeved that she should question my professional judgment, I explained the basis for it. 'Well, you saw what happened. Just after I got here, her bladder broke, and while I was in there with her a minute ago, her liver came out and is now lying on the floor. How can she possibly get well after all that?' "

To get back to Dr. Tilden's letter, in it he told me that some twenty years earlier he had stopped prescribing drugs for his patients and put his trust in hygiene and diet. He sent me a couple of his books on diet and an invitation to come to Denver and see what he had there. The idea interested me, but other matters occupied me then, and I had to turn down his invitation.

In 1924, a patient of mine afflicted with imaginary heart disease met one of Tilden's former patients, who sold her on his institution, and she announced her intention of going there. So I wrote Tilden about her, and in his reply, he repeated his invitation. This time, I accepted.

I can't recall what I expected to find when I left for Denver, but I do remember my surprise to find an institution covering a city block on Fairview Place, directly across the street from Highland Park. Tilden's office and the offices of the administration were housed in what appeared to be a nineteenth-century mansion. The other buildings seemed new: two three-story brick apartment buildings and a long hospital-like building, which housed kitchens and a large dining room, a sun parlor, a lecture hall, and about fifty patients' rooms, most with private baths. A central plant provided heat for the buildings, and the grounds were beautifully landscaped, requiring the attention of a flock of gardeners.

When I introduced myself to a receptionist in Tilden's office, she immediately took me into the inner sanctum. Tilden, who looked a lot older than I remembered him (as, indeed, he was), greeted me cordially. Something in the glint of his eye suggested that under the camouflage of a foxy grandpa there resided a personality as hard-boiled as a ten-minute egg. He was jovial, could swear by note, and enjoyed recalling people we had both known in Illinois. He told a number of amusing anecdotes, and when we had talked ourselves out, he called in his receptionist and told her to find quarters for me that suited me. As we parted, he said I could have the run of the place.

I chose a room in the main building and went through some of the health school's literature, which contained a number of statements that didn't quite make sense to me. I nosed around and found an orderly who filled me in on how the place was run. A horde of employees included stenographers, a battery of practical nurses under command of a graduate, cooks, waitresses, chambermaids, painters, gardeners, and swampers, all of whom seemed to be going in high.

Back in the central office building I found a business manager and two other doctors on the staff. One seemed to be temporary, like myself, but the other, Dr. Brown, had been on duty for some time. He took me under his wing, and I accompanied him on his rounds of the patients, of whom there were many since the summer rush was on.

In conversations with Brown, I learned that Tilden had begun to apply his method twenty years before when he was still in general practice. After he began attracting patients from outside Denver, he remodeled a stable and housed his patients there. When that overflowed, he formed a joint stock company and built the plant on Fairview Place. Patients came from all over the world but mostly from the English-speaking countries of Canada, Britain, Australia, and New Zealand and, of course, from the United States.

I don't believe there was any out-and-out advertising. Most matriculants came on recommendation of former patients and from hearing Tilden lecture. Just before I arrived, for instance, he had made a tour through the South and along the Atlantic Coast, speaking at luncheon clubs which had invited him. He also published a monthly magazine, formerly known as *The Stuffed Club*, a name recently changed to *The Philosophy of Health*, in which he waged a ceaseless war of words against the skeptics.

His theory was based on the notion that the body naturally tends toward health, and deviations from that tendency are the result of enervation and toxemia. The treatment indicated for every affliction was relaxation of the nervous system and removal of waste products. At the health school, relaxation was induced by applied psychology and the cleanup accomplished through fasting, accompanied by stomach washes and high enemas each day. With renovation complete after a couple of weeks, the patient received instruction in diet and how to maintain the regimen. Then, after a month or so, the patient was discharged and sent on his or her way.

Within limits, the system seemed to make sense. Most people obviously eat too much of the wrong things, drinkers drink too much, and smokers smoke too much. At the very least, Tilden's treatment did no harm as long as it was not applied to patients for whom surgery was indicated, and he guarded against that by giving every entering patient a thorough examination.

Tilden's theory of disease appealed to people from every walk of life but especially to those who could read. No patients were accepted for less than a four-week stay, and the cheapest accommodations went for $250 a week, cash on the barrelhead.

One trouble with the system was, as Tilden later admitted, that few patients did as they were told. Tilden put it graphically, saying, "When one of them complains that his old affliction has come back, I tell him, 'Why you God damned son of a bitch! You didn't do what I told you.' And of course, he hadn't and knew it."

All patients had to undergo an introductory regimen of fasting for at least twelve days, during which they took nothing but limited quantities of water. Some fasts were extended for thirty days, and I heard of one that had continued for forty-two days. Such extensions were, however, imposed with circumspection.

If a patient became frightened and could not be reassured, the fast was ended. Patients were kept warm with stone jugs filled with hot water at their feet, and all were checked daily by an assigned physician.

At the end of the fast, the patient took gradually increasing quantities of fruit juice or fifty-fifty, a mixture of half whole milk and half hot water. When he became ready for a full diet he was assigned a seat in the dining room, but supervision continued.

The food in the dining room contained a lot of roughage, including the "Tilden salad," which was merely a combination salad, but served in quantities that would founder a cow. There was meat, fish, and poultry, all cooked without salt and mostly steamed or boiled. Tea, coffee, and sugar were banned.

The effect of the treatment was astonishing to someone like me who had never missed a meal unless he was broke or in the wrong place at the right time. There was no question about the treatment being eliminative, as the stench arising from the skins and lungs of former gluttons would knock an olfactory nerve for a row of swill barrels. And the enemas often dislodged old debris even on the twelfth day.

Maybe the oddest thing about the treatment was that it seemed to work. Asthmatics would arrive gasping for breath and on the second night of their fasts would sleep like logs. One asthmatic, if he told the truth, had taken more than $700 worth of adrenalin with only temporary relief. Sinusitis that looked hopeless to me would improve. Hypertension would diminish. Chronic skin diseases would disappear. Limping kidneys would revive and dispose of dropsical effusions like magic. There was even a story of one patient recovering from a brain tumor with resulting restoration of his eyesight. The last I doubted and suspected that the patient's visual troubles had been psychosomatic; and I also wondered if the apparent initial improvement in the others would continue.

While making my rounds, I decided to do a little research on myself. Except for some mild fudging on weekends, for six weeks I ate nothing except what the patients ate in the dining room. I wound up losing seventeen pounds and having an attack of colitis from so much roughage. When I mentioned it to Tilden, he exploded. "You God damned fool!" he exclaimed. "You're not eating enough!" I didn't contest the first count of his indictment and accepted his diagnosis. I went back to my regular diet and in a few days was hitting on all three cylinders again.

Aside from its therapeutic accomplishments, I liked the system. The duties were exacting, but the hours were only from eight in the morning until five in the afternoon. There were no night calls and no enslavement to the telephone. There was no mileage to be covered, and you didn't have to earn your fees twice—first, by rendering the service and, second, by collecting for it.

One thing that interested me was the lecture hall with about two hundred seats where the patients assembled each evening except Sunday. There, staff physicians and others, including an excellent dentist, offered instruction in diet and hygiene with a little physiology thrown in.

The big night was Friday, when Tilden took the stage. Various Denver musicians opened the festivity in a way that reminded me of a medicine show. Then, when the psychological moment arrived, Tilden strutted down the aisle. Banks of flowers bordered the platform, and Tilden always stopped and ostentatiously sniffed at them. One woman patient who didn't care much for that part of his act told me, "No dyed-in-the-wool egotist, which Tilden is, ever cared a hoot about flowers."

Tilden would have made a good medicine man. He knew when to make his sale, which medicine men called a "joint"; he never talked too long; he injected a little humor; and he never talked over the heads of his listeners. When he was a little short on logic, he filled the gap with enthusiasm and seemed to believe what he said. He was a practical psychologist of the first order.

When patients began to arrive in droves, a few of them were assigned to me. One was an old cattleman from Wyoming who tried to sell me some beaver skins he had brought with him. He bellyached continuously about his fast and about the provender he got after it ended. When I told him one day that his menu called for meat, he said, "Oh, yes. And I'll get a piece about that big," estimating it with a thumb and forefinger. "Hell! At home, I eat more than that while I'm getting supper!"

While making my rounds, I often saw the grandmother and mother of an infant, named John, who was in a go-cart under the charge of a trained nurse. I understood that John's nourishment consisted entirely of huge quantities of fifty-fifty, and his plaintive whine indicated that he was hungrier than hell. I had an urge to kidnap him and fill him with pot liquor.

Another patient, being wheeled around the park across from the health school in a wheelchair operated by a nurse, was the wife of a veterinarian from Texas. From brief conversations I had with her, I thought her main trouble was lack of calories. But she was fanatical about limiting her intake of food. I guessed that whatever ailed her would be cured if she took a course of high-caloric feeding at an institution run by Dr. Arthur Jones in Portland, Oregon, on lines diametrically opposite to Tilden's, but I kept my mouth shut.

About this time, I noticed a stranger flirting around the administration building. After awhile, somebody introduced me, and I found out that he was one of a trio who came from Cincinnati and were buying a controlling interest in the Tilden Health School.

He was an M.D. and one night took the stage in the lecture hall where he actually *read* a lecture. It was the damnedest conglomeration of big words I had ever heard and one that made no sense. He waved his arms and gestured while he read on and on and, when he finished, looked as satisfied as the cat which has just eaten the canary. I wondered how he would have reacted if one of my old hecklers from medicine show days had grabbed him by the leg. I was willing to take a small bet that he would have lost his place.

Before I could assay him further, I received bad news from home in the form of a thirty-day legal notice to vacate my office rooms in the Masonic Block, which the Masons intended to remodel as a lodge hall.

When I told Tilden that I would have to leave, he paid me what I asked for my services, but I thought he didn't think they were so hot, since he didn't ask me to return. I learned later, however, that he had other things on his mind.

I was up a stump when I got home. The only other office rooms possible were on the second floor of a hotel and could be reached only by a stairway as steep as a ladder in a barn. A dentist who was being ousted with me accepted them, but I refused. A patient with an aching tooth could climb the stairway but not one with a broken leg.

I kidded myself into believing that I knew Tilden's racket, and I was fed up on general practice. The office problem was the last straw. So I made a heap of all my winnings and bet the pile on a move to Kalispell, Montana.

Chapter 19

A Hard Winter in Kalispell—Camas Hot Springs—I Join the Tilden Health School Staff—I Resign and We Return to Salmon

Of the many boners I have pulled during a long lifetime, I believe the move to Kalispell was the worst. I deluded myself that I understood and could work Tilden's racket, and Kalispell, where I had made a couple of successful stands in the medicine show game seemed to me to be a good place to try.

Kalispell in 1924 was a pleasant town of about five thousand people in the Flathead River Valley, surrounded by mountain lakes and streams and largely inhabited by people who were convinced that health came in the form of pills and the contents of medicine bottles. That belief was made to order for a medicine show stand or the old army game of general practice, but trying to sell the Tilden method there was like trying to sell New Testaments in Mecca. Besides that, I didn't have enough capital for a long pull nor any place to take care of patients if I got any.

Right at the start, I shoved aside a life preserver that the Eagles Lodge tried to toss me in the form of an appointment to serve as their physician, which would would have given me three hundred families to whom I might sell myself. The trouble was that I knew some of the founders of the order and retained a low opinion of it.

The winter of 1924–25 proved a tough one from the standpoints of cash shortage and rigorous weather. One Sunday evening in January as I was getting ready to go to bed, I noticed that it was raining. By morning, the rain had changed to snow, and the wind was blowing. Since our house was warm, I didn't grasp the full impact of the change, although after breakfast I did put on a fur coat, balaclava cap, and gloves before I started for the office, six blocks due north.

I had got about half way there when I began to debate whether to turn around and go back or keep on plowing through snowdrifts into a howling wind that felt as though it had come directly from the north pole. I decided that the office was a little closer than home, and I half expected that the storm would blow itself out before afternoon; so I kept on past cars which seemed to have been abandoned in the street, not realizing what I was up against until I came to a thermometer hung on a storefront and saw that the mercury had gone down to the bottom of the scale, which was thirty degrees below zero. When I got to my office, I found that I had frosted my cheeks and nose, with a little spot under my chin which Boreas had added for good measure.

Instead of going home for lunch as I usually did, I ate in a restaurant. That evening, although the wind at my back helped me along, I had a tough time getting home. The storm kept up for two days, with everything but the wind at a standstill. It blew in windows on the north side of the high school and even blew a boxcar off the track at Cut Bank, a town across the mountains to the east of Kalispell.

I floundered through the winter, keeping in condition by going on foot to the homes of the few patients I had. When spring came, I was a thousand dollars in the red, with little prospect of changing the color of the ink.

I decided to take a crack at a sort of health resort called Camas Hot Springs, a place south of Kalispell and twenty miles or so west of the lower end of Flathead Lake. I rented a small house for an office, moved my equipment into it, and got ready to take on any prospects. I soon learned that most patrons of the resort were short of cash and preferred sulphur water and mud baths to the fasts, dietetics, and applied psychology that I offered them.

Mr. and Mrs. Crowley, who ran the hotel, did their best to help me, and, through them, I did land one patient. He was a Frenchman, a hard-rock miner from Butte and a guest at the hotel, where I also stayed. For several days, I watched him drag himself back from the mud baths, looking as though he wouldn't make it even by hanging onto the fence. He had been going the rounds of all the health resorts in Montana, and when somebody told him I was a doctor, he asked if I thought I could help him.

After I examined him, I told him that I might be able to do something for him if he would do what I told him to. "I do anything! Dese no good!" he replied, taking several bottles of pills from his pockets.

My examination showed that he was in an advanced stage of heart failure, with grade-2 albumen in his urine, and completely waterlogged with dropsy. He was not a very good prospect for a patient to whom I could later point with pride.

I wanted to see what a fast would do, so I put him in bed at the hotel and served as both doctor and nurse. I cut out all food and allowed him only enough water to satisfy his thirst. It was three days before the fast began to have any effect, and then his crippled kidneys began to work. I weighed him each day, and by the ninth day, he had lost thirty-four pounds, mostly of water. The patient was as amazed as I was, saying, "By God, I eat nothing; I drink nothing! But I piss, piss all day long just like a steer!"

At the end of twelve days, I terminated his fast and got him up and around. Although he looked like a different man and was no longer gasping for each breath, I wasn't very hopeful. What he needed was a new heart and a new pair of kidneys, items that I was unable to supply. I never learned what became of him, but I think I would need but one guess to win the Kewpie Doll.

While twisting on the hook at Camas Springs, I met a remarkable character named James Breen, an Irishman and a mining engineer from Butte. Neither of us had much to do, and I nearly walked him to death, literally. The walks, which didn't bother me, almost had him on the rocks before I realized that he had a weak heart. I put him to bed and had many bad moments before he whipped out of it.

He had a fund of stories about early days in Butte and was one of the best storytellers I have ever listened to. But his stories, amusing though they were, buttered no Stratton parsnips. I got more and more depressed and just didn't know what the hell to do.

Then came a letter from the mysterious doctor who had read his lecture at the Tilden Health School in Denver. He wrote that he and his associates had bought a controlling interest in the health school, he was to be the director, and he wanted me on the staff if we could reach an agreement.

I described my correspondent to Jim Breen, told him about the lecture, and showed him the letter. When he had read it, Jim said, "Well, if you'll knuckle down to this bird and lay flattery on him with a shovel, you can get about anything you want out of him. Of course, you may have to bend over for an occasional ass-kicking."

A year later, I wrote to Jim that he must have been psychic, but at the time, I was willing to put up with everything in his assay except the ass-kicking. So, before long, I left for Denver.

There the new director offered me a satisfactory salary, along with two apartments to house me and my wife and younger son. An article in *The Denver Post* told of the new management's intention to branch out both east and west, establishing additional schools. That, obviously, would require considerable investment, but the investors were said to be well heeled.

What interested me more than plans for the future was that the new director couldn't have treated me better than he did at the start. I was the third doctor on the staff, and shortly afterward another man came. I was soon going in high, examining new matriculants, and attending those already installed.

The new director was a well-qualified physician and worked like a dog, up early and late. I think he was of Dutch ancestry, but he had the browbeating instinct of a German. When I thought Tilden was an egotist, I hadn't seen the new director. Compared to him, Tilden suffered from an aggravated inferiority complex. Woe betide the underling who absorbed even a flicker of the limelight. Flattery mixed with soft soap was the coin of the realm.

The director revealed in various ways that he felt a venomous animosity toward Tilden, who had been retained in a sort of consulting capacity. Such animosity was strange because the current influx of patients was due to a lecture tour Tilden had just made through the southern and eastern states, a fact that I knew because I made a point of asking each new arrival why he or she had come.

This was my first experience in more than thirty years of working under a boss, and, although I kept my mouth shut, I took no pleasure in it. Tilden seemed to be shunted to one side, although the $75,000 he was said to have received probably soothed his wounded pride. With him on the sidelines, however, the arrival of patients soon fell off to a trickle.

I got through the fall and winter, but in the spring the handwriting appeared on the wall, and there was no need to send for Daniel to read it. Dr. George Brown, who had been on the staff when I was there before, paid a friendly visit to Tilden and got fired without notice. A little later, Dr. Gage, the new man, got his walking papers and a separation package that I wouldn't have given a dog.

I figured I was next, so I handed in a two-weeks' notice of my resignation. That seemed to surprise the director, who offered me a two-year contract if I would continue. But I knew that if he decided it was desirable to break the contract, he could make it so unpleasant for me that I would quit. So I turned the contract down and hung on for the two weeks while my younger son finished his junior year in high school. Immediately after that, we returned to Salmon.

Chapter 20

I Tell a Competitor Where the Bear Went Through the
Buckwheat—Hard Times—A Letter from Jim Ferrell—I Feel
Like the Parrot Attacked by Crows—Politics

In June 1926, as I dragged back from my latest fiasco, about all I had left was backbone and my ability to look any man in the face and tell him where to head in. I soon found need for both.

A former patient delivered my first bad news. She had overheard a conversation in the post office, which, as she reported it to me, sounded as though two of my competitors were preparing to run me out of town. That didn't surprise me, but I *was* surprised at their collusion, since I knew that they hated each other's guts. I didn't pay any attention to that rumor, but when I heard that one of them had been telling around that I had not made an equitable division of a fee for surgery, I was fit to be tied.

I knew that I had him in a cleft stick since I kept a file of cancelled checks that ran back for years. I quickly found the needed evidence, and then called on my detractor.

"I've just heard," I said, "that you've been telling around town that I didn't make a fair division of the McDonald fee. And I also understand that you said that if I claimed that I had made a fair division I would be a God damned liar."

He could see that I was hot under the collar and answered as though butter wouldn't melt in his mouth. "Why, doctor, I never said anything like that. And I'm certain that I didn't because you're quoting an expression I never use."

"Well, Dr. Adams just told me that you had."

"Why he's a God damned liar if he said that!"

I bowed and said, "Yes, I see. You never use that expression. Anyway, I'm going to tell you a few things!"

I threw down on his desk a check for fifty dollars bearing his endorsement, the check representing his share of the fee for doing nothing more than give the anesthetic. Then I showed him another check for a hundred which bore the other doctor's signature. He couldn't avoid acknowledging that both were correct, and I then told him in no uncertain terms where the bear went through the buckwheat, a scouring that he took like a hound pup. After I had blown my top, however, I bore him no grudge because he was one of those constitutional liars who couldn't help being the way he was.

My luck wasn't all bad, however, because I was able to rent rooms in an apartment building which had just been remodeled, where I have had my office for more than twenty years. Also I found that two graduate nurses were operating a hospital in a house I had formerly owned, using my old equipment. They didn't exactly welcome me with open arms, since they were boosting for one of my competitors. But they did accept my patients, which was all that mattered.

While the urban part of the country was ripping along during the boom of the 1920s with a chicken in every pot and two cars in every garage, Lemhi County, like a lot of agricultural counties was in a state of depression. One of our two banks failed in 1928, and a lot of people were going around with the seats out of their pants. It got worse in 1930 after the crash of 1929, and I had hard sledding for a number of years, borrowed on my life insurance, and kept the sheriff from taking my home by annually paying the year's taxes longest in arrears.

I had once made a good stand with a medicine show in Hamilton, Montana, which is about seventy-five miles north of Salmon in the Bitterroot Valley. Thinking it might be a better location than Salmon, I went to look Hamilton over. When I got there, however, the place seemed full of doctors, and people were as bad off as they were in Lemhi County. My wife and I spent the night there and drove back to Salmon the next day, arriving with just about enough money in my pocket to fill the gas tank. Before going home, I stopped at the post office to pick up the mail and found in my box an envelope containing a money order from a man I had almost forgotten about in payment of a bill for $180 that he had owed me for years. That was another one for the books!

Things got bad enough at one point that I toyed with the idea of making a lecture tour and wrote some literature on the Tilden method, thinking I might peddle that. My better judgment intervened, however, and I gave up the idea; but I did write to Jim Ferrell, who had started me out in the medicine show game thirty years before, outlining my idea and enclosing some of my literature. He replied from Hollywood as follows:

Dear Friend. Your letter and litature rec'd. Your System and advertising looks good. But after a carefull Physico Analysis of same I find its all wrong. First a lecture tour of its kind where you form clases cannot be done in 3 free lectures. It takes 12 lectures to get acquainted and confidence in order to convert prospects. And 2nd it takes 5 inch double column in newspapers with sensational reading. 3rd material must be no medicine or doctor ad. But of a semi religious matter. How to make money, attract love, and the fountain of rejuvenation and to make human dynamos out of weak saps and develop their hidden powers.

I and old Dr. Tilburn worked two small towns and was a big success but I couldn't handle him as his weakness for opposite sex got him in trouble. So I closed.

I presume you have heard and read of Willshire Tonica Health Belts. It has taken the coast by storm and making a fortune. I mean big money. It retails for

$65.00. It is a magnetic field. Now I have an old German man here who makes a similar Health Belt and magnetic cushion. It is marvellous. You attach it to a electric socket and put the cushion to your back and it magnetizes the whole body. You can ring a bell, light a light through your body or through a wall or a glass window. Now if you can come here on first train I will show you how you can take the State of Idaho or Montana and land agents and offices in every town. I think you could open a state with from three to five thousand dollars and I believe you could clean up fifty to a hundred thousand in from 6 months to a year as I would get you exclusive rights to any state. Now if you can spend a little time and money to come here and let me teach you and show you. So wire me at once if you can come. I would come up there but it is impossible as my time is taken up here in my various business.

Now Strat old boy I've got something for you. Perhaps you could get a partner with the money. But I want you to come and investigate first and I am sure you will be convinced. Now old boy as this is all for the present and you can bet I was glad to hear from you. So with best wishes I remain yours truly. Jim.

Sometimes I felt as though I was on an island in a sea of adversity swarming with creditors. The *Journal of the American Medical Association* even put my overdue subscription into the hands of a deadbeat collection agency. This was my reply to that, written on July 16, 1933:

Dear Sirs:

Have just received a communication from a man named Sweeney in which he asserts that I owe you $7.00, and if it was not for the fact that he is simply brimming over with the milk of human kindness, he would tear down all the credit I have painfully erected during a lifetime of nearly sixty five years. That is, of course, if I do not promptly send him seven smackers pronto and p. d. q. with ten cents added for personal check.

Well, he had just as well get out his wrecking car for three reasons. First, according to postal regulations, you should have stopped my subscription when I did not pay it in advance, so legally I owe you nothing. Second, I have been broke to lead but not to drive. Third, when it is convenient for me to do so, I will make payment, but I will not be hurried by such tactics.

That is the first letter I have ever received from a collection agency, and it comes with ill grace from you, when a reference to your records will show that I took the Journal for nearly a quarter of a century, and up to last year, always paid on the nose in advance. During the past three years I have hypothecated everything I had, striving to continue service to people unable to pay, and here you come trying to bludgeon me out of your seven dollars worth of flesh. No doubt your method succeeds with many a poor medico who is frightened into half-soling his trousers in an attempt to keep your come-on publication appeased.

But let me tell you one thing: if I get any more touching appeals from Dr. Sweeney (I suppose he is the same one who used to treat men only) or if anything more is done to hurt my credit, as he threatens, I am going to do what I can to make you jump through a hoop.

I suppose the American Medical Association is proud of its collection methods, but it is my guess that if the ones who instituted them are as low in stature as they are in principle, they can kiss a rat's hind end without bending the knees.

I was much like the parrot who for many years had occupied a perch on the top of Popcorn George's circus ticket wagon. The parrot had been there so long that he had learned the patter of the ushers directing the crowd through the entrance to the big top. In one town, the parrot disappeared from his customary roost. Discovery of his absence caused a lot of excitement, and the equivalent of a "Hey, Rube!" was yelled. The canvasmen and roustabouts organized themselves into a search party and after a good deal of hunting, found the parrot in a grove of trees, where he had become the center of attraction of a big flock of crows. They filled the air with raucous caws as they dived and swooped, plucking the parrot one feather at a time.

The parrot was squawking, "Take your time, gents! One at a time, as there is no need to hurry. There's plenty of time, gents! Don't push, gents. Don't crowd, as there's plenty of time to see the big show. Here, you! Get back in line! One at a time, gents! There's plenty of time for all of you."

In spite of the parrot's advice, the crows were hurrying and having one hell of a time. When his rescuers arrived, they had the parrot about as bare as old Toby's behind. Although my creditors were polite enough not to caw, they had me picked about as bare as the crows had picked the parrot. As time passed, however, the parrot and I both grew new feathers and survived into old age.

It was during this period that I got into politics, and if anybody has read this far without being persuaded that my head was full of liver instead of brains, my political career will convince them.

Without really thinking about it, I had always regarded myself as a Democrat, and, one day, when somebody asked me, I said that was what I was. Shortly after that, some member of the Lemhi County Democratic Committee offered me the position of committee secretary. I turned it down, but a day or two later, as I was passing a group whom I had pegged as Democrats, I heard one say, "It beats hell that we can't have anything in this town without a damned doctor being mixed up in it." He may not have been referring to me at all, but I jumped to the conclusion that he was and that he was sore about my proffered appointment. So I shifted into reverse and accepted it as soon as I could find the man who offered it to me. "Whom the gods wish to destroy, they first make mad."

Since I was supposed to be neutral, I didn't take part in the primary election, not even voting. But when that was over, the committee met to plan the campaign. The county was normally Republican, and I could see that the committee members had little hope of winning. But I made it clear that as far as I was concerned, there would be no trading and that the tail of the ticket would go along with the hide.

At the start we had a little luck. Trying to get the party together, I got them to give a banquet in honor of George Tannehill, of Lewiston, the Democratic candidate for United States senator, who was running against Senator Borah, a tough number, able to walk a political tightwire without benefit of balancing pole. I didn't think much of the so-called Lion of Idaho then nor in the years following, and I thought my judgment of him was confirmed when it was reported after he died that his cache held a quarter of a million bucks, including forty one-thousand dollar bills. Anyway, we beat the drums for our banquet, and the unterrified and unwashed came in such numbers that our much-impressed guest of honor gave our committee a check for $1,000. With that, we card-indexed the voters of Lemhi County and printed and distributed a little booklet, which I wrote.

At the start of our campaign, the State Democratic Committee sent in a spellbinder from Twin Falls to do some stump speaking. When he was pointed out to me on the street, I saw a ponderous looking individual, who evidently felt his weight. He wore a plumb-colored Prince Albert, its tails hanging nearly to his ankles, and a black sombrero on his head. While assaying him from a distance, I asked the county chairman why, if he needed a speaker, he didn't hire me. He looked startled and replied with another question as to whether I could make a speech. "Well," I answered, "if I can't do better than that blatherskite, I'll jump in the lake."

The upshot of my proposal was that the committee sent the import back to Twin Falls and agreed to pay me a hundred dollars and expenses to stump the county for a week. We advertised and held rallies in all the halls and schoolhouses in the county, and I attended every one of them, along with as many of the candidates as I could get to come with me. Sometimes we had more actors in our show than we had members in our audience. But at each assembly, no matter how small, I gave them the works. It was a new field for me, but I found that I could still think on my feet.

We elected every Democratic candidate for county office except one, and his opponent had so many relatives that he was invincible. Although I doubled my small bankroll by betting on the outcome, I now realize that I would have been better off if we had lost the election, because that might have nipped my political career in the bud. As it was, I became the county Democratic leader and held that post for many years.

In 1930 our candidate for state senator backed out, leaving us only a few days to fill the vacancy. I appointed two committee members to interview some ranchers in an attempt to get one of them to run and made the mistake of adding that, if all the prospects refused, the committee could write my name in. They didn't bother to see the others, and I became the candidate. I made no attempt to be elected but won, hands down.

As that suggests, I had not run on any kind of platform, but I did have a sort of an idea that I kept to myself. In the Noble Experiment of trying to save fools from their own folly, Idaho had gone whole hog and had prohibited liquor not only in the statute books but also in the constitution, notwithstanding that there wasn't a town or hamlet in the state in which a stranger couldn't find a bootlegger fifteen minutes after setting foot there.

During the 1928 campaign, I made up my mind that Prohibition was on its way out. But our candidate for governor couldn't see it and tried to carry water on one shoulder and booze on the other. When he came to make a speech in Salmon, in my role as master of ceremonies, I ballyhooed him a crowd and got him up on a dray on Main Street. Believing him to be a "wet" like Al Smith, I had most of his "dry" guns spiked by the time I finished introducing him. That forced him to confine his speech to "the invisible government," whatever the hell that may have been. He made himself few votes in Lemhi County and went down to defeat along with Smith, but for different and less creditable reasons.

After my election and before I started for the legislative session in Boise, I made up my mind to attack Prohibition if I could figure out a way to do it. Montana had wisely not gone overboard and had a law that permitted doctors to prescribe alcoholic beverages for medicinal purposes. I tried to get two lawyers to draft a bill that would do the same thing for Idaho, but both of them shied away from the enterprise, even though each was a boozehound from way up the creek.

When I got to Boise, I became acquainted with H. H. Miller, a reporter who wrote a column in *The Idaho Statesman* under the name of Cato the Censor, and Miller found a Republican lawyer in Gooding who was willing to draft a bill if I kept quiet about his authorship. His bill was a marvel of intricacy, with more whereases and to-wits than a sewing machine contract, but it drew a bead on my target of Prohibition and allowed physicians to prescribe alcohol for therapeutic purposes.

After I dropped my bill into the legislative hopper, the reporters descended on me. I referred them to Senate Bill No. 74 and permitted it to speak for itself.

When the legislature met, no member knew less about its mechanism than I. One thing, however, that distinguished me from many of my colleagues was that I knew that I knew nothing, and during the first six weeks, I contented myself with showing up for every roll call and looking and listening. By keeping my mouth shut, I kept my feet out of it.

When my bill came up for third reading, I had to speak in explanation and defense, and I think I surprised a good many of my colleagues. Unfortunately, the luncheon adjournment interrupted my speech, and I was afraid that during the interlude, the air might hit my audience and make me lose my "joint." Evidently it held together, however, for the final vote was 23 to 20 in my favor with one senator absent.

Of my speech, one newspaper reporter wrote: "Waiting to fire his volleys until the bill was actually up for third reading, Stratton uncovered his batteries ... in a verbal effort termed by veteran legislative observers one of the finest speeches ever delivered under the senate dome, and by sheer power of his argument forced a reluctant and fearful senate to approve its terms." The House turned out to be even more reluctant and fearful than the senate and laid my bill on the table, where it expired.

My election to the senate in 1930 gave me a hand in a game that a country doctor was sure to lose. For over a month while I attended the legislative session, all I had coming in was five dollars per diem, which didn't even pay for my meals. Unlike a lawyer, a doctor's cases don't pile up until he is present to deal with them. He has to be on the scene or he has no practice.

My economic rashness continued in 1932 when I ran for the Democratic nomination for United States senator. With no money and no machine, my one-man army didn't get very far. There were four other candidates, and even though I got four thousand votes, I didn't show in the race.

I might have done better, although not enough better to win, if I had not had some bad luck. On a swing around the state in the early part of the campaign I picked up a streptococcal sore throat. A debate on Prohibition had been scheduled in the Boise high school auditorium between

Harry Kessler, a dry candidate, and me, and since the debate couldn't be postponed, I faced a crowd of a couple of thousand people while I ran a temperature of over 101 degrees.

I had never before engaged in a formal debate and didn't even know the rules. The platform was high, and it seemed to me that I was about half a mile from my audience. If my mind hadn't been so fuzzy, I would have come down to the floor, where I could relate to the crowd, but I didn't think of that and stayed on the platform, where I turned in a sorry performance, although I had the right side of the question.

I passed up another debate with a preacher in Twin Falls and headed for home, where I battled my malady for three weeks while my campaign was on the rocks. Then, as if that weren't enough, the local bank went broke, leaving me with checks outstanding and no cash with which to meet them.

While I flirted with the big league, the Republican who had run against me in 1930 was nominated on both tickets for the state senate. He could qualify on only one, so the county committee wrote my name in on the Democratic ticket, and I beat my opponent once more. That must have been very discouraging to him.

In 1934, for the third time, I ran for the state senate. Although I was elected, I failed by four votes to carry one precinct. That failure made me think I was slipping, so I swore that I would never run again, and I have kept the oath.

Editor's Epilogue

One reason for my father's 1911 decision to locate in Salmon was what Percy Anderson had told him about the excellent hunting and fishing in Lemhi County.

Percy had told the truth. In those days there were no dams on the Columbia or the Snake, and the Salmon River and its main tributaries carried runs of steelhead and chinook salmon that are probably unequaled today anywhere in the United States outside Alaska. Large numbers of native cutthroat trout inhabited the many creeks, including Jesse Creek, which ran back of the house where we lived from 1919 on. And the Lemhi River, which joined the Salmon River near the town of Salmon, was an almost perfect fly stream.

The Lemhi wound through flat ranch country, and long stretches of the river consisted of short riffles between deeper holes. Dense brush covered the banks with only occasional breaks where fields came down to the river; but the brush was easy for fishermen to avoid by wading the shallow stream between the numerous gravel bars.

About once a week during the summer months, my father would come home from the office around four in the afternoon and change to fishing clothes, which, since he waded "wet," included wool pants, heavy wool socks, and shoes with leather soles studded with cone-shaped Hungarian nails that would hold on wet rocks. From the time I was eleven or twelve until I was seventeen and away from home during the summer, I put on similar clothes, and then we would drive over gravel and dirt roads a few miles up the

Lemhi and fish until dark. When we came back to the car, we changed into dry clothes and drove home, where my mother had kept supper for us.

I had a fly rod and fish basket of my own and for several years tried with little success to imitate my father's casts and fly handling. Although it seemed to me that I continued to do the same things, I suddenly began to catch fish—not as many as my father and fewer one- and two-pound redsides, but a respectable catch, even so.

Although he didn't fish with dry flies and probably never heard of a rolling cast, my father was a skilled wet fly fisherman, the only sort of fishing that interested him much. Fishing with bait or underwater lures didn't appeal to him, probably because it was too long between strikes and most of the action, when there was any, took place out of sight.

In August the sage-hen and grouse seasons opened. Although people said that sage hens were like gold in being where you found them, we usually hunted them and found them around irrigated alfalfa fields. We found grouse in spring gulches where they fed on wild rose pips, chokecherries, and serviceberries.

One Sunday afternoon during sage-hen season, when I was about eleven, my father and I walked a couple of miles up a dry gulch to some springs called Badger Springs, called that, according to my father, because there weren't any badgers there. There were, however, some sage hens.

My father carried what he called Old Meat in the Pot, an L. C. Smith double-barreled 12-gauge. I carried a borrowed single-shot 410-gauge, a caliber so small that it wasn't good for much except shooting rattlesnakes, which was the first use I made of it that day, when I killed my first rattlesnake.

Not long after the rattlesnake, a bird rose from the sagebrush, making a great noise with its wings. I fired my 410 and through purest accident killed my first sage hen. I can still hear my father's voice as he exclaimed, "Good boy!"

When September came, the duck season opened. On Sunday afternoons, my father and I and a friend of his would leave our houses around 2:30 and walk through fields down the Salmon River Valley for two or three miles, jump-shooting ducks that rose from cattail ponds and warm spring creeks. A little before dusk we would arrive at a slough we knew and wait there for ducks to come in to spend the night. When it got too dark to shoot, we walked back to town, carrying our ducks in our hunting coats.

My father was an accurate rifle shot and occasionally went deer hunting, sometimes successfully. But deer hunting, like bait fishing, lacked appeal because it lacked action.

Bird shooting was different, and for that he retained his enthusiasm into old age. In October 1944, ten days after his seventy-sixth birthday, he wrote in a letter to my brother, "I have gone duck hunting three times on the Norton ranch. Got seventeen ducks with fifty-two shells, which shows how rotten I shoot. The pheasant season opens next Sunday, but it looks like it will be hard to find birds. I think I saw but six on my three duck hunts, even with Boo along."

Boo, whose full name was Boo Burns of Hightell, was a pedigreed golden retriever my brother Paul gave our father in 1939. Boo quickly became a member of the family, although one who refused to enter the house and took his meals and slept outside even in thirty-below weather.

Toward the end of his life, my father wrote: "Boo has been a good friend and a great hunting dog, although he does have one peculiarity. For some reason, cattle scare him, and he will go a mile out of his way to avoid one, which can cause difficulties when we are hunting on a cattle ranch.

"Boo and I are getting old together, and it is a question as to which of us will poop out first."

When I visited Salmon in July 1950, my father had diagnosed himself as having cancer of the colon and of the prostate. He had decided against surgery. Although he didn't say so, I am sure that his reason was partly that he distrusted surgeons he couldn't watch and partly that he judged the few extra months of life that surgery might give him weren't worth their cost.

When he got up on the morning of August 24, he was unable to urinate. He had expected the blockage to occur before long and had told me that when it did, it would be "curtains."

He stood in his pajamas at the kitchen sink and took some pills. When my mother asked him what he was taking, he answered, "Oh, just some pills I've got here. And I'm taking plenty. I'm going back to bed, and don't let anybody wake me up."

He went to the front door and spoke to Boo, who lay on the front porch, and then went back to bed. After giving him enough time to die, I went into the bedroom and found him dead.

On August 31, the weekly Salmon *Recorder Herald* reported:

> Dr. Owen Tully Stratton, 81, a prominent citizen of this community for nearly forty years, passed away at his home on the bar Thursday afternoon following a brief illness. His sudden death came as a shock to his many old time friends over the county, who were deeply grieved at his passing.

Boo outlived him a month, and my mother died two years later.

Glossary

Bigmitt artist: I have been unable to find *bigmitt* in any dictionary, but according to Ramon Adams, *Western Words*, a *mitt-joint* is "a gambling place where marked cards are used."

Blanket stiff: A *stiff* was an unskilled laborer. For example, a laborer on a railroad or highway grade (roadbed) was a grade stiff. A *blanket stiff* (same as a bindle stiff) was a laborer who moved from one job to another, carrying a blanket roll.

Booster: *See* shell game.

Cayuse: An Indian pony. Originally, one bred by the Cayuse Indians of eastern Oregon.

Coon shouter: I am unable to find *coon shouter* in any dictionary. *Coon* is a nineteenth-century derogatory term meaning a black person. According to the *Dictionary of American Slang*, a *shout* is "a slow blues sung by a jazz singer in the traditional manner." *Coon shouter*, therefore, may have meant a black blues singer.

Coupstick: A stick carried by a Plains Indian, used to strike a fallen foe. The auther, however, used the term to mean a stick on which each victory over a foe was recorded by a notch.

Deadfall: A *deadfall* is a trap in which a weight falls upon and kills the animal beneath it. Western U.S. slang for a low gambling house.

Doggery: A low drinking house.

Dominant minority: The leaders of a community. The phrase is from *A Study of History* by Arnold Toynbee.

Fixer: According to the *Dictionary of American Slang*, one meaning of *fixer* is "a negotiator between criminals and officials." The word probably also meant a negotiator between officials and people who were not precisely criminals but who were engaged in illegal activities such as gambling and the operation of carnival games.

Garrison finish: Named after a nineteenth-century jockey, Snapper Garrison, who became known for holding his horse back and moving up only when entering the home stretch. He won most of his races in the last eighth mile.

Hank Monk: According to Mark Twain, *Roughing It*, volume 1, chapter 20, Hank Monk was a stage driver for the Overland Stage Company who was supposed to have had Horace Greeley as a passenger from Carson City, Nevada, to California. Greeley told Monk "that he had an engagement to lecture at Placerville and was very anxious to go through quick. Hank Monk cracked his whip and started off at an awful pace. The coach bounced up and down in such a terrific way that it jolted the buttons all off of Horace's coat, and finally shot his head clean through the roof of the stage, and then he yelled at Hank Monk and begged him to go easier—said he warn't in as much of a hurry as he was awhile ago. But Hank Monk said, 'Keep your seat, Horace, and I'll get you there on time'—and you bet you he did, too, what was left of him."

Mark Twain said he had heard of that "deathless incident four hundred and eighty-one or eighty-two times. . . . Drivers always told it, conductors told it, the very Chinamen and vagrant Indians recounted it. I have had the same driver tell it to me two or three times in the same afternoon."

Katzenjammer: A German word meaning severe hangover.
　　　Dr. Park's katzenjammers probably approached de-
　　　lirium tremens.
Kerry Patch jeer: I have been unable to find this term in any
　　　dictionary, but the context of the term as used in
　　　Medicine Man suggests that it was the equivalent of a
　　　Bronx cheer.
Kid McCoy: World welterweight champion from 1890 to
　　　1900. According to the *Morris Dictionary of Word and
　　　Phrase Origins*, so many second-rate prize fighters
　　　called themselves Kid McCoy that the champion had
　　　to bill himself as *the real McCoy*.
Pot-metal revolver: A cheap revolver.
Prince Albert: A double-breasted coat with skirts that fell
　　　below the knee.
Riel's Rebellion: In 1885, French-Indian mixed-bloods
　　　led by Louis Riel rebelled against the Canadian
　　　government.
Shell game: In a 1949 letter my father wrote, "A shell game
　　　was worked with half of three English walnut shells
　　　lined with putty to make the insides smooth so the
　　　pea would roll out easy. Actually, it wasn't a pea at all
　　　but a small ball made of soft rubber. A sucker bet
　　　that the pea was under a certain shell and won if the
　　　pea was there and lost if it wasn't. In the game's most
　　　deadly form, a booster or shill among the onlookers
　　　would pretend to surreptiously remove the pea from
　　　under a shell, press it into the hand of a sucker, and
　　　whisper to the sucker, 'Bet him that it isn't under any
　　　of them.' If the sucker made the bet, the shellman
　　　would tell him to pick up the shells himself. Low and
　　　behold, there would be the pea which the sucker
　　　thought he had in his hand.
　　　"In Skagway in 1897 a highbinder called Soapy
　　　Smith was the brains of as tough a gang of goons as
　　　ever came down the pike. They had a saloon named
　　　The Klondike in which they operated all the sure-

thing games known to wolves. When an incoming steamship announced its arrival by a blast from its whistle, Soapy's henchmen would yell, 'Fresh Fish!' and head for the landing, where they would pose as a welcoming committee and try to steer the new arrivals into their trap.

"They also ran shell games on both the Skagway and Dyea trails. One day when I was hiking from the foot of the trail to Skagway, I saw one of these shell games operating on the wagon road. The shellman was a big Irishman named Dan Daley. He had his little table set up in about four inches of snow, and the boosters all carried dummy packs on their backs.

"I halted to see how they worked, believing that with my whiskers and mackinaw clothing I looked like any come-on. It seemed, however, that I didn't, because I hadn't stood there more than a few minutes when Mr. Daley looked up and advised, 'Better run along and peddle your papers, young fellow. You can't make any money around here.' I, not hankering for a punch in the nose, took his advice and moved on."

Skookum: A Chinook jargon word meaning *good*. Chinook jargon was a lingua franca made up of Indian, French, English, and other words developed by Indians and traders along the Columbia.

Slapstick: According to the *Oxford Reference Dictionary* slapstick is knockabout comedy. What is knockabout? Loud, boisterous. The Morrises in their dictionary say the comedy got its name from two sticks fastened together at one end so that they would make a slapping sound when the comedians struck each other with them. Exactly what the medicine show comedians did in their slapstick will probably never be known.

Spiritus frumenti: Spirits distilled from grain, i.e., *whiskey*.

Squaw man: A white man living with an Indian woman.
Tapeworm: A ribbonlike parasitical worm infesting the alimentary canal of its host.
Tyhee: Chief or headman.

Index